Cinema Babel

Cinema Babel

Translating Global Cinema

Abé Mark Nornes

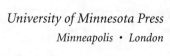

University of Minnesota Press
Minneapolis • *London*

Portions of chapter 2 were previously published in "Pōru Rūta/Paul Rotha and the Politics of Translation," *Cinema Journal* 38, no. 3 (1999): 91–108; copyright 1999 by the University of Texas Press; all rights reserved. Parts of this book were previously published in "Toward an Abusive Subtitling: Illuminating Cinema's Apparatus of Translation," *Film Quarterly* 52, no. 3 (spring 1999): 17–34; copyright 1999 by the University of California Press.

Published by the University of Minnesota Press
111 Third Avenue South, Suite 290
Minneapolis, MN 55401-2520
http://www.upress.umn.edu

Library of Congress Cataloging-in-Publication Data

Nornes, Markus.
    Cinema babel : translating global cinema / Abè Mark Nornes.
        p.   cm.
    Includes bibliographical references and index.
    ISBN: 978-0-8166-5041-5 (hc : alk. paper)
    ISBN-10: 0-8166-5041-1 (hc : alk. paper)
    ISBN: 978-0-8166-5042-2 (pb : alk. paper)
    ISBN-10: 0-8166-5042-X (pb : alk. paper)
    1. Motion pictures—Titling.   I. Title.
    TR886.6.N67   2007
    778.5'2344—dc22   2007030755

Printed in the United States of America on acid-free paper

The University of Minnesota is an equal-opportunity educator and employer.

15 14 13 12 11 10 09 08 07   10 9 8 7 6 5 4 3 2 1

For Hideko,
who both discussed it
and put up with it

Contents

Acknowledgments

This book has been a pleasure to write, thanks to my colleagues at University of Michigan and around the world. I am particularly grateful to Ueno Toshiya, Iwamoto Kenji, Lucia Saks, Nancy Florida, Luc Van Haute, Ulrich Straus, Yamanouchi Etsuko, Minako O'Hagen, Sarah Frederick, Scott Simmon, Karen Strassler, Roland Domenig, Donald Richie, Yomota Inuhiko, Anne McKnight, Jane Gaines, Mitsuhiro Yoshimoto, Chika Kinoshita, and Sharon Hayashi. My work on subtitles has benefited greatly from the critical comments of translators Gabriele Pauer and Yamamoto Naoki. I thank Jennifer Lindsay, Sheila Skaff, and Jon Jost for sharing their work with me at critical stages of the writing process. Over the years, a number of friends read the manuscript, and their feedback has made the book immeasurably better; they include Tessa Dwyer, Darrell Davis, Alex Zahlten, Giorgio Bertellini, Christi Merrill, Eric Cazdyn, Aaron Gerow, David Desser, and an anonymous reader. I extend a special thank you to Alan Tansman and Dennis Washburn for inviting me to the Dartmouth/Berkeley Translation Workshop, an interdisciplinary setting that was extremely thought-provoking each time out.

Research for this book was supported through grants from the Japan Foundation and University of Michigan Center for Japanese Studies. My digs into the archives would not have been productive without the help of generous bibliographers like Scott Dennis and Phil Hallman at University of Michigan, and Barbara Hall at the Academy's Margaret Herrick Library. Thanks go to the Kawakita Memorial Film Library and the National Film Center of Japan for opening their collections to me.

Makino Mamoru, as always, trotted out a few select items from his closets that boosted me over a number of seemingly insurmountable hurdles. Temperance Bonner helped me explore many film periodicals through an Undergraduate Research Opportunity Program grant at University of Michigan. My research into the present-day situation would not have been possible without the help of Jirina Hradecká in Prague and Luise von Flotow, Robert Paquin, Herbert Fielden-Briggs, and Hélène Lauzon in Montreal.

I probably would not have expanded my initial essay on subtitling into a book were it not for the enthusiastic support of Lawrence Venuti. I was particularly impressed by his sharp comments when I revised said essay for the *Translation Studies Reader*. An equally strong force propelling me along was filmmaker Sato Makoto. I subtitled three of his films over the years, and thanks to my research I came to each job with a slightly different perspective. Makoto was open to trying new things, allowing me to port my theoretical inclinations into subtitling practice. It was great fun and always fed back into my writing.

Finally, I have appreciated the support of the fine people at the University of Minnesota Press, especially my editors Jason Weidemann and David Thorstad. And I must not forget the Yamagata International Documentary Film Festival, which gave me so many opportunities to translate, be translated, and hang around translators.

INTRODUCTION

Translating Traffic

Every film is a foreign film, foreign to some audience somewhere.
—Atom Egoyan and Ian Balfour

All of us have, at one time or another, left a movie theater wanting to kill the translator. Our motive: the movie's murder by incompetent subtitling or dubbing. The death of a text through translation is an age-old trope, but it takes on new meaning with its transposition into cinema. The very possibility of that death implies a state of animation, a state that is, after all, essential to the moving image. As in the case of literature, that death is a discursive condition, but with film it also constitutes a perceptual category. Spectators often find cinema's powerful sense of mimesis muddied by subtitles, even by skillful ones. And dubbing is simply beyond the pale. The original, foreign, object—its sights and its sounds—is available to all, but it is easily obscured by the graphic text or disconnected speech through which we necessarily approach it. Thus, the opacity or awkwardness of film translation easily inspires rage.

I began thinking about the vagaries of film translation when I translated my first subtitles for Ogawa Shinsuke and Iizuka Toshio's *A Movie Capital* (*Eiga no miyako*, 1991). It was an experience filled with surprises. Here was an extraordinarily close form of textual analysis where every element of verbal and visual language is read off the image, repeatedly, line by line, even frame by frame. I was fascinated by the way this particular field of film analysis naturally raised theoretical problems in the course of working out practical solutions to seemingly simple problems.

1

Figure 1. Sven Nykvist's brilliant black-and-white photography rendered the subtitles of *Persona* (1966) notoriously invisible. The subtitles censored the film, which was far more sexually explicit than British and American spectators imagined. This film was among the first to be retranslated for high-quality DVD releases.

But nothing is simple when it comes to subtitles; every turn of phrase, every punctuation mark, every decision the translator makes holds implications for the viewing experience of foreign spectators.

After this first subtitling job, the issue of translation doggedly followed me wherever I went. As a coordinator for the Yamagata International Documentary Film Festival in Japan, I regularly worked with translators. I edited their work for catalogs and newsletters, and occasionally performed translations myself, both for print and for subtitled films. When filmmakers or critics visited Japan, I lent a hand as one of many informal liaisons. The festival itself is utterly dependent on interpreters, both highly trained professionals and bilingual liaisons at the bars. In my other life as a professor of Japanese film studies, my debt to translators of theory, criticism, and films is obvious. Not a day goes by that my students and I don't depend on some (usually anonymous) translator to study a work from somewhere in the world. Over the years, I increasingly found myself in the curious—and frankly uncanny—position of standing on a foreign stage, speaking to an audience through the mouth of an interpreter. In short, I came to recognize my own life in translation.

Naturally, I began to wonder why so little attention is paid to the work of film translators. The reasons are multiple and ultimately have to do with a more generalized devaluation of translation, but one is that the industry itself has historically discounted their contribution. Few translators get credit for their essential work and they generally receive no residuals, a clear indication that their authorship goes unrecognized. The same is often true for voice actors who ply their specialized skills for dubbing. The following example is revealing. When the American Screen Actors Guild filed a claim during a contract dispute with Saban Entertainment over the dubbing of *Digimon: The Movie* (2000), the Guild's lawyer proposed a rather tortured definition of performance art: "The dialogue that the performers are recording for the film does not merely substitute for the original Japanese dialogue; rather, the original dialogue is significantly altered by revisions, deletions, and modification such that the employment no longer constitutes 'dubbing' as defined by the dubbing agreement."[1] This dubbing agreement conceded all manner of rights and privileges to the studios, essentially drawing a line between dubbing and acting, instrumentality versus creative genius.

How strange it is that the tasks of the translators of the film world have gone largely uncommented on for the past century. It is strange because they have been active participants in most aspects of film culture. That they create subtitled and dubbed prints of foreign films is certainly obvious to all. However, what of all the translators who helped move those prints from a creative idea in one part of the world to a finished film projected in a foreign land? Every step in this process involved the drawing up of complex contracts, many of which required translation. The amount of interlingual communication in an international coproduction is astonishing. Distribution deals always involve some degree of translation and interpretation. To pave the way for a film's release, interpreters help directors and stars on junkets to the major markets and far-flung festivals. They sit alongside artist and critic in the interview scene and are hardly set dressing, even if they are treated as such. All manner of publicity materials—posters, press packs, Web sites, print and television advertisements—must be prepared in the target market's language. Outside of film production and distribution, ideas and theories about film circulate the globe in translation, alighting in a certain place to be rejected, rearticulated, or assimilated. Further-more, we must not neglect the role translation plays in canon formation, and the establishment, development, and maintenance of an academic discipline like film studies, especially in its national cinema subfields.

However, despite the rich complexity of the film translators' task and their singular role in mediating the foreign in cinema, they have been vir-tually ignored in film studies.[2] Within translation studies, in contrast, there has recently been a proliferation of work, but it has almost exclu-sively concentrated on practical issues for translators, linguistic analysis, or the physiology of the peculiar brand of speed-reading demanded by subtitles.[3] Scholars in either discipline have yet to explore in depth the historical, cultural, and ideological issues I will attend to here.

Indeed, it is impossible to fathom a film world without all these trans-lators toiling away in the background. What on earth would it be like? In sum, a major premise of this book is that moving-image media was (unevenly) globalized from the start and this was only possible thanks to tens of thousands of anonymous translators. Funny so few have noticed.

The Global Traffic System

This book is about traffic in and out of translation. "Traffic" is qualita-tively different than "movement" or "circulation" because it indicates regulation. In its most basic terms it points to the propelled directional-ity of textual sources and targets, of films imagined in the built world of one language transported to be reimagined and reconstructed within another. "Traffic" also refers to the journeys of people: to the American sound technician in 1930s Tokyo, to the French disciple on a pilgrimage to Hollywood to meet his master, to the actor bringing her talent to a foreign coproduction, and all the other production personnel that travel around the world. These examples also suggest the importance of mi-grating ideas, whether aesthetic, technical, critical, or philosophical.

The term also gestures to the global system of channels that shuttle around film prints—and now bytes—appended with translations of one sort or another, from one national cinema to many others. This developed side by side with other modern information networks such as the telex, telephone, and postal system. Cinema was one of the first globalized art forms, if we mean by this a mode of production so thor-oughly internationalized that it predicates itself on translation and traffic.

Even the slightest of national cinemas keep close watch on their international dimension.

In its most basic sense, globalization refers to a vision of history emphasizing a steady intensification of interconnection and intercommunication between peoples over the last several centuries. "The world" comes to be a planetary space linked by economic, social, and even cultural forces. In the last decades of the twentieth century the character of these links underwent extraordinary transformation. Today, the networking of these forces is so supple and sensitive that events on one spot on the Earth can swiftly affect faraway places, or even achieve global reverberations.

A driving force behind these interlinkages has been an ever-evolving capitalism, which now circulates finance across political borders with astonishing ease and instantaneous speed. Concomitant developments in transportation systems allow businesses to easily achieve transnational structures, creating products in one part of the world with favorable conditions—too often meaning cheap, unorganized labor and lax environmental laws—and assembling, marketing, and selling those products virtually anywhere else. The labor force itself has become remarkably fluid as workers follow the jobs and show a willingness to leave national homes for widely scattered immigrant communities, where travel and communication technologies allow them to forge and maintain new relationships to home.

The nation-state system appears to be disintegrating, displaced by transnational organizations and corporations, and for all these reasons and more we find ourselves immersed in talk of borderlessness and globalization. The latter term itself excises the nation from earlier discussions of "internationalism" or "transnationalism." This erosion of the nation-state and the felt emergence of a homogeneous planetary space implies a threat to local cultures, or what has recently been dubbed "McWorld" or "Planet Hollywood."[4]

As the latter appellation implies, the movies play a key role in all this. Communication technologies provide an architectural undergirding for the forces of globalization, most particularly all the digital media that use electrons to effortlessly traverse political borders. The Internet gets all the attention, but film prints have also moved around the world with remarkable speed, even within years of cinema's invention. This trafffficking in imagery expanded forcefully through broadcast television. Today, the global circulation of moving images is increasingly intricate and saturating, thanks to videotape, satellite television, VCDs, DVDs, and the Internet, not to mention in-flight movies and the ubiquitous video screens of our urban spaces.

Cinema and television study has been at pains to account for these developments. Despite the obvious importance of these space-collapsing, homogenizing distribution technologies, critiques of globalization never achieve quite the force they have in many other fields of inquiry. Although introductory classes and textbooks assume a universalizing stance, "national cinema" was long the dominant paradigm for the study of foreign film. This began with the search for "national character" as expressed in a country's filmmaking, but the category of national cinema itself came under forceful critique in the 1980s and 1990s. Despite this, we seem unable to slough the category off completely. That "cinema" maintains a special relationship to globalization helps explain why most studies of global film and television focus on new technology, transnational industrial structures, or relatively small immigrant communities, while, at the same time, most people continue to think, study, and watch in modes substantially similar to, say, the heyday of the foreign art cinema of the 1950s and 1960s.

Aside from the persistent pressure of the nation-state in our daily lives, two reasons stand out to explain the durability of the national cinema model. First, as Eric Cazdyn notes in a fascinating essay on subtitles, people erroneously assume that the cultural and ideological dimensions of globalization are marching at the same breakneck speed as its the sociopolitical structures: "When it comes to national identities and ideologies—the primary unit by which people locate themselves in the world—the nation's stock is still sky high. We still root for our own teams in the Olympics and our own armies in war while the political-economic stakeholders—without any nostalgia—focus on the bottom line."[5]

We can add that for all the transnational developments in the film world, people persistently slot films into the national cinema rubric. Furthermore, the majority of the world's film and television industries continue to be organized at a national level. We may find spectacular exceptions at the extreme ends of the production spectrum, most notably the Hollywood action blockbuster and the "accented" independent work by diasporic artists. However, we still attach great importance to where films come from. To my knowledge, no "international" film festival catalog eschews the category "country of origin." And when that line lists more than one country it merely indicates multinational financing, often from governmental grant agencies and nation-based television networks with few of the transnational structures of major corporations. Significantly, the vast majority of actors and stars are either confined to a nationally defined industry or identified with one; indeed, one would be hard-pressed to list many more transnational stars from today than in the age of the talkies.

If we extract the mechanisms for financing from the equation, today's industries themselves appear fundamentally continuous with the organizational structures and practices of the past. Films come from one nation (no matter how they were financed or where they were shot) and they are distributed to many other nations (through more conduits, but in substantially the same manner as during the silent era). Thus, the phrase "international coproduction," which we will closely examine in chapter 1, only reiterates the national cinema framework. Furthermore, industrial protectionism is advocated or protested by nationally organized unions and trade associations and legislated, enforced, or combated by states. Censorship laws and rating systems are nearly always organized at the level of nation. In fact, outside of copyright, most law governing the production and distribution of moving images is the domain of the nation-states.

The second reason for the persistence of the national cinema category underlies all the factors already listed: language itself. Unlike the pen I write this with or the (made in China) "Japanese" *Finding Nemo* (2003) toy I just bought my son, moving image works cannot be localized by merely changing the label or translating the instruction manual. Once they cross linguistic borders, they are marked as foreign. When the language gulf is deep enough to require translation, that translation is always imperfect and all spectators know it. At the very least, they see the reduction of the subtitles or register the lack of lip-synch. Advocates of the domesticating translation often say that the best translation is one that reads as though it was written in the local tongue. Indeed, translations of written texts can be crafted in such a manner; they can effect something close to a perfect substitution or displacement; exceptional moments—whether planned of serendipitous—are labeled "culture bumps" or "the remainder."[6] By way of contrast, I contend that moving image translation inevitably sports the bumps of a jeep trail, and is flooded by so much remainder that we should probably come up with a different term. Subtitles and dubs, even at their finest, hold something in common with the rocky translation of the instruction manual for a cheap VCR from China: they are legible, but inescapably foreign.

Language exerts a particular, delimiting pressure on cinema. Language, combined with visual signs like gesture, physiognomy, and billboards, marks a film as foreign. This delimiting pressure is what makes translation an instrumental mechanism for prophylactic measures like economic protectionism and censorship. It is what drives Hollywood, in its quest for the most massive of markets, to eschew translation for the remaking of perfectly wonderful foreign films—the ultimate free translation (examples include *Queer as Folk* [1999, U.S. version 2000–2005], *Shall We Dance* [1996, U.S. version 2004], *The Ring* [1998, U.S. version 2002], and the like). Although some viewers run from the foreign film, others find themselves deeply attracted to the pleasures awaiting them there. As Koichi Iwabuchi would put it, foreign films have the "cultural odor" of their country of origin, and scents can be anything from fetid to fragrant.[7]

For all the global developments in the world of film and television, the moving image is inexorably marked by Babel. Hollywood stars and American visions of the good life may threaten to displace local cultures into McWorld. However, as Miriam Hansen points out, this displacement can also dislodge constrictive social and gender roles at local sites. What's more, as each of the subsequent chapters demonstrate, any time translation enters the motion picture, a negotiation process begins with the translator and ends with the spectators. Cazdyn points to the place and potential of art in this paradoxical situation:

> The unevenness of the different levels of the social formation produces one of the great contradictions of our time: between the persistent power of residual national forms and the emerging influence of transnational ones. The force of this contradiction paralyzes our capacity to exist squarely in either dimension. Rather, we exist dead-centre in the contradiction and must wait for the movement of history (which is based on both our individual acts and its own structural logic) to transform the situation... Yet socio-political limits and contradictions always presuppose aesthetic possibilities and solutions. The aesthetic, in other words, offers a realm within which formal escapes are posed— however much these experiments might never directly engage the problem at hand.[8]

Cazdyn argues that one of these experiments is CNN's "running sub-title," the pastiche of news crawling across the bottom of the screen on cable news networks in the United States. He contrasts the multiple temporalities and complex articulation of text, voice, and photoelectronic imagery in moments of crisis, such as 9/11, with the straightforward subtitling of the controversial Osama bin Laden tape produced by the Pentagon. Cazdyn is particularly interested in the running subtitle as a symptom, unconsciously produced, of grappling with the paradoxes of globalization. However, we must note that his running subtitle is monolingual.[9] How the language difference raking the globe fits into his argument is left unclear.

This book is my attempt to write film history in that sweet spot Cazdyn identifies, that dead-center position between the "persistent power of residual national forms and the emerging influence of transnational ones." While never losing sight of aesthetic potentialities, I emphasize language and its translation. In the pages that follow I will examine how the reading processes of both translators and spectators are hybrid, something most readily visible in the interstitial spaces of diasporic communities, but ultimately true of all foreign film audiences. Reception may be directed, but it is never unified, nor will it be identical to Hollywood's domestic reception context.

The question then becomes, how do translators direct reception? What is their role in this global traffic system? What should or can their role be? Helmut Lethen points out that intellectuals in Weimar Germany were equally fond of the trope of "traffic." In 1924, Helmut Plessner contrasted the imperial era's suffocating community and attachment to hierarchy with Weimar society's "open system of traffic among unconnected individuals."[10] The New Objectivity writers such as Bertolt Brecht, Carl Schmitt, Ernst Jünger, and Walter Benjamin discovered a pleasurable egalitarianism in the rush of movement through spaces like Alexanderplatz. In contrast to the warm communitarianism of before, people now had to be civil to make it work, negotiating their spatial relationships within the anonymity of the public sphere. Among the Weimar traffic motifs, the most compelling is Siegfried Kracauer's description of a taxi driver catching the eye of a cop directing traffic:

> It is scarcely possible to measure how fleetingly the greeting is accomplished. The policeman is occupied with difficult arm movements, which he must execute according to rigorously standardized stipulations. The

driver, let us call him A., must divide his attention between the steering wheel and the official arm movements of the policeman ... What connects the driver with the traffic police is the constant utilization of the roadways for the sake of the generality of traffic. These two categories of work contribute more to maintaining the flow than any others.[11]

In this image of traffic, the state's police force has transformed into a dispersion of traffic cops, interacting with private drivers in a new form of communication. Kracauer captures the mode of being in urban encounters, which he and other New Objectivity intellectuals and artists associated with regulated flow and civil conduct. In his book *Cool Conduct* Lethen argues that this is the way these vulnerable intellectuals reacted to the suffocating communitarianism and hierarchy of the Wilhelmine era, while dealing with the interwar period's social and political crises—traffic navigated by an "armored individual." In contrast, my model of traffic works against armoring, particularly because such cool conduct in an intercultural and interlinguistic context invariably involves the more proactive violence of domestication. Indeed, this study zeros in on historical and emerging circuits of traffic that demand contact. In short, I celebrate the nonlethal collision—the equivalent of a linguistic fender bender.

Translation provides a special perch from which to view the global circulation of moving image media, of images on the move. All traffic in the film world is subject to myriad strategies to regulate movement. The most overt of these are inscribed in the legal system through tariffs, taxes, and censorship. However, much of this book is devoted to uncovering the way in which translation also regulates traffic through literary conventions, domestic cultural norms, and even language itself. As the nexus of transnational traffic, translation reveals the *inter*action at play, the negotiation of meaning and all it implies: appropriation, affect, diversion, rejection, embrace. I propose approaches to translation that embody the hybridity in this contradictory social formation of national cinemas and transnational traffic. These are "abusive translations" by translators with attitude that allow reception possibilities to proliferate.

Sub versus Dub

Although this book will attend to many aspects of film translation, subtitling and dubbing will be a major concern. It is likely that no one has ever come away from a foreign film admiring the translation. *Variety*'s Tom Rowe provides a typical, if crude, sentiment: "The meanest man in the world was the guy who said, 'I'm goin' home now, and if dinner ain't ready, I'm gonna beat my wife. And if it is ready, I ain't gonna eat it.' In the film biz, 'dubbing' is the wife."[12] As Rowe exemplifies, subtitling or dubbing attracts comment only when it inspires a desire for reciprocal violence, a revenge for the text in the face of its corruption; for, as we shall see in chapters 5 and 6, most spectators are quick to grudgingly champion one while disparaging the other, but dubbing and subtitling share one thing in common: widespread corruption.

Interestingly enough, one man's corruption tends to be another's pure-felt contact with the foreign original. At least this is what is suggested by the endurance of the sub versus dub debate. There is little trace of this disagreement among film aficionados in the prewar era, although, strictly speaking, the debate sinks its roots in the chaos of the talkie era, which we will explore in detail in chapter 4.[13]

The debate in the United States really seems to heat up in the 1950s with the rise of the auteur-driven art film and the explosive growth of television, with its insatiable hunger for moving image content. It appears that the first mainstream dubbed release in the United States was *Bitter Rice* (*Riso amaro*, 1949) with Silvano Morgano. An experiment to appeal to viewers who found subtitles annoying, it proved a big hit and brought in patrons who usually avoided foreign films. Across the Pacific in Japan, dubbing started out for children's shows like *Superman* and animation; however, when they dubbed *I Love Lucy* and *Alfred Hitchcock Presents* in 1957, the first post-talkies sub versus dub debate began and it fell into a familiar pattern.[14] The basic positions in both places were simple, and nicely summed up by this quote from a sub versus dub Web site: "Intellectuals, who love to hang breathlessly on the subtle supra-segmental vocal inflections, even of languages they don't understand, like films in the original language. Clods, like me—people who just want to enjoy the film and who don't want to bounce their eyeballs constantly up and down from picture to subtitle to picture to subtitle—generally like their films dubbed."[15] Many years before this and not long after the debate began in the United States, a writer from "the other side" sent this less humorous letter to the editor of the *New York Times:*

> Some despot in the upper echelons of the imported film industry has apparently decreed that pictures in languages other than English may be shown in the original with printed subtitles on the film only in first-run Manhattan theaters. This same tyrant has at the same time ruled that

when these films are screened for us yokels in the neighborhood houses or the suburbs, the sound-track and the subtitles must be ruthlessly erased and the original dialogue replaced with English spoken by an American cast reading from a script in which great ingenuity—but an appalling lack of creative imagination—has been exercised to match the original cast's lip movements... [he gives many examples of many sins] For those of us who retain a little of our high school or college French, German, Spanish or Italian, an occasional good foreign film used to bring values over and above its function as entertainment. There was the challenging sense of first-hand contact with another culture. There was a stimulating and painless form of educational refresher. The dubbed versions give us none of these while, at the same time, perpetrating a most sickening form of artistic vandalism.[16]

Obviously, a class dimension underlies these two examples. One aspect of the foreign film market in English-language contexts is its diminutive size. While the vast majority of national cinemas have always been dominated by foreign-language imports, the United States, the United Kingdom, and Australia show mostly English-language films. Because these audiences are inclined to purchase tickets for Hollywood films, foreign-language film audiences tend to be elite and well educated. Proponents of dubbing invariably emphasize this class dimension.[17]

This was certainly true for the most famous champion of dubbing, Bosley Crowther. He served as a film critic for the *New York Times* in the 1950s and 1960s, precisely when the foreign film enjoyed an air of prestige thanks to the international success of such directors as Kurosawa, Godard, and Fellini. These figures were celebrated as "auteurs," granting privileged authorship to their collectively created work by virtue of having left their personal stamp on their films. Therefore, it is no wonder that the issue of translation came to the fore, as the translator obviously mediated the genius of the auteur and implicitly competed for the authorship of a film. Crowther initially wrote about the merits of subtitling, but made a public volte-face in 1960 and, in the words of Paul Rotha, "began a one-man vendetta, quite illogically, on behalf of dubbed films as opposed to sub-titled ones."[18] Pointing to the increasingly complex use of language in the dense scripts of directors such as Ingmar Bergman, Crowther argued,

the English subtitle is itself a thoroughly inartistic thing, when you come right down to thinking hard about it; [the majority of American people] are compelled to accept a mechanism that inadequately and often ineloquently imparts what should be a very important element of the communication in a talking film ... Now that the medium of motion pictures is becoming more internationalized, more eclectic in its expansion across geographical, artistic and commercial lines, it is foolish to hobble expression with an old device that was mainly contrived as a convenience to save the cost of dubbing foreign-language films when they had limited appeal. Now that the American market is crying out for more and varied films and more international producers are seeking wider scope for their films, it is particularly foolish to saddle the foreign product with an obsolete device ... It is time we abandon the somewhat specious and even snobbish notion that foreign-language films (some of which have even been dubbed in their own language!) are linguistically inviolable. Let's give the general audience a chance to hear what they are saying. Subtitles must go![19]

Crowther's article, which took its title from the last sentence of this quote, provoked a firestorm of criticism, but he refused to back down. There were scandalized responses in the letters to the editors, and the debate spilled into the theaters. Stanley Kauffman, the equally powerful critic for the *New Republic,* launched a counterattack: "If he had written his article 30 years ago and if it had succeeded in its purpose, I would never have heard the voices of Louis Jouvet, Raimu, Edwige Feuillère, Shimura Takashi, Vittorio De Sica, and Victor Sjöström ... Certainly, too, I prefer to see Miss Bardot's bosom without typographic obscuration. But the subtitle gives you the gist of the dialogue and allows you to enjoy the actor's whole performance."[20]

Over the years, Crowther continued to counter these critiques and give nuance to his position. He analyzed the differences between the dubbed and subbed versions of the same film. He compared the irregular flow and semiotic impoverishment of subtitles to the intertitles of the silent era. Advocating the use of highly skilled actors whose voices matched their characters' type and body build, he noted how dubbing allowed viewers to concentrate on the visual aspects of performance and celebrated dubbing's liberation of the eye from the edge of the frame. He suggested that subtitles turn the mass of Americans away from films they would otherwise flock to, and dismissed many advocates of subtitling as elitists. And he argued that one reason people dislike dubbing is that they have never seen a masterful one.

On the last two points, Crowther was particularly perceptive. In the postwar era, foreign film distributors dub when they strive to compete with Hollywood for the mass market, while the core audience for such films almost invariably demands subtitles. In this respect, the box-office and critical success of Ang Lee's *Crouching Tiger, Hidden Dragon* (2000) is revealing. This was perceived to be a historic exception to the rule that a subtitled film could never be a popular success, let alone a block-buster; it seemed to herald a new era in translation practice. However, no subtitled film has followed in its wake. Furthermore, it is notable that, for explicitly commercial reasons, the DVD contained a dubbed version in additional to the original subtitles.

At the same time, there is Crowther's assertion that few lovers of sub-titles have ever seen an accomplished translation using the dubbing method, and here again *Crouching Tiger, Hidden Dragon* is instructive. The DVD's translation was undertaken by Ang Lee and the film's co-screenwriter James Shamus. Great care went into every aspect of the process, from translation to performance, and the bilingual stars per-formed their own English lines. If all dubbings were this superb, this finely crafted, the subbing versus dubbing debate would likely play out in unpredictable ways.

However, most screenwriters and directors never participate in the translation of their work. The film's producers take responsibility for supervision, when it happens at all. In the majority of translations, the distributors (who generally see films and television more as product than art) and their translators take total control and typically cut, censor, and revise the original text to suit local cultural whims and mores. When this kind of revision emerges into public view in the United States, it is usually when the distributors and their translators are gloating about their skills in tailoring the original film to "American sensibilities."[21] This appears to be the situation in many parts of the world.

It would be a mistake to assume that the translation of subtitles is in-variably more refined or rigorous. As I will argue in chapter 5, a subtitled film may grant access to the original aural universe of the text, but this does not necessarily indicate that the translation avoids domesticating moves, or even that an admirable amount of effort or intelligence went into the process. The other problems with subtitles are simple to see. In an article citing Crowther, but championing subtitling, *New York Times* critic Vincent Canby wrote in 1983:

It is undeniable that subtitles alter our perception of any film, which becomes a kind of high-class comic book with sound effects, something to be read while looking at the pictures. Subtitles can shield us from certain banalities as often as they destroy the subtleties. They also distort the image, cluttering the bottom of every shot with strings of words that not only obscure a substantial portion of the frame, but also prevent us from seeing much of what is in that part of the frame not scribbled on.[22]

This is to say that the conception of translation undergirding the practices of dubbing and subtitling is essentially the same, but inflected differently across the globe. In an article comparing British, Flemish, and German versions of Gabriel Axel's *Babettes Gæstebud* (1987), Egil Törnqvist comes close to relativizing subbing and dubbing by arguing that "both systems have their advantages and disadvantages." However, in his concluding paragraph he suddenly comes down on the side of subtitling: "For all things considered, subtitling has two fundamental advantages compared to dubbing: it shows respect for the art of acting, and it counteracts linguistic and cultural isolation. For once, economic interests harmonize with aesthetic and ideological considerations."[23] Although I admire Törnqvist's open mind, especially regarding dubbing, his essay teeters on logic oblivious to the value systems generating his "commonsense" conclusion. For example, it can easily be argued that a careful and skillful dubbing pays more respect to the craft of the actor, and that subtitling does not necessarily liberate us from cultural isolation. And here we should return to Bosley Crowther for some sage advice:

I urge that dubbing be faced up to as an evolutionary mechanical method, comparable to the innovation of sound, and required by critics and public to be as proficient as possible. True, I do take the position that dubbing can be done so artfully that, as a means for conveying verbal content, it may be superior to the also inconsistent and sometimes more disconcerting device of English subtitles. There is an esthetic issue here that needs to be discussed in a more sophisticated way.[24]

This is precisely a major aim of this book. In the following chapters, I hope to confound the logic of the sub versus dub debate. I will demonstrate how subtitles produce a new text, offer limited access to the original, and the translation itself is usually domesticating. As for dubbing, it is far closer to subtitling than one would think and offers distinct advantages that are not readily apparent. Furthermore, the resistance to one or the other is culturally informed and people can change preferences with training. Both require new forms of translation, which ultimately demand new translations of old films as well. Indeed, the recent retranslation of old films for DVD (Figure 1), evidence of new modes of subtitling, examples of superb dubbings like *Crouching Tiger, Hidden Dragon*, and the DVD's invitation to critically compare and analyze multiple translations, all intimate changes in our midst. To the extent that skilled translators disregard conventional practices and creatively work through translation problems—both typical ones and those arising from the specificities of dubbing and subtitling—the outlook and possibilities for moving image translation are both hopeful and intriguing. We appear to be entering a new era in the history of film translation.

Fans and Scholars/Misprision and Metaphor

For the time being, spectators will most likely continue to lock away translators in the darkest spaces of the film world, letting them out only to berate them. Whenever I present this work, a large segment of my audience invariably trots out their favorite examples of misprision, or mistranslation. They take perverse pleasure in committing the more delicious mistakes to memory, waiting for an opportune moment to share them. As Mike Nowak points out, bad translations can be delightfully "disterbing"[25] (Figure 2). We can actually trace this fun back to the silent era when early film critics ridiculed sloppy intertitles.[26] It would seem as though some cataloging of misprision is called for here, so as not to incur the wrath of the reader. So here you go—some red meat found on an Internet shrine devoted to bad subtitling in Chinese movies. Get it out of your system:

> "Beat him out of recognizable shape!" *Police Story 2* (*Ging chaat goo si juk jaap,* dir. Jackie Chan, 1988)
> "That may disarray my intestines." *Eastern Condors* (*Dung fong tuk ying,* dir. Sammo Hung, 1986)
> "Don't come back forever." *Comrades, Almost a Love Story* (*Tian mi mi,* dir. Peter Chan, 1996)
> "It takes turn to tango." *Once a Thief* (*Zong heng si hai,* dir. John Woo, 1990)
> "Are you painful?" *1941 Hong Kong on Fire* (*Xiang Gang lun xian,* dir. Chin Man Kei, 1995)
> "Be careful of your nostral hair." *Forbidden City Cop* (*Daai laap mat taam 008,* dir. Stephen Chow and Vincent Kok, 1996)

"You two must be te steaming dollops he Tree Men that grew after
   my fertilization." *The Eight Hilarious Gods* (*Siu baa sin,* dir. Jeffrey
   Chiang, 1994)
"My brother is not easy to deal with, he is tear and I have mucus." *Tiger
   on Beat* (*Lo foo chut gang,* dir. Liu Chia-Liang, 1988)
"Fat head! Look at you! You're full of cholesterol." *Diabolical Erroneous
   Monk* (n.d.)[27]

Admittedly good fun, however, this list does not take us far. I am
interested in misprision primarily to the extent that it is semiotically or
aesthetically productive. This will be a major concern of chapter 2 on the
translation of theory. As for the examples above, they are typical and
fundamentally uninteresting. However, one aspect intrigues, and that is
the camp attitude driving their collection and online publishing. This is
a peculiar subculture among collectors of misprision and explicitly linked
to the fandom surrounding Hong Kong cinema and its love of the ado-
lescent pratfalls, spectacular violence, and bathroom humor of the former
colony's cinema. Stefan Hammond dubbed the mistakes "hex errors," a
term borrowed from computer programming referring to glitches where
"something goes in one way and comes out the other."[28] Note the ambivalence built into this camp appropriation. It conveys a will to dominate, a cultural arrogance, but all the while laced with a twisted and wink-
ing respect. Here mistranslation offers an entry point for exploring the
meaning released by dumb mistakes and, ultimately, this particular community's relationship to the foreign.

By now my own positioning should be fairly clear. Coming from film
studies, I am primarily interested in the ideological and aesthetic issues
connected to translation practice. The routes I take to address these problems involve everything from industrial history to theoretically driven
close textual analysis. This puts me in a particularly interdisciplinary,
but readily identifiable, camp within translation studies. The study of
translation goes back two millennia. Much of the key writing came from
introductions to translations, making it a field of study where theory
and practice are intimately and inextricably intertwined. At the same
time, when translation studies coalesced as an academic institution in the
last few decades, it has been predominantly social-scientific or practice-
oriented. This explains why, although there has been enough work produced on film translation to fill a book-length bibliography, few articles

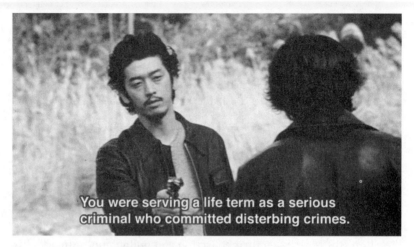

Figure 2. *Versus* (2000): bad subtitles can be disterbing.

ask the questions that draw me to the topic. In the most general sense, my disciplinary home focuses on how films make meaning, and for a global audience riven by difference.

Film studies has, at least since Eisenstein in the 1920s, always been cognizant of the fact that inquiry into narrative form cannot be divorced from questions of power. For this reason, the translation scholars I identify with most closely are those who look at the role translation played in empire building, such as Tejaswini Niranjana, Eric Cheyfitz, Douglas Robinson, Lydia Liu, and Vicente Rafael—scholars who may feel as little kinship to academic translation studies as I do.[29] As with film studies, much of this work is deeply indebted to poststructuralism. I have also found inspiration in the writings of George Steinar, Lawrence Venuti, and Antoine Berman, who reread the German Romantics and Benjamin to argue for a translation approach that respects the foreign and integrates difference into translated textuality.[30]

Film studies itself has had little to say about translation, this despite having regularly deployed a film-as-language metaphor throughout most of its history. Vachel Lindsay compared film to hieroglyphs in his 1916 *Art of the Motion Picture* to argue that film embodied a kind of visual Esperanto.[31] Years later, Christian Metz and other cinema semioticians brought the language metaphor to its apotheosis in 1970s screen theory. Subsequent scholarship critiqued screen theory's reliance on a monolithic spectator by emphasizing the radical heterogeneity of the reception context. Much of this latter work studied interstitial spaces such as immigrant communities and, curiously enough, these scholars often refined the language metaphor by focusing on translation.

For example, Miriam Hansen's influential work on vernacular modernism examines how silent cinema offered a "sensory-reflexive horizon" for the dizzyingly complex experience of modernity. Unlike a tradition of film study going back to Lindsay, she argues that Hollywood cinema and its continuity system of narration succeeded because it was an "idiom" that meant different things to different people—both domestically and internationally. American cinema dominated most national cinemas of the world since World War I, and certainly acted as a homogenizing force complicit with mass consumer capitalism. At the same time, Hansen points out that it also "challenged prevailing social and sexual arrangements and advanced new possibilities of identity and cultural styles."[32] She also points to how the reception context exerted pressure on the films themselves, through "censorship, alternative endings, marketing, and programming practices, not to mention subtitling and dubbing." She asserts, "To write the international history of classical American cinema, therefore, is a matter of tracing not just its mechanism of standardization and hegemony (screen theory + neoformalism) but also the diversity of ways in which this cinema was translated and reconfigured in both local and translocal contexts of reception."[33]

This constitutes a central thread of the book in hand, which examines the film translation practices of every era, as well as extra-cinematic forms such as interpretation and publishing. However, notice how Hansen adds the two standard mechanisms of interlinguistic traffic, subbing and dubbing, only as an afterthought, and for her, *translated* and *reconfigured* are basically homologous. There is a vast and enormously exciting literature in film studies built on the metaphor "cultural translation"— what Hamid Naficy has called "accented cinema."[34] All these authors recognize the centrality of actual translation practices, yet for some reason few give it sustained and nuanced attention. I see my own project as picking up where they left off. That is why I offer this nod in their direction before striking out on my own.

The Mystic Translation Machine

Walter Wanger was a Hollywood producer of note. In 1939, he wrote, "Here is a fact worth pondering. No one forces these pictures on any public. Weary feet carry patrons to the box offices. Millions of hands of

every hue extend clutched earnings. Every tongue—outdoing Babel—
says for American pictures, 'Two tickets, please.'"[35] This quote comes
just after an impressive bit of math: the United States exports roughly
six hundred films a year, with each film averaging about two hundred
prints. That means that 120,000 "American ambassadors" set out for
every region of the world yearly. For Wanger, American cinema "outdoes
Babel" by virtue of being entertaining, plain and simple. We will see
how it is, in fact, rather more complex than this. Throughout this book
I will emphasize the specificities of film translation. One of the key aspects will be the system of narration identified with Hollywood. The
chapter on silent cinema will examine its emergence in American film
and its swift proliferation across national and linguistic borders. Essentially, it is a form of narration that strives for a realism built on legibility,
where time and space are linear and homogeneous. Nothing is out of
place; anything appearing in the film is motivated by the story, or allowed
in through a complex apparatus of rules. Intertitles, for example, were
utterly foreign to the silent film's diegesis—the world of the story—but
were made acceptable through an incrementally changing set of conventions that regulated their every aspect.

This approach to cinematic narration met novel challenges with the
introduction of sound and the language difference it reinserted into the
cinema. Both the subtitle and the imperfect sync of dubbing were as
potentially disruptive to diegetic illusion as intertitles. Over the years,
filmmakers imagined a variety of ways to avoid them altogether, when
foreign characters appear in a film or when characters travel to foreign
settings. We see this strategy in nascent form in Josef von Sternberg's *Blue
Angel* (*Der Blaue Engel,* 1930; English version 1931). This was produced
in both German and English with the same actors on the same sets, a
phenomenon examined in depth in chapter 4. With its German story,
the German-language version was unproblematic; however, how could
all the foreign language be accounted for in the English version? Von
Sternberg provides the motivation—the justification of its inclusion in
the diegesis—by converting the class into an English lesson and putting
the line "Speak my language" into the mouth of Marlene Dietrich. Shortly
thereafter, filmmakers would stop worrying about motivating the switch
through such diegetic devices in the screenplay. As Ella Shohat and Robert
Stam suggest (in a quote that effortlessly reveals the arrogance of Wanger's
enthusiastic humanism), "Hollywood proposed to tell not only its own

stories, but also those of other nations, and not only to Americans but also to the other nations themselves, and always in English. In Cecil B. DeMille epics, both the ancient Egyptians and the Israelites, not to mention God, speak English."[36]

Thus, by the 1950s, everyone in the world in every era of history speaks English, and diegetic devices designed to motivate and explain away language difference become the domain of science fiction. My favorite example is *Doraemon* (1973, 1979–present), the adorable robot cat from the Japanese TV *anime*. Whenever he meets a foreigner, alien, or caveman, he reaches into his Fibber McGee–like pocket and pulls out his "*honyaku konyaku*"/"translation *konyaku*." This is doubly delightful, as *konyaku* is a block of stiff jelly made from the tuber of *Amorphophallus konjac*, otherwise known for its otherworldly flower as "Devil's Tongue." One also recalls the "Translation Microbes" in *Farscape* (1999–2003) that are inserted into the back of one's brain (and often stumble on metaphors and American slang to interesting effect). However, the most famous diegetic translation device is certainly the Babel Fish from Douglas Adams's *Hitchhiker's Guide to the Galaxy* (TV version: 1981). In one episode, the droll BBC-style narrator explains how they work:

> The Babel Fish is small, yellow, leech-like and probably the oddest thing in the universe. It feeds on brain wave energy, absorbing all unconscious frequencies and then excreting telepathically a matrix formed from the conscious frequencies and nerve signals picked up from the speech centers of the brain, the practical upshot of which is if you stick one in your ear you instantly understand anything said to you in any form of language. The speech you hear decodes the brain wave matrix. Now it is such a bizarrely improbably coincidence that anything so mind-bogglingly useful could evolve purely by chance that many thinkers have come to see it as a final and clinching proof of the non-existence of God ... Meanwhile, the poor Babel Fish, by effectively removing all barriers between communications between different cultures and races, has caused more and bloodier wars than anything else in the history of creation.[37]

Perhaps it is no accident that Adams, Stam, and Shohat point us to the heavens (and Doraemon to hell!). Throughout most of its history, cinema has functioned as a mystical translation machine, making peoples from distant lands transparently comprehensible. We could mark the beginning of this role in the 1930s with the addition of sound to the classical Hollywood continuity style, effectively amplifying its remarkably

Figure 3. A gadget capable of magic from the James Bond film *From Russia with Love* (1963). Sean Connery points to an image-recording machine and says, "Talk into this. Answer my questions—quietly, but clearly." The Japanese subtitle simplifies the utterance and dilutes the paradox of talking into a camera: "I'll record with this. Talk clearly."

powerful ability to fathom other worlds—what filmmaking manuals aptly call the "suspension of disbelief." Thanks to this elegantly simple apparatus of lights, cogs, and lenses, combined with the complex of rules of continuity style narration as described in tomes like the perfectly titled *The Screenwriter's Bible,* billions of people over the last century have ritually bought those tickets and assumed the contemplative position for their out-of-body experiences in the theater.[38] The films they see and hear—whether as practical and matter-of-fact as Zen or as ecstatic and symbolic as Tantra—enable a transcendent experience discontinuous with the usual categories of empty time and contiguous and delimited space. The individual soul is rendered moot as audiences surrender to the foreign on-screen Others whose Babel becomes perfectly legible through the pure language of cinema.

The pleasures made available by the foreign film are difficult to quantify, and just as difficult to account for. They exceed mere narrativization, and invite comparison to the "attractions" of the early cinema. Indeed, Linda Williams has suggested that the popularity of Tom Gunning's concept of the "cinema of attractions" had to do with the way it pointed to aspects of cinema that were dismissed, overlooked or vilified by previous theories of the gaze: "The reason, I suspect, relates not only to the undeniable importance and relevance of this concept to the attractions of early cinema... but also to its ability to point to aspects of spectatorial relations that have been ignored under the dominance of the gaze paradigm and that are perfectly applicable to all forms of spectatorship, not only those early sensations. Gunning's notions of *attraction* and *astonishment* have caught on, in other words, because, in addition to being apt descriptions of early cinema, they describe aspects of all cinema that have also been undervalued in the classical paradigm."[39] The mystic translation machine of cinema taps into these feelings of fascination, astounding us with its ability to transport us to a foreign world with such vivid, palpable immediacy.

When they point out that in Hollywood even God speaks English, Shohat and Stam mean to throw a monkey wrench into the cogs of the mystic translation machine. They remind us that the pleasures and promises of the machine hide certain acts of violence. Adams makes the same point through his paradoxical war imagery, and his parodic rewriting of the philosopher's reductio ad absurdum attack on mysticism. In this light, *Doraemon*'s darker *honyaku konyaku* is more revealing than it appears at first glance.

Laura Marks writes that "The further [a film] travels... the more its meanings become rarefied and distanced from their material origin."[40] Marks is most concerned with how intercultural cinema builds cultural and linguistic difference into the very fabric of the film. Similarly, I will ask how subtitling and dubbing might do the same thing, even (or especially) for mainstream cinemas. In one sense, this is also what the science-fiction creators of *Doraemon, Farscape,* and *Hitchhiker's Guide the Galaxy* were striving for by refusing the Cecil B. DeMille model and building translation into the materiality of their narratives.

Note the way the Babel Fish, *honyaku konyaku,* and translator microbes are all organic tropes. In comparison to the icy cold silicon of *Star Trek*'s combadges or *Star Wars*' C-3PO, they figure the mystical translation machine in warm and lively biological terms.[41] Conferring biological or human qualities to machines has a long history; however, one pertinent and particularly useful example is television. We will continually revisit the innumerable connections between conventional cinematic narrative and translation strategies, but let us end this introduction with the curious dubbing we find on television news. It hints at many issues I will attend to in the following chapters.

Television news is of particular interest because, of all forms of moving image media, its design comes closest to reproducing the scenario of human beings in dialogue. Margaret Morse has parsed the terms of this machine-mediated human exchange in her book *Virtualities*.[42] She points to the uncommon power of the television news format and its global adoption around the world, and asks why, of all the possible ways television producers might have communicated the events of the day, they settled on a hierarchical textuality pivoting around a single person. Everything in the televisual text revolves around the figure of the "anchor," who is invariably charismatic and almost always a man on whom society confers great respect and authority. This anchor is rendered in a highly legible manner, generally seated at a desk and framed in a head-and-shoulders shot. He addresses the viewer—the target, as it were—directly, as if speaking to the viewer across a table, separated only by the transparent glass of the television screen.

From this primary discursive level, the anchor introduces secondary and tertiary levels. Acting as a shifter, he signifies the switch with gestures such as the chair swivel or the head twist. His gestures are accompanied by verbal cues: "And now we turn to our national security reporter, so and so." The reporter thanks the anchor; they may speak to each other directly for a moment, establishing that the reporter is speaking to the anchor and only indirectly to the millions watching their televisions. In other words, while the reporter is also shot in a legible, full-frontal pose and speaks in direct address, *she or he can only address the anchor and not the viewer*. Finally, when the reporter introduces a third level by interviewing a "regular person," this subject is invariably photographed at a 45-degree angle, addressing the offscreen reporter and edited down to an evidentiary sound bite.

Morse demonstrates how these levels represent a *spectrum of discursive authority*, which places the anchor at its undisputed seat of power and control. She notes how the only people on (American) television that can address the viewer directly are the anchor, the sitting president of the United States, and representatives of the corporate sponsors during commercial breaks. At the core of her argument, Morse suggests that humans harbor a deep-seated need to engage other humans. We require and desire experiences of intersubjectivity, and in the modern era these experiences have become increasingly available through machines and in virtual forms. This helps explain why, in the latter half of the twentieth century, television displaced cinema as the most powerful and ubiquitous of these devices.

It is in this complex textual system that televisual voice actors insert themselves to transform television into a translation machine. They either completely erase the original voices of the anchor, reporters, and interviewees, or they hide on subchannels of the audio track, awaiting the viewer's thumb, which can summon them up with a click of the remote control. The typical approach in many contexts is akin to the notorious dubbing styles of certain Eastern European televisual cultures. A single actor speaks over the image, making no attempt to synchronize voice to lips. The delivery is monotone. The genders of the dubber and caster need not correspond. Needless to say, someone had to *choose* to use a monotone, to select a man to voice a woman, and to ignore the gestures on-screen, as well as most of the visual text.

These choices place value on "information" and implicitly discount all other aspects of the exchange of meaning and textual features enabling the transmission of sense. Their passionless delivery and disregard for gesture, sync, and everything occurring on the visual track is symptomatic of the form. This is News. It is the information itself that is important, not the package—"Hear me, but do not listen," says the dubber of TV news. Paradoxical and nonsensical though this may sound, we could also say it is the typical pose of the film world's translators. Whether they stand before an audience at a film festival or leave their trace in the nonsync of dubbing or the visual marks of the subtitle, their basic stance amounts to the quiet assertion, "(You can see me, but) I am invisible." These other translators, most notably subtitlers, play their vanishing act more convincingly. However, they too are both visible and naked. The audience, the critics, and the film scholars obediently avert their gaze (unless mistranslations are too egregious or mistakes too "disterbing"). However, if you shut your eyes and cover your ears, you'll miss the show. It ultimately requires tremendous effort to ignore the translators, no matter how hard they try to hide.

With their inclination toward monotonous nonperformance and their indifference to sync, it would appear that TV news translators are the exception to the rule. Only they refuse to hide and are content with full exposure, perhaps amounting to some kind of reflexivity that refuses and debunks the mysticism of the machine. However, they are ultimately no different. The voice actor = translator of television news tells us, "Hear me, but do not listen; I am legible, but inaudible" through his *performance of sobriety* and dull, dry transmission of meaning.[43] "This happened," is his simple stance. Perhaps it did, but of all the modes of moving image translation, everyone agrees that this is among the most frustrating and obnoxious. This is because he failed to learn the lessons of his source text. Television news represents "what happened" in the elaborate trappings of charismatic, authoritative (and aesthetically pleasing) personalities, gesture, music, spectacular graphics, and multiple levels of discursive power. Simply put, the translator disrupts this fine-tuned system.

The translators of the moving image world disavow their tremendous power over the text. The exposure of this power can have a remarkable effect. For example, in November 2004 the certification of Prime Minister Viktor Yanukovich's dubious victory in the Ukrainian elections was being reported on state television. This was only days after five hundred thousand people demonstrated against the election, and negotiations to resolve the crisis broke down. A translation for the deaf was, as always, provided in a small inset by interpreter Natalia Dimitruk, an important figure in the deaf community as its single and trusted source of news. Ignoring the burgeoning protests over vote rigging, the anchor reported the prime minister's victory. Dimitruk suddenly left the all-powerful anchor's script and signed, "The results announced by the Central Electoral Commission are rigged. Do not believe them."[44] News of Dimitruk's act of resistance incited widespread criticism of state-sponsored journalism and contributed to the onset of the Orange Revolution. Her silent rebellion was controversial among interpreters the world over, some of whom questioned her ethics. We will not shirk these ethical questions in the pages below, especially when it comes to matters of propriety and censorship. For the time being, we simply note how her example indicates the vast power concentrated at the scene of translation, a power in constant circulation but always under a stealthy cloak of mystical invisibility.

Morse enables us to grasp how the textual system we know as television news gives us great and varied pleasure, how it enables economic exchange, how it confers and regulates power, and how it engages human consciousness at the deepest of levels. Likewise, *Cinema Babel* seeks to recognize what happens when such systems cross linguistic frontiers and require the facilitation or the addition of bilingual interlopers. The first two chapters make a case for the far-reaching significance and intricacies of translation within film culture by focusing on the unlikely sites of the film festival and the work of film theory. The frontiers awaiting us beyond the sub versus dub debate will immediately become evident. From there, the two middle chapters turn to the history of film translation. They chart the development of early practices and the prehistory of the contemporary methods of subtitling and dubbing in order to highlight the heterogeneity and complexities that reside in these techniques. In the final two chapters, I switch to a more polemical mode and return to the sub versus dub divide in order to dismantle it. The stakes are high. The situation is bad and getting worse. And what we need are translators who are unruly, not transparently naked. Not sober, but intoxicated—and, as I will argue in the final chapters, positively *abusive*. We want translators with attitude.

CHAPTER ONE

Interpreters with Attitude

The Traders and Traitors in Our Midst

The Panoptic Visibility of the Interpreter

Most spectators probably assume that film translation starts and ends with subbing and dubbing. This book ends there, but begins at a far more expansive place in order to lay out some practical and theoretical groundwork. The first two chapters consider the contributions to film culture made by interpreters and translators of written texts. "Interpreters with Attitude" charts out the wide variety of roles assumed by interpreters at each stage of a film's life: preproduction, principle photography and editing, distribution, and exhibition.

The figure of the interpreter probably appeared shortly after humans acquired speech; millennia later, electronic technologies enabled the speed of translation to accelerate to "simultaneity." The birth of simultaneous interpretation is generally identified with a scene of power: the International Tribunal for the Far East, otherwise known as the Tokyo Trial. The example is fascinating and instructive, providing one looks closely at the material conditions of the translation scene. The theater that hosted the trial, as well as novelist Mishima Yukio's ritual suicide, belonged to the Japanese military, and has been preserved on the grounds of the current Self-Defense Forces headquarters (the equivalent of Japan's Pentagon).

Although not necessarily evident in movies and photographs of the trial, the layout of the court was sideways. The jurors sat along one side of the theater, facing the defendants on the other. Viewers on official business watched from low bleachers before the stage, and the public sat opposite in the balcony. The stand and a bevy of lawyers and clerks were positioned in the middle, converting the conventional auditorium into theater-in-the-round. Naturally, the interpreters were relegated to as peripheral a place as possible, ensconced in plywood boxes at the back of the original stage (see the top of Figure 4).

There is a telling irony hidden in this layout, as this is not an ordinary theater. Backstage, two parallel sets of stairs provide access to the stage. One leads to the back of the stage, where the interpretation booths were installed. Walking up this stairway is a strange experience; the risers are noticeably shorter than usual, and that is because only one person was meant to use them: the diminutive Emperor Hirohito, who presided over military ceremonies from a special spot at the back of the stage. This is to say, the interpreters for the Tokyo Trial sat in the very seat of imperial power.

Although it is unlikely anyone has appreciated the irony of it all, this was surely the most appropriate of seating arrangements. It was those interpreters who sat in the nexus of postwar power as the geopolitical map was being redrawn through an interrogation of both history and high-profile prisoners. However, despite the life-and-death stakes of the interpreters' singular mediating presence, the seating layout was meant to sideline them, to render them invisible.

Lawrence Venuti has forcefully argued that the value of "invisibility" has underwritten English-language translation practice from the eighteenth century to the present. This explains the translator's despised position as mediator in textual traffic, and the discursive feints that render the translator's prose "transparent." Venuti suggests:

> The absence of any linguistic or stylistic peculiarities makes it seem transparent, giving the appearance that it reflects the foreign writer's personality or intention or the essential meaning of the foreign text— the appearance, in other words, that the translation is not in fact a translation, but the "original." The illusion of transparency is an effect of fluent discourse, of the translator's effort to ensure easy readability by adhering to current usage, maintaining continuous syntax, fixing a precise meaning. What is remarkable here is that this illusory effect conceals the numerous conditions under which the translation is made, starting with the translator's crucial intervention in the foreign text. The more fluent the translation, the more invisible the translator, and, presumably, the more visible the writer or meaning of the foreign text.[1]

Figure 4. The Tokyo Trial, considered the first significant use of simultaneous interpretation. The interpreter booths were placed at the back of the main stage (top), the space once reserved exclusively for Emperor Hirohito when he presided over military ceremonies. Photograph courtesy Ulrich Straus and U.S. Signal Corps.

This fluency is enabled through the production of what Barthes called a "readerly text." The translator avoids any literary devices marked by reflexivity, archaicisms, or phonic effects like alliteration, assonance, and rhyme. He or she assumes a coherent authorial intentionality at the heart of the text to be translated. This nugget of coherent and stable sense is recovered by the translator, who then guides it unproblematically through the traffic of the translation process and renders it as natural and self-evident meaning.

This model of translation reigns supreme in much of the world and is closely compatible with the social-scientific thrust of many areas of translation research. Here the study of translation too often naturalizes the values of invisibility through the iterable description of empirical science. Where the researcher ventures gingerly into prescription, it is usually for the sake of pedagogy, disciplining practitioners, and reproducing the model. The conception of language and textuality on which this approach to translation is based has come under fire in recent decades, particularly as translations of Jacques Derrida's and Roland Barthes's writings enabled the rethinking of many disciplines. Here the intention of the author is placed into brackets, and the text and its reader are brought under intense scrutiny. Whatever the author meant, it is always already deferred and slippery. Meaning is never stable or unified and thus is ultimately beyond the control of the author or the translator. The reader may consume a translation and assume that he or she has had unmediated access to some original, pure product; however, this would only be thanks to the fluency strategies adopted by the translator to veil her semiotic labor and remain invisible.

Film studies digested this critique of textuality and language early on, in the late 1960s and 1970s. It brought the analogous transparency strategies of cinematic realism under rigorous critique for the way they tended to naturalize the ideological assumptions imbuing cinema. For some time, it celebrated modernist filmmakers such as Godard, whose writerly texts hampered easy consumption through experimentation and self-reflexivity and demanded an active viewer. These theories themselves came under reevaluation with a new emphasis on the reception context of the reader/viewer.

What sets Venuti's strain of translation theory apart from the early poststructuralist film theory is the invariable fact of foreignness. It is not uncommon for film scholars to invoke the trope of translation to describe the semiotic process of rendering a script or the world into cinematic space and time (for example, documentary as a "translation" of lived reality). However, this deployment of the trope usually disengages the key element of the foreign, in effect reducing language to structures divorced from the cultures and politics they are inextricably embedded in and co-construct. Both Barthes and Venuti are suspicious of the transparent, readerly text, but the latter is also concerned with cultures of reading, the inequalities of languages, and, indeed, the geopolitics of textuality. This explains Venuti's emphasis on foreignizing strategies that render the translator visible, and why he disparages readerly translations as "domesticating."

I will have much more to say about this in subsequent chapters, especially when I turn to the matter of subtitling in chapter 5. However, there are curious ways in which the bodily presence of the interpreter is analogous to the scene of writing. Here, however, difference is made spectacle. Source and target stand face-to-face, but never toe-to-toe because there would not be room for that third body of the interpreter. The mediation of the translator is obvious, as is the deferral of meaning through the temporal delay of the translator's relay. We recognize the "imperfect" mediation of the interpreter. That is why we laugh in *Lost in Translation* (2003) when a director assaults Bill Murray with a barrage of instructions and the interpreter reduces his lengthy utterance to a few curt phrases. "Is that all he said?" asks Murray quizzically.

Things get even more interesting when interpreters show up as characters in dubbed films and translators are forced to transform two source languages into a single target track for the dubbing. The Spanish dubbing of *Tombstone* (1993) resolved this problem with an innovative idea. When an Arizonan interprets between two warring gangs, he talks to the gringos in Castilian Spanish and in a Mexican accent for the gang from over the border.[2] Unlike the literary translator, the interpreter, cinematic or flesh-and-blood, cannot pull a disappearing act. The interpreter is like Claude Raines's invisible man, only she is condemned to committing her treachery swathed in full view, unable to unwrap those strips of cloth that render her visible. So perhaps a more apt comparison is the mummy, that *unheimlich*, living corpse. The text the mummy delivers has a similar undecidability straddling vibrant life and abject death. Everyone is fascinated with the magic that animates the mummy or the invisible man, just as surely as they harbor the desire to destroy them.

Needless to say, this visibility of the translator puts the interpreter in a precarious position. Popular (and many pedagogical) conceptions of interpretation analogize the translator as a machine—a conduit through which meaning cleanly passes from sender to receiver. In recent years, even researchers antagonistic to poststructuralism point to the myriad problems with the conduit metaphor. For example, in his analysis of the Spanish interpretation captured in the television broadcasts of the O. J. Simpson trial, Anthony Pym assails the assumptions behind this model.[3] He points out that people tend to think that interpreters belong to the target language and culture—a natural conclusion in a domesticating discourse—but they actually sit in the nexus of a radically intercultural space. People also assume that interpreters work for people who do not know the source language, but allegiances are complex, and from a different perspective we could say that target institutions provide interpreters to advocate for people and level the linguistic playing field. Furthermore, it is not unusual for participants to know varying degrees of the other's language and still use an interpreter.

A significant shift in the study of interpretation was inspired by the introduction of sociolinguistics, particularly the work on politeness by Erving Goffman.[4] This is the region of linguistics that acknowledges the relevance of politics and power in language use (and curiously cannot own up to the violence of its own commitment to scientific method and value-free description—just look at the discursive gymnastics necessary to defend "natural speech" from the contamination of difference). The strength of sociolinguistics is its thoroughgoing attention to the dynamics of power in linguistic interaction. Taking a cue from Goffman, students of interpretation began pointing out how the interpreter is anything but a machine or piece of plumbing.[5] Rather, they often run the show by determining turn taking and pacing. In translating dialogue (as opposed to the presentational, one-way flow of conference interpreting), they choose who gets translated when speakers overlap. They can also control the length of utterances through interruption, and even what to stress or what to excise (especially when a speaker starts droning on at excessive length). The translator is thus seen as a present participant and intercultural mediator.

At the same time, this active participation has a flip side. The visibility of the interpreter transforms the translation scene into a panopticon. Interpreters are always under surveillance and they know it. Their intercultural nexus is surging with the flux of power as well, and the translator is caught in the spotlight. Their translation is monitored, often from multiple sides, and they often operate under immense pressure. Mistakes can be singled out and corrected. Participants can address the translator directly, even say things not meant to be translated. It is a precarious position to say the least. Francesco Straniero Sergio notes that in one common interpretation scene of the moving picture world, the rules of the game capitalize on the panopticonic aspects:

> [The interpreter of the television talk show] must be aware that the "text" he or she delivers can become a form of pre-text for the presenter (and other participants) to develop and manipulate—in short, "media-tize"... At the level of register, an interpreter who expresses something in an unmarked language may find it being reformulated by the presenter in a more colloquial and television-friendly way. The interpreter's text may also go beyond the limits of the event itself and become part of the media discourse in general. Not only are interpreters' performances commented on, (mis)quoted, praised and criticized in the press, but their blunders, facial expressions or gestures, individual utterances, un-witting comic or bizarre situations in which they may find themselves, are also re-contextualized into comic TV collages through skillful editing. There are even now comedians who mimic interpreters in satirical programmes. More recently, these events have become more personal, with one comedian in Italy impersonating a popular TV interpreter.[6]

This quote vividly evidences the importance of what sociolinguists have called footing. This refers to the paralinguistic aspects of the inter-pretation scene, and recent research has convincingly shown how this material context bears down on the traffic of meaning. Goffman called footing "the alignment that people take up to each other in face-to-face interaction."[7] It has to do with the gazes, postures, gestures, body lan-guage, tones and volumes of voice, and even the seating arrangements of participants. Although simplistic notions of interpretation see a dyad involving a speaker and listener (with the translator put in brackets that render her magically "invisible"), the analysis of footing reveals a dy-namic, ever-shifting process that involves everyone in the room—and that includes the silent and immobile audience members.

As a counterexample to the television talk show, imagine the common seating arrangement for film festival interpretation. If the translation is consecutive, the speaker is positioned at center stage and the translator is shuttled off to the side, often by the curtains, as if waiting for a large hook to emerge from backstage. If the translation is simultaneous, the translator is literally made invisible, stuck in a box and plugged into a complex electronic apparatus. She wears headphones that pipe the source sound into her ears. She feeds her running translation into a microphone, which sends a signal to a radio transmission box that bathes the theater with the translation. All auditors wear a device in their ears that reconverts the signal to speech. Here we have the translator as networked cyborg. The ideological positioning of these two translators is obvious. It is usually informed by the desire to keep the interpreter invisible—a clean pipeline for the transmission of stable meanings from the genius of the artist to the audience.

In its unquenchable thirst for spectacle, television often turns the footing of the interpretation scene into the carnivalesque (Figure 5). The translator for the news anchor may be trapped in a sub-audio track, but *information* takes a back seat to *situation* in most television. As a television interpreter himself, Straniero Sergio has convincingly written about how the special "lightness" of meaning, the pleasures of slippery communication, set this form of interpretation apart:

Figure 5. Interpreter (left) on Japanese television, translating for an offscreen star from Korea. The host (right) continually jokes and flirts with her, finally leaning over to ask, "OK, how about giving me your phone number later." This is a typical example of the intralingual subtitles of Japanese television since the early 1990s, which always use different colors, fonts, and sizes; by the early 2000s, many were also animated. See also Figure 25.

Talk show interpretation requires a specific job profile and special skills compared not only to conference interpretation but also to other forms of dialogue interpreting . . . A distinctive feature of the talk show, particularly in multiparty settings, is that there is not necessarily a logical or consequential development of the *content.* Topics continually shift, and what counts is the development of the *situation.* It is the latter which gives rhythm to the show and keeps viewers glued to the TV screen. Local attention is focused not so much on propositional as on relational aspects: to cause a reaction, to embarrass someone, etc. . . . No wonder then that broadcasting organizations expect interpreters not just to have the relevant linguistic skills but also to be good "performers."[8]

We can learn a lot from television, despite what elite critics have been saying for decades. The television talk show is hardly a unique form of interpretation. Rather, its rules of discursive interchange release the translator from the strictures of invisibility. Put another way, it takes a scholar to point out that all interpretation involves dynamic participation, even when the rules of their game attempt to restrict the translators to plumbing or cybernetic apparatuses.

In the spirit of unstrapping and flushing out the interpreter, let us look at the life of a film. For the stages of preproduction and principle photography, the storied production of *Tora! Tora! Tora!* (1970) shall exemplify the absolutely essential and remarkably heavy burden shouldered by interpreters for international coproductions. With the completion of a film, the project is handed over to a new set of interpreters. Thanks to the personality cult of the star system and auteurism of fan culture, the interview has a special place in the film world. For this next life stage, we will examine what is probably the most celebrated interview in film history—the remarkable meeting of François Truffaut and Alfred Hitchcock—to find a particularly impressive and instructive instance of interview interpretation. The chapter ends with the last stop films take before their dissemination through local theaters and video decks: the international film festival. It is in the lively context of the festival that the interpreter's contribution is rendered so *visible,* and this visibility in turn raises many of the basic problematics that run through this book.

International Coproductions and the Traitors in Our Midst

Major feature films are remarkably complex undertakings. Adding translation to the mix complicates every aspect of the process. Money, strong personalities, cultural differences, and tight shooting schedules can make for a decidedly unglamorous and potentially explosive situation. Translators that facilitate such coproductions are both powerful and powerless. In this section, I take an extended look at the controversial production of *Tora! Tora! Tora!* (1970) and the translator at the heart of all the production's troubles, Aoyagi Tetsuro. This film provides an excellent example of the wide variety of roles played by translators, as well as a textbook case for the many ways bad interpreters can both precipitate and intensify very expensive problems.

Tora! Tora! Tora! was modeled after *The Longest Day* (1962), another Twentieth-Century Fox film produced by Elmo Williams that was celebrated for its realism. Aside from its spectacular rendering of modern warfare, the film was notable as one of Hollywood's first efforts to let foreign characters speak (subtitled) foreign languages for scenes on the other side of the front lines. On the heels of this success Darryl Zanuck turned to the Pacific War. He would re-create the attack on Pearl Harbor at the same scale, with the same commitment to historical and linguistic accuracy, and hire none other than Kurosawa Akira to direct the Japanese half.

It is clear from the archival record that, for both sides, this project was explicitly about reconciling the relationship of the United States and Japan, two short decades after the occupying forces executed the defendants of the Tokyo Trial. The producers thought a film like this could help people surmount their violent past and inaugurate a new era in the Japanese–American relationship. The equality of their coproduction was a prominent plank of their public relations. A handwritten letter, in English, from Kurosawa Akira to producer Elmo Williams states, "The Americans had thought that the Japanese were completely different from them and much inferior race to them. The Japanese had thought that the Americans were superior people in a country with a background of limitless resources and had a hostile feeling against them. There, however, was nothing different between both countries except the smallest difference of way of thinking. Here was how a big tragedy of Pearl Harbor had happened."[9] These would prove to be, shall we say, famous last words.

The cultural differences and translation problems immediately became apparent during preproduction, but were simply accepted as part of the process. In June 1967, only months after starting the screenwriting, producer Williams wrote Darryl Zanuck, "Working with Orientals is a new experience for me. So far, I have managed to get along. And so

Figure 6. Kurosawa Akira greets producer Elmo Williams at the press conference announcing the coproduction of *Tora! Tora! Tora!* (1970). Photograph courtesy of the Mainichi Newspapers.

far, my education in this direction has reached stage one. This means that I now understand why there is *NO* understanding between the Occident and Oriental peoples, which is an integral part of our story. Therefore, it will be worthwhile going on with the Japanese because the difference in points of view when it reaches the screen will be a plus factor for this film."[10]

It was in this self-consciously open attitude that they began the production. At the same time, language difference was conceived of as a *barrier.* Notes from a story conference between Williams, Kurosawa, and Aoyagi record one participant's assertion: "Don't forget that the Japanese people will have to suffer through subtitled English dialogue. Americans will have to suffer through subtitled Japanese dialogue. Therefore, let us tell as much of our film in the visual medium as possible."[11]

Despite their cognizance of cultural and linguistic difference, both Fox and Kurosawa Productions relied on a single figure to mediate their relationship. Aoyagi Tetsuro was the new general manager of Kurosawa Productions, but in fact he was also the primary translator for *Tora!*

Tora! Tora!'s complicated production. He originally worked in the foreign film division of Toho in New York, and once worked as an assistant director to both Naruse Mikio and Kawashima Yuzo. His father was director Aoyagi Nobuo, a family friend of Kurosawa's going back three decades. Aoyagi's credentials were strong. He had comforting connections with Kurosawa's old studio and old friend, and he was one of the few people in the film world who could operate in both Japanese and English. The deals he brokered for Kurosawa's *Runaway Train* (1985) and *Tora! Tora! Tora!* were proof enough that Aoyagi had skills Kurosawa needed for his entry into international coproductions, as the era of the Japanese studio system was clearly coming to an end.[12]

Writing the scenario in two languages and between writers who could not freely communicate with each other was understandably difficult. Each side took responsibility for the scenes in their own language. Kurosawa began writing in early 1967, when he retreated to a hot spring resort for three months with collaborators Oguni Hideo and Kikushima Ryuzo. In early June they returned to civilization with a 401-page script. Writing on the American side was undertaken by a variety of people, with producers Elmo Williams and Richard Zanuck, studio head Darryl Zanuck, director Richard Fleischer, and screenwriters Larry Forrester and Mitchell Lindman all working on various drafts. By June 1968 they were on their fifteenth version of the script. Each time the script crossed the Pacific, it had to undergo a translation. At one point, Aoyagi sent a memo to his American colleagues describing the elaborate procedure they devised for translating all the writing:

1. I check the story structure first and make a list of scenes order from Scence-1 *[sic]* through the end.
2. Our translators tape-record the entire translation, so we can get the first whole contents quickly by saving hand-writing time.
3. Using two tape recorders simultaneously for reproducing the recorded-tapes, our production staffs put the contents on paper.
4. Then we send the first written script in Japanese back to the translators who worked with recorders to check on paper. An assistant director works on one copy of the same sent back to translators, so the assistant director can very roughly compare your script with Kurosawa's.
5. When our translators complete checking from beginning till the end, we always have two different translators double-check separately and afterwards they exchange each one's material for triple check.

6. Then we send all completed materials to one of our present technical supervisors, Mr. Genda or Mr. Yoshida or Mr. Kobayashi to check anything inaccurate.

7. Then one copy of the completed translation script comes back to our office, then I check the translation completed and precisely checked comparing with your English script and our Japanese script and make a list of differences between your latest script and our last script, then when each one of them who worked on translation agrees with me, on his own responsibility, to send it to Kurosawa, then we have the first meeting on the script from you. Now, once when we have Japanese materials, we have to take the entire procedure just reverse from Japanese into English to send them to you.[13]

Fox was frustrated with the slow pace of this system and complained to Kurosawa Productions. Aoyagi wrote a defensive letter back to producer Elmo Williams, pleading, "Please always be aware that all our correspondences and every single process of the making of 'Tora, Tora, Tora' between Fox and us have been being done in your language, not in our language. It means that our job is always double."[14] Aoyagi was pointing out the obvious, and one could imagine impolitic ways of writing the same thing. Despite their rhetoric of equality and the emphasis on the "co" of the coproduction, Fox displayed the typical arrogance of the hegemonizer in its deferral of the task of translation to the Japanese side. Every sea crossing of the script meant a doubling of the work for the Japanese staff. The Americans expected all communication to be conducted in the comfort of their own tongue. As we will see, the demand for these double crossings was a nearly fatal mistake.

In the course of preproduction, all manner of complications arose. At this stage, timing of the script's utterances was all important, as every minute of running time cost tens of thousands of dollars. This naturally determined what could be rendered on screen. Kurosawa's timing of the script came to three hours and twenty minutes, but Williams clocked it an hour longer. He suspected that linguistic difference might be a factor, that speaking the Japanese sections of his English-language script might actually take less time. But he cut the script unilaterally all the same.

Williams was also tired of the constant changes demanded by Kurosawa but was going out of his way to give the director his creative space and the benefit of the doubt. In his weekly report to the studio executives, he mulled over the issue of equivalency: "Monday—ready to despair. Two weeks ago, Tetsuo sent us what he called the *final* markings for our modified aircraft. Today we receive yet another final batch of instructions for the painting of the aircraft, and of course they differ from the ones we received earlier. Somehow I don't think final in Japanese means the same as it does in English."[15] All of these problems were eventually surmounted, and in early December 1968 they began principle photography—"*kuranku in*" as it is nontranslated into Japanese.

Zanuck and Williams watched Kurosawa start production at the Toei Studios in Kyoto. He immediately fell behind schedule, and there were certain irregularities that they both attributed to Kurosawa's perfectionism. Still, when they saw him shooting, they were impressed that he seemed to be getting exactly what he wanted. Worried that Kurosawa's apparent nervousness might have something to do with the famous Hollywood mogul looking over his shoulder, Zanuck retreated to Hollywood and Williams flew to Honolulu, where Richard Fleischer's crew was in the midst of the complicated battle scenes at Pearl Harbor. However, reports to Williams immediately signaled trouble in Kyoto. In mid-December the Japanese crew walked off the set, staging a strike to protest their mistreatment by Kurosawa. The American line producer phoned Williams to report that Kurosawa wasn't acting "normal," forcing Williams to return to Kyoto. "To Japan," he wrote in his diary. "It's supposed to be a quaint place. I always wanted to go there!!!"[16]

Upon arrival, Williams found chaos. He immediately negotiated a truce between Kurosawa and his crew. In an attempt to save the production and protect Kurosawa's health, he brought in director Sato Masamichi to act as Kurosawa's assistant. The young director would set the lights and cameras in the morning so that Kurosawa could go straight to shooting and soften the stress of production. It worked for a day or two before Kurosawa resumed his mystifying antics.

On December 24, Fox announced that Kurosawa was ill and would have to be replaced by a new director.

Kurosawa's departure from the production "for medical reasons" was announced at a press conference the same day. In his interpretation for the Japanese press, Aoyagi used the word *hossa* three times to describe Kurosawa's condition. He explained that it was a translation from the materials Fox relayed to Kurosawa Productions. *Hossa* refers not to a specific clinical condition, but "fit, spasm, attack, or stroke." This was probably a conveniently vague term designed to protect Kurosawa from what should be a private matter. However, that very vagueness allowed journalists giving Kurosawa the benefit of the doubt an opening to question the seriousness of his illness and assume the worst about Fox. This set the tone of all subsequent histories of the incident. After completing more archival research and interviews than any other writer to date, Stuart Galbraith III concludes, "In retrospect, Kurosawa was no more demanding than most great artists."[17] This is actually what the Japanese refer to as a *teisetsu*, or "fixed explanation," that goes back to the initial scandal.

In an interview given at the height of the incident, assistant director Sato gave his own take on the situation: "Kurosawa himself faced an intense dilemma between his intent as producer for Kurosawa Productions to 'finish the first true Japanese–American co-production according to the American way of doing things,' and his position to 'absolutely work at his own pace as an independent director.'"[18] And, as Sato saw it, the independent director side won. This became the commonsense explanation in the film world for what happened. The auteur's dedication to film art at all costs and the Hollywood penchant for rationalization of production came to loggerheads on the Toei set.

The media was clearly operating under the assumption that the imprecision of *hossa* was a code word for "firing." Kurosawa was being let go for being his usual angrily demanding and impeccably precise self. Aoyagi amplified these suspicions over the question of *hossa*'s translation. A journalist from the English-language *Yomiuri News* asked Aoyagi the term Fox used in their original documents. He told her that his secretary was gone for the day, so she should call back on Monday. When she called on Monday, he told her to come to his office that afternoon. When she came to his office, he told her the documents were in Kyoto somewhere so there was nothing he could say.[19] This kind of behavior—coming from someone who seemed to remember everything *but* the illness that supposedly started it all—only fed the fires. In point of fact, Kurosawa had been fired, but Fox was careful not to reveal the specifics behind the story for fear of damaging Kurosawa's reputation. At the same time, Kurosawa's crew kept to Sato's line about cultural and methodological differences, probably out of either loyalty to the great director or dread of his famous temper.[20]

However, in preparation for potential lawsuits and insurance claims, Williams made a painstakingly careful record of Kurosawa's behavior on the set. The insurance adjusters were the first historians here. The problems seemed to start when a chandelier fell onto the set and very nearly hit the director. From that moment on, Kurosawa began displaying signs of paranoia. He was sure someone on the crew was out to kill him, and suddenly appeared with eight armed bodyguards. They were stationed outside the set or his hotel room, and even escorted him to the hotel bath. He once asked Aoyagi to call the prime minister of Japan to complain about the number of police in Kyoto. He asked Fox for money to put bulletproof glass into his car, and then buy a 50 percent interest in Toei so that he could wall off his half the studio to ensure his safety. This was the golden age of *yakuza* gangster films at Toei, and all the rough-looking extras walking around the lot with shades and punch-bowl perms apparently unnerved Kurosawa.

On the set, Kurosawa's behavior was often inexplicable and excessively abusive by any standards. He forced everyone to wear Kurosawa Productions jackets, and when one crew member forgot his jacket at lunch he was immediately fired. When he disapproved of the way the clapper boy did his job, Kurosawa beat him with a roll of rice paper. Kurosawa handed the roll to an assistant and ordered him to beat the entire crew; when the man refused, Kurosawa fired him. At night he was drinking, and had been thrown out of three Kyoto hotels for tearing his rooms up.

The auteur legends favored by film buffs often have to do with directors like Kurosawa and Visconti's penchant for creating a realistic atmosphere for the actors. Visconti, for example, famously placed costumes into drawers that were never opened. Kurosawa brought this to a new level for *Tora! Tora! Tora!*, one that would seem parodic (or the creativity of a great artist!) if it were not so serious a situation. For one thing, he demanded set dressing for areas that would never be photographed, but this was to be expected from any self-respecting auteur. He also blew up when he found a stack of twenty letters where ten were addressed to the character and the rest were props from a *yakuza* film. Only the top two were visible to the camera and none were legible on film, but he lectured the crew for two hours about carelessness and then fired three assistants.[21] One day Kurosawa decided the dressing room for the actor playing General Yamamoto was shabby and thus inappropriate, so he had the set for the general's bedroom dismantled, reconstructed in the actor's dressing room, and then ordered a replacement set built. He also

pronounced the floors unworthy of Yamamoto and ordered them car-
peted, including a red carpet that started at the entrance to the building
and ran up four floors to the dressing room. Two days before being fired,
Kurosawa took the auteur mythology of authenticity to heights worthy
of burlesque. In his insurance report, Williams writes:

> When I arrived, I found a large, red carpet laid out in the doorway. A
> fanfare of music was played, and I was asked not to remove my shoes but
> to walk the red carpet to the set. This I did, as an honor guard, dressed in
> sailor uniforms with rifles, etc. were ordered to come to attention even
> though they were standing well off the set where no one could see them,
> and to remain at attention throughout the filming of each take. Eventually,
> nine takes were made before Kurosawa printed one. At this juncture, he
> announced that shooting for the day was over. The guard was brought to
> the entrance of the stage, ordered to attention by Kurosawa, who put on
> his crash helmet and white gloves. He then called Kagitani—Yamamoto—
> and extended a military salute to Yamamoto, then screamed at the honor
> guard and some of his assistants to do the same, everyone snapped to
> attention, saluted, and Kurosawa escorted Kagitani off the set, again
> screamed an order to the honor guard who snapped to attention and
> saluted as Kagitani was helped into his car. Another guard outside the
> studio, dressed as policemen in white helmets, also snapped to attention
> and were ordered to salute. This they did, and they stood at attention
> along with Kurosawa in a salute position as Kagitani drove away. Kuro-
> sawa then repeated the performance by coming back to the stage, called
> a command to the balance of the cast—three naval officers. These were
> Yamamoto's aids [sic] in the scene that had just been filmed. Again
> Kurosawa extended a snappy salute and ordered everyone else to do
> the same. The three naval officers—actors—were escorted off the stage
> and again the guards outside the stage were ordered to salute as they got
> in their car and drove away. Kurosawa then came back to the set and
> cautioned me to wear my white crash helmet and warned me again that
> there was danger from falling lamps, etc.[22]

Naturally, Williams found this all rather odd, but he reported to Zanuck
that they had a good day of filming in any case. However, Williams felt
that Kurosawa stepped over a line the next day (December 23) when he
had the entire crew, even senior technicians, repaint a set because it featured a shrine to the emperor, explaining that the actual battleship crew
from World War II repainted it every week and also that he wanted a
whiter white because it was a space containing the emperor's shrine.
This incident particularly bothered Williams because Kurosawa had

been in the business long enough to know that white photographs as many colors thanks to the characteristics of filters, film stocks, and the color temperatures of lights; it only looks white thanks to postproduction color correction; this was clearly a costly waste of time and technical talent. To make things worse, Kurosawa abruptly ordered the rental of a screen, at great expense to Fox, to cover up the white wall his entire crew had just repainted. When it arrived, he had the entire crew appreciate its artfulness, and then ordered an assistant to send the screen to the imperial palace to ask Hirohito himself if the screen was worthy of being in the same space as the shrine dedicated to him.

Put simply, Kurosawa was courting insanity. But all the while Aoyagi's secret duplicity was as serious a problem.

Williams's production diary indicates that they perceived Aoyagi as a particular concern as early as the fall before photography began. They attributed some of the frictions developing between the Japanese and American crews to him. In November, they reached the point where Williams had to fly Japan to keep things from spinning out of control. He dreaded the trip, especially when one of his location producers told him, "Stan [Goldsmith, producer] expects you to slay Tetsu for a start."[23] When he arrived in Japan, he was shocked to discover that they were farther behind schedule than he had imagined. They were only weeks away from shooting and no sets had been built at Toei's Kyoto studios. The schedule was Aoyagi's responsibility as the Japanese producer. When Williams pressed for an explanation, Aoyagi told him that they still didn't have a contract with Toei finalized—this despite the fact that they had already built a new building at Fox's expense and 75 percent of their crew would come from Toei. When the carpenters held a strike a week later over money, Aoyagi told him that there was still no contract with them. However, for reasons that were never clear to Williams, a Fox lawyer sent to Japan after Kurosawa's departure to sort out the books and mop up the financial mess discovered that Aoyagi did indeed have a contract with Toei Studios. Why he chose to hide that information from Williams remained a mystery to the producer himself.[24]

Aoyagi's position was the result of a new approach to management at Kurosawa Productions. The entire industry was on the cusp of great structural change, as the insular and stable studio system crumbled and left independent production companies and free-agent talent competing for fewer and fewer films. Kurosawa Productions adopted a forward-looking stance that recognized international coproduction as a survival strategy for not just him, but the national cinema itself. As one of the most celebrated directors on the international film scene, Kurosawa was ideally positioned to forge ties with the big money in Hollywood. But he lacked the linguistic ability to do this on his own. He was utterly dependent on the translation skills of someone as green as Aoyagi Tetsuro.

Tsubota Sadahiro, a core member of Kurosawa Productions, was once asked how Aoyagi was as a producer, and he replied, "He was wanting in terms of both knowledge and experience, but had fantastic English."[25] He recalled that everything from Fox, both correspondence and money, went through Aoyagi exclusively. Once when Tsubota opened up a letter from Fox, it was a big to-do.[26] This was a new style of management in Kurosawa Productions, an effect of their new reliance on someone with linguistic skills.

This anecdote reveals the intensity with which Aoyagi protected his domain as producer through an instrumental exploitation of his dual role as translator and producer. As they approached photography, the Americans began to worry about Aoyagi's singular role. In notes to a December 4 meeting, Williams wrote, "I am worried that too many things have to go through Tetsu."[27] When he returned to Japan, he had his own, independent translator sit in on meetings to surveil Aoyagi's translation.

It took longer for Kurosawa to come to this conclusion. He was understandably concerned more about the complex details of rehearsals and photography than the nitty-gritty of money and scheduling. However, it is also likely that he was blinded by his dependency on Aoyagi's interpretation. The rift between the two did not begin until December 27, several days *after* Kurosawa had been let go. Why is uncertain, but Aoyagi was clearly undermining Kurosawa from his powerful position between English and Japanese worlds. Kurosawa wanted to take back the production, even if it meant putting his own money down as a stake in the film's success. Richard Zanuck sent a telegram to Kurosawa Productions announcing a visit to Tokyo on a certain date and a willingness to meet. Aoyagi intercepted the telex and for some reason failed to pass the information on. Zanuck arrived and contacted Kurosawa's office asking if they were going to meet. A suspicious and confused Kurosawa asked his secretary to find out what he wanted. By the time Kurosawa realized what was going on Zanuck had left Japan. Kurosawa's staff tracked down a copy of Zanuck's telex, and found Aoyagi's signature on it. When confronted,

Aoyagi claimed he knew nothing. "What telex?" They handed him the copy. "Oh, that one . . ." Kurosawa started contacting Darryl Zanuck directly. At the very same time, Aoyagi wrote to Williams that "Kurosawa has no intent to make the film with his own money. He recognizes he is sick, and also consents to be replaced by a new director."[28]

The scandal escalated on January 20, 1969, when Aoyagi and two others gave a press conference at which Aoyagi did most of the talking. They announced their resignations from Kurosawa Productions. The following day Kurosawa himself called a press conference to give his side of the story, lambasting Aoyagi. Kurosawa said, "Trusting Aoyagi, who had never worked on even one of my films, was a miscalculation."[29] Journalist Murayama Yoshikuni suggested that the difference in Zanuck's and Kurosawa's approaches was the source of the problem; however, "Aoyagi put on a good face for each side and tried to make his stories for the two consistent, in that peculiarly Japanese way, but he couldn't mend things in the end. I don't think he was malicious from the start, but in the end he was simply too small a person."[30]

Kinema Junpo's Shirai Yoshio said the situation reminded him of Kurosawa's *Rashomon*.[31] He went on to write thirteen lengthy investigative reports about the scandal, yet still ended up with only contradictory stories and countless questions.

Among the most serious were the ones dealing with money. Aoyagi never once showed anyone at Kurosawa Productions their contract with Fox, claiming that an American entertainment lawyer was vetting it. He assured them the lawyer thought the conditions were extraordinary, even by Hollywood standards, but they actually entered production without signing a final contract. Aoyagi had assured Kurosawa that he had the final edit of the film and was "overall director," but when he finally saw the contract in the spring he discovered that Richard Zanuck had the crucial right to the final edit. And because there was no signed contract, the terms of Kurosawa's release had to be negotiated by Fox lawyers. Indeed, when the Fox lawyer arrived to sort out the mess left in Kurosawa's wake, he discovered that Aoyagi had failed to sign contracts with many of the Japanese artists involved.

Even more perplexing, Aoyagi deposited a $600,000 infusion of Fox money into Kurosawa Productions coffers on January 8, 1969, six months after the money arrived and a couple of weeks after Kurosawa left the film.

After Aoyagi quit Kurosawa Productions, he aligned himself with Fox. The situation was complicated. Each side had assumed the other was paying Aoyagi; however, it turned out he had actually forgone a salary to insert his name in the writing credits, probably expecting a perpetual bonanza from the percentage of profits that residuals promised. Concerned about lawsuits and bad press, both of which could destroy their investment at the box office, Williams was not sure what to do. He contacted Zanuck on January 29, saying it was evident they had to get rid of Aoyagi. In early February, he wrote in his production diary:

Another difficult situation is Tetsu. We are in a way stuck with him since he jumped on our side when we broke with Kurosawa. However, no one here in Japan trusts him and Stanley Goldsmith just abhors the idea of having to ask Tetsu for information. So something has to be done about that . . . Another strange phenomena [sic] is that everybody is accusing everybody of lying and cheating. Tetsu, who is known to be devious, said without flicking an eye that "I must say it in all honesty. My people, the Japanese people are not honest. You cannot trust them. They lie. However, I wish they would lie like adults and not like children. What do they take us for, children, to believe their lies that are the lies of children."[32]

As for Kurosawa, he was no less dependent on translation after Aoyagi's departure. He clung to his unreasonable dream of returning to *Tora! Tora! Tora!* while simultaneously negotiating with Fox lawyers about his release. Despite this disaster, he knew that more international coproduction was in his future. Kurosawa turned to an acquaintance for help with translation matters. Matsue Yoichi could reportedly speak several languages, and Kurosawa asked him to be a "pipeline in various senses of the term."[33] Matsue became one of the conduits for leaks and interviews to the Japanese press on matters relating to the scandal. For example, in a February 1969 interview with *Kinema Junpo* critic Shirai Yoshio, he described a meeting between Kurosawa, Matsue, Aoyagi, and an executive from Embassy Pictures about the script for *Runaway Train*. The Embassy producer gave one budget figure, and Aoyagi translated a completely different number and without batting an eye. Upon hearing this, Shirai gasped, "That's an unimaginable story, isn't it?"[34]

As such scandalous stories must be read with care, however, Kurosawa Pro was deploying Matsue to defend the company's reputation in the face of a very embarrassing rejection by the Hollywood bigwigs. This is to say that Matsue was Kurosawa's attack dog. At least one of the problems he publicly attributed to Aoyagi was clearly Kurosawa's doing, according to the internal memorandum circulating at Fox.[35] Furthermore, there are questions about his ability to judge Aoyagi's interpreting skills. Matsue's credentials were based entirely on his supposedly grand command of foreign languages. He studied in Italy, and could reportedly speak French, Italian, and English. However, a letter he wrote to Elmo Williams on July 15, 1969, is absolutely incomprehensible, and makes Aoyagi's linguistic abilities look impressive indeed. Williams wrote back to Matsue, "I am in receipt of your letter, the contents of which baffles me."[36] Even after all the problems with Aoyagi, Kurosawa was clearly choosing people without vetting their qualifications for translation and interpretation.

As mediating translators, both Aoyagi and Matsue were able to amplify the dissonance of the scandal through disinformation. This is largely because the Japanese film press was, and remains, remarkably monolingual. Yoshii Michiko, a reporter for the *Yomiuri News,* seemed to be the only journalist around who could speak English well enough to interview Williams himself. When she asked him what he thought the source of all the problems was, he responded, "There were various misunderstandings. Also, you understand both Japanese and English so I think you know, but the difference in languages means an incompleteness in translation and interpretation. And because of this problem we've ended up in this situation."[37]

Here is an extreme case of what Friedrich Schleiermacher admired about the translator, that the translator confronts us with the incommensurability of languages. Williams started out mildly pessimistic about the possibility of translatability, and he ends up convinced of the impossibility of equivalence. Of course, we might join his extreme theory of translation had we experienced the chaos he had just survived, or had we been reading impenetrable letters from Aoyagi like this one:

> Elmo, do you think we can eliminate a war in future? Of course not. There will be more and more war. You may not believe it but if I were a strictly translator between you, Mr. Zanuck and Kurosawa, we could never and never reach to that point. I am sure you and Mr. Zanuck hated him long time ago. Since I knew how significant to let him direct the picture for Fox's and his benefit, I really had hard time to bring up to that point. As a result, Mr. Zanuck liked him very much. Both you and I had always known very well how important to keep a nice relationship

between two. But Elmo, I could not expect nor count his sickness. I could not help it. Well, anyway, let's forget the nonsense. It was a nightmare and a child story which they do not appreciate.[38]

Aoyagi's point is difficult to extract, somewhat lost in translation as it is, but he seems to be emphasizing his mediating, advocacy function over meaning. Had he kept his translation strict, he suggests, it would have been Pearl Harbor all over again. However, above and beyond his role as translator and mediator, Aoyagi was clearly working both sides for selfish ends. However visible Aoyagi was as the sole interpreter, he had many balls in the air and he rendered them invisible to both sides. This meaning remained hidden from all involved thanks to the differences of languages. It enabled Aoyagi to keep each side from understanding and knowing the conditions of the other.

Users of translation services generally assume a stable condition of translatability and equivalence, even if they may debate the theoretical details. They also assume that the translation, while subject to misinterpretation at every step of the way, has been delivered by the translator in good faith. Williams emphasized the "incompleteness" of interpretation and translation because he entered the relationship with Kurosawa Productions assuming that the translator would render his Japanese partners legible, transparent. However, nonprofessional translators often bring ulterior motives and unknown agendas. Despite any assumptions about the conditions of translation, we also know that the potential for treachery, linguistic or otherwise, always lurks in the shadows. This is why translation theorists love to cite the Italian proverb that plays on the synonym of translator, *Traduttore, traditore*—"Translator, traitor." Of course, these theorists refer to the way the translator betrays an author despite his or her best efforts. Here in the example of Aoyagi Tetsuro, we discover other forms of translator treachery.

In March, the production got off on a new footing. After negotiations with actor Mifune Toshiro and director Ichikawa Kon broke down, Williams hired two eminently competent directors in Fukasaku Kinji and Masuda Toshio. After recasting the film, they completed the photography in good time. The finished film was rather mediocre. We can only guess if Kurosawa could have done better. He probably could have.

The last translation issue for this saga was the subtitling of the Japanese for the English version of the film, which was always the *original* despite the rhetoric of equality. This helps explain why the subtitling process was so unusual. From the archival record, it is difficult to say if any Japanese were involved at all. It appears that Williams simply took their full translations in the English-language version of the script, and had them simplified according to the subtitling companies' spotting and spacing guidelines. The translations also went past Darryl Zanuck, who shot off the following telex to his producer: "Received your March sixth list of English titles for the Japanese sequences and in my opinion they are at least 80 percent correct, but I have shortened a few of them."[39] I suppose participation in the translation of a language one does not possess is the prerogative of Hollywood studio moguls.

In one of Aoyagi's last letters to Williams, he reflects on the entire experience as producer and translator: "I ignored myself getting bad reputations by protecting him and Kurosawa Productions even when I found that he did not make any sense. Well, Elmo, I do not want to think nor talk about all the past. All I want to do toward the past is to spit on them."[40]

Interviewing Hitch: The Question of Involvement

After a film is completed, the crew goes on to the next production while the core creative staff members begin the task of publicizing the film and paving the way for distribution and exhibition. During a series of premieres, parties, and foreign junkets, the director, actors, and other artists usually sit down for a parade of critics and offer interviews. For the most popular filmmakers, these interviews are often held in hotel rooms, with staff ushering in reporters one after the other for short fifteen- to twenty-minute "dialogues." Interpreters are often on hand to facilitate these discussions, cutting them down to a few minutes of interaction of questionable substance. This section will feature an interview at the other end of the spectrum. It is the conversation between directors François Truffaut and Alfred Hitchcock. Most film scholars would single this out as the most famous interview in film history. It is exemplary not just for the quality of the translation, but also for the nature of the interpreter's *involvement* in the interview scene.

Aside from the celebrity fame of the two participants, a factor in the interview's fame has to do with the agenda driving Truffaut's passion as interlocutor. Truffaut began his career as a critic under the wing of André Bazin (in fact, he was the adoptive child of the elder critic). Along with other young critics in France, Truffaut celebrated the genius of directors, and helped forge *Cahiers du cinéma*'s "policy of auteurism." Put simply, this emphasized the individual genius of directors, attributing a new measure of authorship to certain directors that left their personal stamp on what was by nature a collective enterprise. Above all, Truffaut and his colleagues admired directors who managed to do this in the strict confines of popular film and its studio systems. Before their intervention it was startling to celebrate the work of mainstream directors like Howard Hawks, John Ford, and Alfred Hitchcock. In his introduction, Truffaut writes:

> Inasmuch as his achievements have, until now, been grossly underrated, I feel it is high time Hitchcock was granted the leading position he deserves. Only then can we go on to appraise his work; indeed, his own critical comments in the pages that follow set the tone for such an objective examination . . . If, in the era of Ingmar Bergman, one accepts the premise that cinema is an art form, on a par with literature, I suggest that Hitchcock belongs—and why classify him at all?—among such artists of anxiety as Kafka, Dostoyevsky, and Poe. In light of their own doubts these artists of anxiety can hardly be expected to show us how to live; their mission is simply to share with us the anxieties that haunt them. Consciously or not, this is their way of helping us to understand ourselves, which is, after all, a fundamental purpose of any work of art.[41]

Hitchcock loomed large in Truffaut's world. He figured in nearly fifty critical essays Truffaut wrote in the 1950s.[42] He had already interviewed Hitchcock once in 1955 with Claude Chabrol, an interview Truffaut describes in an amusing anecdote to his introduction. The invitation to engage in a major interview came to Hitchcock in a June 2, 1962, letter from Truffaut. It arrived with a typewritten translation in English. In it, Truffaut wrote, "The ensemble would be prefaced by a text written by me, and the essence of which can be summed up as follows: If cinema was to be deprived of sound overnight, and were once again to become a silent art, many directors would be doomed to unemployment. But among the survivors, the towering figure would be Alfred Hitchock who would inevitably be acknowledged as the best director in the world." Truffaut continued, "I would spend some ten days at whichever place is most convenient for you, bringing along Mrs. Helen Scott, who is the ideal interpreter: Her simultaneous translation is so rapid that it would be as if we were speaking without intermediary—directly to each other."[43]

Truffaut knew Helen Scott from her work at the French film office in New York City. By this time, she had already undertaken the subtitles for a couple of Truffaut's films (at the time of the interview, Truffaut had produced four features and a few shorts, and Hitchcock was shooting his fiftieth film). Scott eventually moved to Paris in 1963 to work on the manuscript with Truffaut. There she became the head of Universal Pictures' European Division. She was well known as a supporter of the New Wave filmmakers. French film fans remember her as the middle-aged woman playing pinball in a café in Jean-Luc Godard's *Two or Three Things I Know about Her* (*2 ou 3 choses que je sais d'elle*, 1967), or the woman who drives up to Jean Yanne during the famous traffic-jam scene from *Weekend* (*Week End*, 1967) and asks, "Who would you rather sleep with, Mao Tse-tung or Johnson?" Yanne replies, "Johnson, of course." And Scott spits, "Fascist!" and drives off. When Scott met Truffaut in New York, however, he knew her only as a marvelously competent translator.

Hitchcock was on his own. He wrote a positive response to Truffaut's initial inquiry, having his driver take his own letter to Berlitz for translation (and charging the fee to the budget of *The Birds* [1963]—someone has to pay the translator!). After this they routed letters through Scott in New York, and the *Los Angeles Times* reported their arrival that August: "French director François Truffaut is here doing a book on Alfred Hitchcock. They don't speak each other's language, but an interpreter is getting through—they hope."[44] Truffaut describes the translation scene for the *New Yorker*'s "Talk of the Town" column:

> On August 13th, Hitchcock's birthday, Helen and I arrived in Hollywood. We stayed at the Beverly Hills Hotel. Every day Hitchcock would come and pick us up at eight in the morning and take us to his office at Universal City Studios, and we would sit in his office and talk until six at night. We spoke to him with microphones around our necks, and a sound engineer stationed in the next room recorded what was said. We kept the microphones on even during meals. Every day we ate with Hitchcock, and every day we ate what he ate—steak, fried potatoes, and ice cream.[45]

Truffaut said he brought five hundred questions to the interview. The tapes and their transcript remain in the Margaret Herrick Library at the Academy of Motion Pictures Arts and Sciences, and they document an extraordinary conversation. Its sheer length—they spoke for nearly fifty hours—allowed for a patience in letting the three people's relationship develop. Perhaps partly because they dined together, Scott's role bled into the more intimate and participatory role of liaison. Occasionally, she would interject her own contribution to the discussion. At one point, she tells them a strange story about a bra made out of metal; Hitchcock drolly responded, "That's very funny." Scott replied, "I'm sorry to interrupt, really," probably sensing she had overstepped a boundary. But it was an impressive performance. Those curious can hear a snatch of the recording on Criterion's DVD release of *Rebecca* (1940).

After they parted, Truffaut returned to Paris and Scott to New York. A copy of the recording was made and each transcribed the sections in their respective native tongue. That fall, Scott wrote Hitchcock with an update: "The transcription of the tapes in two languages turned out to be as lengthy and arduous as I feared and then some . . . Truffaut claims that the major difficulty was with my diction and I mailed back a scientific argument, pointing out that since I spoke twice as much as either of you . . ."[46] In 1963, Scott moved to Paris and the two worked in close collaboration to produce this book with two originals, one in French and the other in English. With fifty hours of dialogue, the editing job was tremendously difficult. In the process, translation edged toward paraphrase and rewriting. Hitchcock asked for few changes, and then only to avoid upsetting certain people. Scott and Truffaut still rewrote most of his utterances for smoothness and they also added things. During the interview itself, Truffaut's contributions and questions were curt, allowing Hitchcock to do the talking. In the editing and translation process, they are vastly expanded and given a literary quality that was absent in the original text.

Comparing recorded tape and published book, the difference is often astonishing. This was Truffaut's power as a director, critic, and close observer of the cinema, but he certainly could not have done this without Helen Scott. Impressively, he foregrounds her contribution to the book. In his introduction, he writes of her in glowing terms:

> There now remained one last hurdle, the language barrier, and I turned to my friend Helen Scott, of the French Film Office in New York. An American raised in France, her thorough command of the cinema vocabulary, her sound judgment and exceptional human qualities, made her the ideal accomplice for the project.[47]

Truffaut also includes a photograph of the three sitting in dialogue, without either of the directors being privileged by camera angle. The photograph itself (Figure 7) represents them in a kind of graphic equality. Most important, Truffaut acknowledges credit where it is due. The

Figure 7. Truffaut included this photograph of the interview scene with Hitchcock and Scott in his book, without privileging either of the directors in the composition: the photograph represents them in a kind of graphic equality. Photograph by Philip Halsman; courtesy of Magnum.

byline for the book is "avec la collaboration de Helen Scott/with the collaboration of Helen G. Scott."

Involving the Translator: Interpreters with Attitude

In addition to their often invisible contribution to the published interview, interpreters appear up front, onstage, alongside artists at film festivals. In the last half century, the international film festival has become an integral part of film culture in nearly every part of the world. Historically, a handful of so-called A-list festivals have dominated the scene. They include prestigious events like Cannes, Berlin, and Venice. A screening at one of these festivals can launch a career or guarantee some degree of box-office treasure. Even if a film loses in one of these competitions, the prestige of place rubs off on the artists. The potency of this cultural capital cannot be minimized. All filmmakers crave it as much as the glittering trophies and the checks.

Outside of this elite circuit, festivals thrive in every size and shape and every nook and cranny of the globe. Their basic function is to plug spectators into the internationality of cinema. This was most obvious in the wake of World War II, which temporarily halted most transnational film traffic and filled the theaters with domestic propaganda. Writing in 1947, Dilys Powell asserted that the newly revived international film festivals constituted an "escape from the national projection room" where the spectators can see their "native cinema as cinema, not as the mirror of a national consciousness."[48] Some festivals link regions or political spheres. For example, the Asian Film Festival started shortly after the Kurosawa's Venice Film Festival win in 1953, springing from the peculiar market energies circulating within Asia and off the radar of the rest of the world. The International Leipzig Festival for Documentary and Animation Film (1955–present) is another interesting example, having been created to network the Soviet bloc and like-minded filmmakers everywhere. There are film festivals that have played important roles in what could be called the "subcultures" of the film world. The Flaherty Seminar and Margaret Meade Film Festival played a central part in the development of Euro-American documentary. In an analogous manner, the Yamagata International Documentary Film Festival, a Japanese event where I have worked as a programmer, helped renovate Asian documentary. For many years it served as the sole conduit for world documentary into Asia, a traffic in prints, ideas, and people that transformed Asian documentary just as digital video enabled high-quality, low-cost independent work. At the same time, it acted as the networking hub for the new independent filmmakers.

In the 1990s, the number of festivals increased dramatically. They were started up by city governments to stimulate business, enrich local culture, and attract tourism. Others were spearheaded by groups with political agendas, from human rights to environmental crusades. Gay and lesbian film festivals announced the existence of other ways of loving and being. Fans of everything from martial-arts flicks to ski videos hold events tailored to their peculiar obsessions. If distribution is the end point of the filmmaking process, then the film festival and markets represent the crucial segue between filmmaker and filmgoer. The degree of distribution—indeed, the possibility of distribution, in many cases—is determined by a film and filmmaker's performance on this circuit of events.

Needless to say, none of this traffic could take place without vast numbers of translators. They stand on stages next to directors, producers, and actors. Offstage, they ply every party to ensure that artists and programmers and distributors and journalists from here or there can propel the films to their next venues. The same interpreters sit down with artists and critics from far-flung places, enabling the writers to publish interviews and reviews that spark the craving of potential spectators. Deals for distribution are discussed or struck. The importance of this activity cannot be minimized. For some national cinemas, foreign income is absolutely crucial to their survival. In the case of the United States, box office from outside the national borders is precisely what makes its technical polish and impressive scale possible, which in turn guarantees its hegemony over those very same foreign markets. For smaller industries, foreign sales may be small or negligible, but the stamp of approval from international film festival screenings creates cultural capital ready for domestic exploitation. Simply note how many advertisements feature the imprimatur of international film festival awards and screenings. Put simply, the stakes are high.

For this reason and others, the pressure on interpreters can be quite extraordinary. The festival interpreter is in plain view and subject to unusual, conflicting demands. As Susanna Gaultier, a longtime Cannes translator, put it, "We have to be emotionally neutral and mustn't get involved, but we can't be tedious or monotonous."[49] Put another way, the translator must be invisible, but at the same time the show must go on.

Having worked on international film festivals for nearly two decades, I have come in intimate contact with a variety of interpreters and the conditions in which they work. One of the most impressive I have worked with is Tanaka Katsue. Above and beyond her inimitable linguistic abilities, she is an interpreter with a beautiful mind. If you are merely mortal like the majority of us, most information goes in one ear and swiftly out the other. With Tanaka, that input dwells in her mind awaiting her turn, then emerges from her mouth translated and ready for easy listening. The mnemonic abilities of interpreters like Tanaka are breathtaking and her simultaneous interpretation is astounding.

At the same time, she subscribes to the ideology of transparency. Thus, her delivery of the translation sidesteps the paralinguistic aspects of the artists' utterances. Indeed, she seems to prefer the invisible but hardly hidden anonymity (and safety?) of the simultaneous interpretation booth. No matter what an artist says or how he says it, Tanaka's delivery rarely strays from a regular musicality. Thanks to the constant rising and falling tone, her interpretation is never boring, never "tedious or monotonous." However, the disconnect between the paralinguistic performance of the artist and/or the topic at hand is perfectly visible, audible, and sometimes disconcerting. This is why, despite the technical brilliance and superhuman abilities of Tanaka, the interpreter I most enjoy working with is Yamanouchi Etsuko.

I must pause here to point out that film festival interpretation is set apart from, say, film conference settings or business meetings because of the object that brings people together. Film, of course, runs the gamut of human life, from the most vulgar pleasures of popular cinema to the heady heights of the art film. Tanaka, Yamanouchi, and I worked on the Yamagata International Documentary Film Festival, and these interpreters find that the documentary places special demands on the translator.

As Bill Nichols points out, the documentary is by definition an engagement with *the* world, not *a* world.[50] The films often ask big questions, and they do so through representations of living, breathing people. Yamanouchi comes to her task with all the skills of Tanaka yet greets the films and filmmakers with the attitude they demand; whether they are bitter indictments of human folly or thrilling celebrations of the best of humanity, these films demand engagement. As a political person, she keeps an ambivalent relationship to the ideology of invisibility. Yamanouchi is *interested,* and that felt connection and curiosity is palpable to the audience. She is famous for, on very rare occasions, crying while interpreting for a filmmaker with a particularly wrenching story. Audiences recognize and appreciate the way this inflects her essential contribution to the event, her natural participation in the proceedings.

She is also willing to tamper with the conventions of interpretation. In 2003, I presented a program of political parodies from the United States, which she helped translate into Japanese. Humor is daunting, especially when translated on the fly, and particularly difficult when combined with the complexities of politics. I introduced her to the audience as a *collaborator,* and we proceeded to go through some clever and quite hilarious Photoshop manipulations and reedited parodies of George Bush's State of the Union address. Her consecutive interpretation would depart from strict translation of my utterances to include translation and then interpretation of texts embedded in photographs. She laughed at the outrageous things she was translating, giving the audience much-needed cues that are the staple of typical humorous interaction. Where a joke needed a little extra unpacking to release its punch, she had the freedom to leave her "script." This was unlike typical film festival interpretation and closer to what Straniero Sergio finds on the television talk show. With my introduction releasing Yamanouchi from the ideology of invisibility, the audience enjoyed this novel approach to interpretation.

Granted, this is a special case, but the lesson is there for the taking. The interpreter is no conduit trafficking in simple messages. Everything from the arrangement of the stage to the tone of voice to the gestures she may or may not use impinges on meaning. Rather than stand center stage and feign invisibility, interpreters must be the participants that they in fact are. More specifically, they must be allowed to engage.

One of the few venues where this is permitted is the star junket and the television variety show. The most famous film translator in Japan is unquestionably Toda Natsuko. I will take her subtitling practice to task in a subsequent chapter, but her interpretation for visiting Hollywood stars is wonderful. She has a bright face and an engaging demeanor. Toda participates seamlessly in the often carnivalesque atmosphere of Japanese television, making a contribution to the show along with the star. Unfortunately, most venues are not so forgiving, and the engagement of an interpreter can open her up for reprisals. Yamanouchi, for one, has been attacked for showing an emotional reaction while interpreting on stage, but this was her very human, un-machinelike reaction to the tragedy at hand. The fervent dedication of filmmakers dealing with the big issues in life deserves interpretation that embodies that passion.

Other aspects of film festival interpretation cannot escape our attention. Translation is often one of the largest budget lines for international film festivals. The many events whose ambition exceeds their bottom lines adopt a number of compromising strategies to deal with language difference. Some translators are forced to simultaneously act as moderators for question-and-answer sessions. This puts them in an impossible situation. They must compartmentalize their roles as moderator and as translator, but inevitably slide one into the other. Sometimes festivals do not have the money for simultaneous interpretation over earphones, but still have the need to provide translation in two languages. Aside from the great lag required to move from source through one target to a second, there is an inevitable winnowing out of meaning. Other festivals force translators with inadequate training in simultaneous interpretation to step into the booth, and it is not uncommon for them to simply give up. Another cost-saving strategy is to use nonprofessionals. Any handy bilingual will do—for example, an enthusiastic graduate student studying abroad.

Many of these nonprofessional interpreters are bilingual film scholars or critics. A collateral advantage of using scholars is their thoroughgoing knowledge about film. Interpreters often cite film interpretation as particularly challenging because speakers are so apt to cite obscure films (which often have standard translations for their titles) or they deploy the vast technical jargon from film production and aesthetics. These scholars and critics generally accept solicitations to translate for unusual reasons. They are advocates and are willing to translate for filmmakers to transport the films they love to the widest audience possible. At a basic level, one must admire the translating advocate, especially when fees are cut or ignored for the sake of promoting filmmakers and their work.

At the same time, there are potential traps for these nonprofessionals. The more unruly of the bunch may begin discoursing from their vast knowledge base, combining translation with unsolicited pedagogy. A more typical problem is neatly summed up by an example from the 1997 Venice International Film Festival. The Golden Lion was awarded to Kitano Takeshi for his film *Hanabi* (aka *Fireworks*, 1997). This was a big event, as the last Golden Lion won by a Japanese was Kurosawa Akira nearly five decades earlier. That film was *Rashomon* (1950), and its award inaugurated the entry of Asian cinema into the international art-film world, which had historically been hegemonized by Europe. Kurosawa did not give an acceptance speech at Venice because he did not even know the film had been submitted to the festival. Having no foreign-language ability to speak of, had Kurosawa been able to stand at the dais his interpreter probably would have relayed a humble and humanistic message of hope for Japan's reentry into international culture after the disaster of World War II. Nearly half a century later, Japanese filmmakers and their fans across the globe hoped this new award for Kitano would renew flagging interest in Japanese cinema, and perhaps even usher in a new golden age analogous to the 1950s auteur cinema of Kurosawa, Mizoguchi, and Ozu.

Festival organizers were disappointed to learn that Kitano could not speak English. This is typical of Japanese directors and, as we saw with *Tora! Tora! Tora!* much to their detriment. Thanks to their impoverished language skills, Japanese filmmakers are utterly dependent on translators in their communication with the outside world. At film festival parties, they inevitably collect together in a pack as they are unable to communicate to anyone but themselves. Kitano's acceptance speech was to be interpreted by Roberta Novelli, one of the finest scholars of Japanese film. She had spent three entire days interpreting for Kitano, all day every day, and found him shy and kind. As is typical for the interpretation of public events, Novelli met the director before the awards ceremony to discuss the territory he planned to cover. Kitano's explanation shocked Novelli. He wanted to invoke the wartime partnership between fascist Italy and Japan to express how this surely must have contributed to the festival's selection. Novelli told him that such comments would be unwise, perhaps even self-destructive. Say anything but that, she counseled. Film scholars are inevitably fans as well as researchers, and Novelli was thrilled with the potential this award held for Kitano personally and Japanese cinema in general. Who knows how such a proclamation would be received? It certainly did not reflect well on Kitano. He agreed to avoid World War II and keep his remarks simple and short.

However, when he stepped onto the Venice stage and took his trophy in hand, things did not go as planned. The ceremony announcer and the festival director did not understand why Kitano needed an interpreter. Surely he could say a few words in English? Of course, he actually couldn't and was very nervous, even trembling. And so much to the film scholar's horror Kitano reverted to Plan A and began talking about how he felt Japan and Italy had a special relationship, adding for good measure: "Japan and Italy should join forces once again and go start a war with some country."

This comment is quite revealing and is probably significant for understanding Kitano. The film that he had won for was filled with images from the fascist imaginary. Beautiful Mount Fuji and stunning cherry trees served as a backdrop for impending death. Kitano's own rhetoric in interviews was filled with nostalgia for things Japanese, and a lost sensibility untainted by Western ways. Perhaps he is no nationalist in the manner of so many suspicious Japanese politicians, right-wing activists, or gangsters. However, there is no question that the film and his comment expose his impoverished sense of history. Despite the seriousness of his violent cinema, Kitano is among the most famous comedians in Japan. But this was no Japanese talk show with Toda Natsuko interpreting.

Novelli saw her hopes for a renewed Japanese cinema dashed the instant he finished his inflammatory comment. So, for his sake, and the sake of the national cinema, she decided not to translate Kitano's precise words, rendering his joke as an innocuous Italian "Thank you."

As we have seen, the interpretation scene is a panopticon, and Novelli's intentional mistranslation was immediately seized upon. Surprisingly enough, the rage of Italians focused on *her,* not Kitano. The scandalous translation made her the object of scorn, and left her ambivalent and frustrated. She regretted the entire episode, but, as an advocate, still feels it was something she had to do.

This kind of defensive or prophylactic translation does not always spring from political or canonical concerns. For example, when translators (especially nonprofessional ones) are put in the position of moderating, they naturally become concerned about the event's contribution to the festiveness of the festival. It is not unusual for otherwise quite creative filmmakers to have trouble putting two words together on a stage. Feeling the pressure to put on a good show, translators may supplement the broken comments of the filmmaker. They may interpret what they *thought* the director meant to say and repackage it in their own words, provide cultural background, gossip, or the like. After all, interpreters are generally far more gifted than filmmakers at manipulating language on the fly.

Other traps await the nonprofessional translators = advocates of the film world. Take the case of British critic Tony Rayns. Starting back in the 1980s, Rayns became the tireless champion of Asian cinema. He was particularly fond of the independent film—both feature and documentary—which had been particularly ignored in the West. With the steady emergence of "new cinemas" in Taiwan, Hong Kong, China, Korea, and elsewhere, international film festivals began competing for the latest, hottest films from the region. A glowing review by Rayns, along with offstage cheerleading in the small world of festivals and distributors, could pave the way to relative fame and fortune for powerless Asian filmmakers. With strong opinions, yet varied and unpredictable predilections, Rayns made a significant contribution to the development of Asian cinema. He certainly helped internationalize the international film festival, making it decidedly less Euro-American-centric.

As part of his campaign to leverage Asian films into festivals and foreign distribution, Rayns began working as a subtitler. This was on top of his well-established roles as critic and film festival consultant. He thus parlayed his influence and specialized knowledge into a new route for advocacy. Criticism, consulting, translation—each produced knowledge, capital, and cultural capital that synergized the three nodes of activity.

The question is how translation fits into this schema. It was language that provided Rayns his particularly powerful role. Language has always been a bottleneck in the traffic of the international film festival circuit. When festivals in the West started taking notice of the breadth of Asian cinema as opposed to the stray auteur from India or Japan, there were few bilinguals in the film world to rely on for information. Programmers were dependent on a handful of film festivals (like Hong Kong and Hawaii), institutes (like Kawakita in Japan), and critics like Donald Richie, Peggy Chiao, and Tony Rayns. The latter fit in this group uncomfortably on the point of language. Chiao is Taiwanese with an advanced degree in cinema studies from an American university. Richie spent most of his adult life living in Japan. Rayns began studying Chinese relatively late in life, and clearly had to rely on translators and bilinguals for his work as critic and consultant. However, the British critic's name regularly appears in the credits of films under the title "Subtitles by Tony Rayns." This includes films in Thai and Korean. As I will discuss at length in the chapter on subtitling, cinema is one of the few art forms where the translator can be only semilingual. Imagine the translator of a playwright or novelist taking a rough translation performed by the original author or some editor, smoothing it out, and claiming credit for the end product. It happens, but not with the regularity one finds in the film world.

What is the relationship between translation and Rayns's advocacy? Presumably, the true advocate would refer the artists to someone with the requisite linguistic skill set and genius for translation. If those filmmakers are not purchasing Rayns's linguistic and translational skills, then what do they think they are buying in these transactions? Put another way, what does the critic-cum-translator think he is selling?

The trader = translator haunts the film festival world. It is common to see translators maneuvering to interpret for certain directors or actors. Certainly, most do this out of deep respect for the artists and a commitment to guarantee the finest translation possible. Sometimes, it is probably because some filmmakers are more interesting than others. At the same time, the venue of the film festival is different from the typical conference thanks to the stars. When translators start caring about the aura of the speaker they interpret for, an ethical dimension arises. What are the implications when an excellent translator chooses whom to translate for?

Whether they like it or not, translators have taken the first step from advocacy toward gatekeeping. This is because the film festival is a scene of power. Festivals make and break careers. Distributors, critics, and artists all gather at these events to work the network. They are at each other's feet, at each other's throats, and in each other's drinks. Few scenes feature as extreme a combination of vicious backstabbing, starry-eyed worshipping, and introductions followed by the powerful walking away from the powerless. Newcomers find themselves excluded from the party unless they've done something extraordinary. Filmmakers who cannot speak English are at an incredible disadvantage, unless they are powerful enough (or the festival is conscientious enough) to offer them a liaison. Without the help of a translator, they are left isolated, drifting in the babel. When translators join this club, they enter accompanied by many risks.

CHAPTER TWO

The Circulation of Ideas

Trafficking in (Mis)Translation

From a certain perspective, the history of cinema is one of endless border struggles. Not surprisingly, there is always a strong demand for open borders for corporate purposes. Even when a nation establishes protectionist measures to defend its film industry from hegemonic competition, usually American, these actions run up against the strong desire of domestic audiences to see the latest foreign films. There is also a contrasting demand for closed borders when it comes to ideas, evidenced by elaborate censorship apparatuses the world over and generally attributable to fears of cultural contamination, usually American. These would be nonissues were it not for all the translators collaborating with forces on each and every side, facilitating or frustrating desires that reach across linguistic borders.

What would the film world be like without translation? I asked in the introduction. We may find a hint at the answer by looking at the domain of theory and criticism. Of course, there are translated texts crisscrossing the globe in every which direction. However, the volume of the translation of ideas pales in comparison to the highly capitalized business of subtitling and dubbing. Furthermore, as Lawrence Venuti demonstrates, the global volume of translation is marked by inequity when broken down by language group. Statistics restricted to film and television publication simply do not exist. However, it is probably safe to say that most people in the world know more about Hollywood than about their own national cinema. This is only possible through an inequitable flow of translated information from English into other tongues.

This structure is often mirrored at the academic level of film culture. In the late twentieth century, for example, Italy became the undisputed center of silent film study, thanks to yearly events like Aprodenoni and Le Giornate del Cinema (not to mention festivals in Bologna, Turin, and Udine). Despite this, researcher Giorgio Bertellini asks why so little is known about Italian cinema. He writes, "Film scholars on both sides of the Atlantic instead seem to be suffering from what I would describe as a propensity for cultural monoglotism. Historiographic approaches and agendas have long remained attached to national field research and have been informed by domestic and academic trajectories."[1]

Bertellini is speaking in both literal and metaphoric senses, proffering a general critique of the cultural balkanization of national cinema study. If you do Italian cinema, you can ignore Mexico, and vice versa. This situation is also connected to tendencies toward linguistic monoglotism in film studies, especially its manifestation in the U.S. academy. Unlike all other disciplines of the humanities, it was possible until quite recently to do specialized research into the arts and culture of a foreign cinema without the "requisite" linguistic skills. Although German and French cinemas may be exceptions to the rule—the geopolitical status of these languages is exceptional—thumb through the bibliographies and footnotes of most pre-1990 publications on foreign film and nearly all the references will be in English.

We can attribute this phenomenon to the unique textual and industrial specificity of cinema. Canonical films are usually available in subtitled or dubbed versions that are rarely translated by scholars. In the case of literature, the sense that translations are new texts that displace the work of the author compels scholars to learn the language and work with original texts. Thus, translation itself became highly regarded and the stuff careers were made of. Philosophers want to understand how ideas and arguments were articulated in the cultural and historical contexts from which they emerged. Anthropologists want to talk to people, read what they read. By way of contrast, film scholars had subtitles. If they were a little less fortunate, they had dubbings, and in a pinch a bilingual informer could whisper in their ear while watching the film. In other words, they sensed privileged access to the original, which unspooled before them in the theater. This is to say that the authorship of the film translator was doubly disavowed. Furthermore, film scholars often had an industrial advantage, because governments, cultural institutions, and the industries themselves underwrote most subtitle translations.

This changed in the late 1980s and 1990s when area studies finally warmed to popular culture. Previously, research and pedagogy on film often went unrewarded in the tenure and promotion process—amounting to a kind of punishment. Bibliographers for foreign-language books created deep collections for literature, history, and the social sciences, leaving film and television a cavernous hole in most major research libraries. Early on, when area studies scholars taught film because they loved it and thought it was important, they often had to do it covertly under obscure and orthodox-sounding course titles, or they felt compelled to combine it with safer topics like literary adaptation. However, in the 1990s area studies transformed in its contact with cultural studies, opening up many disciplines to the study of popular culture and producing a new generation of scholars working on film and television. Now the bibliography without primary sources is the exception, not the rule. One finds foreign film scholarship integrating translation everywhere, although the promotion process's dismissive attitude toward translation itself is, if anything, worse.

In the midst of this transformation, there were unfortunate attacks on the work of monoglotal film scholars. At one level, there was the erroneous assumption that language fluency was a prerequisite to making any useful critical contribution, or even having the right to offer a contribution. At another level, language and translation may also have become a cover for generational conflict or reactionary rejections of film studies' theoretical and methodological apparatus. Thus, I raise the issue of monoglotal scholarship not to diminish its importance, but to emphasize its inherent productivity. Of course, these are contributions subject to critique, and what concerns us here is the nature of those contributions in the context of translation—or the lack thereof. Having attended graduate school in the midst of that late 1980s and 1990s transformation and stepped into one of the first area studies positions specifically devoted to Asian cinema, I am highly conscious of the context of my own writing, a situation where area studies embraces popular culture and all its baggage, where film studies commits itself to the hard work of becoming polyglotal, where translation studies steps gingerly into perilously interdisciplinary territory.

This chapter is devoted to a case study of misprision in a largely monoglotal world. It tracks an idea that moves from England to Japan in the 1930s. Only a privileged few spoke or read English back then, and the translator who seized upon this idea seemed to possess a rather shaky hold on the language. Her translation suffered from many mistakes, which initially remained invisible to her readership. Although the author's idea transformed upon its insertion into the Japanese film world, this did not stop it from inspiring filmmakers. Indeed, the latter's inability to access the original actually amplified the translation's transformative power. Its example demonstrates what close analysis of translation practices can reveal about an influential instance of "cultural translation."

Poru Ruta/Paul Rotha and the Productivity of Misprision

Open any Japanese book on documentary, and the "theory" of Paul Rotha will be singled out as one of the most influential bodies of thought in the history of Japanese cinema. Although there were translations of all the major Western film theorists, from Münsterberg to Eisenstein, it is safe to say that none of their writing was as fiercely contested and discussed as Rotha. No other theorist or critic had more impact on actual film practice or underwent as much "processing."

Rotha's influence in Japan may surprise the Western film scholar. Upon its release, *Documentary Film* (1935) was widely read throughout Europe and the United States, particularly within the educational film movement. However, it was seen largely as a promotion of British documentary at the time—hardly a theoretical "bible."[2] His place in (our) history is basically as one of the central filmmakers of the British school, as a writer, and occasionally as an antagonist of John Grierson. Despite Euro-American film studies' renewed interest in documentary, one rarely if ever hears Rotha's name invoked. Even book-length histories of the British documentary movement note *Documentary Film* only in passing. This would undoubtedly shock Japanese filmmakers and scholars, as Japanese books about film theory and history mention Rotha's name in the same breath as Eisenstein, Balasz, Pudovkin, Arnheim, Münsterberg, Moholy-Nagy, and Vertov.

Imamura Taihei's 1952 overview of film theory puts Rotha in the privileged position of his final chapter—the author posed with *Documentary Film* for his portrait (Figure 8)—and Rotha's prestige has hardly

Figure 8. Imamura Taihei reading Paul Rotha.

weakened in the intervening years.[3] Thus, in 1960 translator Atsugi Taka offered a completely revised translation of Rotha's 1952 expanded version. This in turn was reprinted in 1976 and 1995.[4] Ironically enough, judging from his papers, Rotha himself appears to have had no idea how influential he was in Japan. This indicates that while we may speak of Rotha's "influence," something was happening in Japan that was disconnected from larger traffic in film theorization.[5]

This apparent imbalance may be partially explained by returning to the time when Rotha's book arrived in Japan in the latter half of the 1930s, an opportune moment if there ever was one. Japan was escalating its invasion of China, especially with the 1937 China Incident. On the home front, the government ensured that the war reached into the daily lives of citizens everywhere, drawing on young men for cannon fodder and increasingly controlling "appropriate" behavior. Police pressure, including mass arrests, imprisonment, and occasional torture, had shut down the noisy left by mid-decade. Many progressive intellectuals underwent ideological conversion to a rabid nationalism and an often racist nativism. Those who refused this course quietly retreated underground or disguised their thoughts in carefully chosen language when in public. At the same time, the government placed elaborate strictures on filmmaking, ranging from intricate censorship mechanisms to nationalizing entire sectors of the industry. This culminated with the 1939 Film Law, which mandated the forced screening of nonfiction films, or the so-called *bunka eiga* (culture film). Along with the pressures of continental warfare, this legislation propelled documentary to a level of prestige comparable to the fiction film. Film journals were filled with articles attempting to theorize a documentary practice appropriate for the times, and included essays by intellectuals as disparate as Hasegawa Nyozekan, Tosaka Jun, Kamei Katsuichiro, and Nakai Masakazu. In this atmosphere, the appearance of Rotha's *Documentary Film*—especially its 1938 translation—electrified the film world, and was greeted with the respect afforded the most authoritative of theoretical systems. This intense interest eventually filtered into filmmaking itself, allowing Rotha to leave a mark on the history of Japanese cinema that few theorists ever achieve anywhere, anytime.

But why Rotha? And, by extension, what did his writing mean in wartime Japan? A hint at the answer lies in the title itself—*Documentary Film*. The manner in which this was translated immediately alerts us to the political ramifications of the translation act and suggests the exceeding complexity of these questions. A variety of words were circulating in the Japanese film world to designate nonfiction filmmaking: *jissha eiga, kiroku eiga, nyusu eiga, dokyumentarii eiga,* and the like. However, the

1938 edition appeared with language on the cover that may or may not be a mistranslation: *Bunka Eiga-ron,* or *On Culture Film.* First, the suffix *ron* (argument, discourse) appended to the title could also render a reverse translation as *Documentary Film Theory.* This may have given Rotha's thought a heft we do not feel when reading the original English text. Second, an intertext for the *bunka eiga* is the *Kulturfilm* of Universal Filmaktiengesellschaft (UFA) in Germany. These were primarily science films, but upon their successful Japanese release some critics began using the term for a variety of nonfiction films by Japanese filmmakers. The word begins to appear in Japanese texts as early as 1933, and all documentary came under the rubric of *bunka eiga* with the 1939 Film Law. Although most readers knew the word *dokyumentarii eiga* (documentary film), the translator chose to use *bunka eiga,* which was strongly connected to propaganda filmmaking by the time Rotha's book appeared. Many of Rotha's contemporary critics pointed out the ambiguity of the film genre to which this title points. Few, however, noted that it firmly inserted Rotha's thought into the discourse raging around the terms of the new Film Law. The translation of Rotha roughly coincided with the announcement of plans for these detailed government regulations over the film industry, and amid the fervent discussion about the new meaning and direction for nonfiction film, Rotha's cheerleading for the documentary found an enthusiastic audience. In one sense, this would appear to sell out Rotha to a radically opposed politics; however, I argue that it could also be seen as an attempt on the part of the translator to quietly shift the terms of the Japanese documentary debate in a certain direction. Thus, the short answer to the question "Why Rotha?" is that Rotha's book meant many things indeed.

The long answer is that because of this slipperiness, a curious situation arose in which Rotha's book appealed equally to the entire political spectrum, with all debate participants claiming Rotha's thought to different ends. The rest of this chapter will examine precisely this struggle over meaning at multiple levels. However, to root out the most important issues underlying this discourse we must look to an arena less obvious than the film magazines, that is, the media through which Rotha's thought came to be known: translation.

Consider this relatively obvious example: the 1938 edition mistranslates "Workers' Revolution" with the more innocuous *rodosha katsudo,* or "Worker's Activities," to return the term to English.[6] Only in the postwar revision did the proper translation appear: *rodosha kakumei*.[7] The reason is unambiguous; this was a dangerous term in 1939, and a text containing it would never pass censorship review. Authors, translators, and publishers had been deflecting such trouble with authorities for nearly a decade by printing obvious synonyms and even substituting problematic words with XX's (called *fuseji*). Readers knew the protocol; when they came across *fuseji* or ambiguous words, they could read past them at the original meanings. The first edition of *Documentary Film* is sprinkled with many examples such as this, but analysis of such simple instances of intentional mistranslation will only get us so far. This is because, first, as the example just mentioned suggests, there were entire communities of readers who were forced to conceal their true relationship to the book, and second, many knew the translator's command of English was dubious at best because it became one of the issues raised in the debates.[8]

We must dig far deeper into the issue of translation to appreciate the complexity of the highly politicized discourses circulating around Rotha's original text upon its insertion into the Japanese linguistic world. After all, this is the medium through which Rotha came to be known in Japan; very few filmmakers and critics could read English well enough to take the original into hand. Furthermore, shifting our analysis from simplistic notions of (one-way) "influence" to the site of translation brings an array of larger issues into focus. For example, looking at the sheer volume of translation reveals much about the relationship between cultures (it follows that a lack of translation activity indicates a discourse stuck in an unhealthy short-circuit of desire). When bringing texts from one language to another, the translator's approach to language and meaning is inseparable from larger historical and ideological currents in the target language. This new linguistic and cultural context often impinges upon the translation while having little to do with the original text itself. In this situation, where competing translations circulated among overlapping readerships, a struggle over authority occurs—after all, can there be a more powerful position over cross-cultural discourse than that of the translator? We must look at the qualities of a given translation, and ask who the translator is, what her relationship is with the original text, the author, and the larger communities of readers. These are all key factors

in the relationship to the other. From this perspective, the difference between translation theory and documentary film theory is very slim indeed,
as both fields involve representations weighed by a debt to an "original,"
whether it be the source text or the world.

Documentary Film Enters the (Japanese-Language) Film World

Originally, Rotha's book was read by Japan's preeminent prewar film
theorist, Imamura Taihei, who passed it on to Domei Tsushin's Kuwano
Shigeru. From there, the book surged into the film community.[9] At one
point, it came into the hands of Atsugi Taka, one of the first female filmmakers in Japanese cinema. Atsugi originally came to filmmaking as a
leading member of the Nippon Puroretaria Eiga Domei (Proletarian Film
League of Japan), or Prokino for short. After the breakup of Prokino
under police pressure in 1934, Atsugi began writing film criticism and
translating foreign film theory. She was also one of the members of a
collective producing the early film theory journal *Eiga Sozo*, along with
other former Prokino members. This gave her concrete links to Yuibutsu
Kenkyukai (Materialism Study Society, or Yuiken), a group of leftist
intellectuals organized by philosopher Tosaka Jun.[10]

Atsugi even wrote a review article of Rotha's book in the society's
Yuibutsuron Kenkyu, probably the first mention of *Documentary Film* in
print. In the late 1930s, Atsugi began a long career in documentary screenwriting, working for Photochemical Laboratory (PCL), Toho, and Geijutsu Eigasha (Art Film Company, or GES). This afforded her the chance
to bring Rotha's theory into practice. Above and beyond her own filmmaking activities, Atsugi's most influential project was a translation of
Paul Rotha's *Documentary Film*, which she took on at the request of her
PCL supervisor; he was moving to JO Studios to become head of production, and wanted to use the book as a textbook for study groups.
Atsugi had been reading the English original, and was glad to use the
translation as an excuse to finish the book. She published the first edition in the fall of 1938.[11]

The translation had an enormous impact, and went into second and
third printings within a year.[12] The book's influence spread in the late
1930s as critics debated Rotha's terms and their implications for documentary filmmaking, often offering their own translations of the original in their quotations. Soon an alternative translation by Ueno Ichiro
appeared in *Eiga Kenkyu*, a film studies series put out by the magazine

Eiga Hyoron.[13] There were study groups devoted to Rotha's book in the production companies and film studios. Toho's staff called it the documentary filmmaker's "bible", and their Kyoto studio actually circulated its own handwritten, mimeographed translation within the company.[14] Before Atsugi's translation appeared, the original English-language book was even used for English practice at JO Studios.[15]

About the same time, the original text came into the hands of Omura Einosuke and Ishimoto Tokichi, and their reading of the book had a great impact on the formation of GES. Thanks to Rotha's ideas, the company's early films, such as *Snow Country* (*Yukiguni,* 1939) and *Train C57* (*Kikansha C57,* 1940), strove to surpass the usual public relations film and bring documentary to a new, independent level.[16] Geijutsu Eigasha's own film journal, *Bunka Eiga,* published enthusiastic debates over Rotha's book, as did most of the other serious film publications.

One of the major responses to the Rotha translation involved a knee-jerk reaction to his disdain for the "story film" that "threatens to stifle all other methods of cinema" and "tends to become an anesthetic instead of a stimulant."[17] The most vociferous of these critics displayed a near uncontrollable anger. For example, in his book-length, bibliographic survey of film literature, Okuda Shinkichi passes Rotha off with a flourish: "I—and others—can only recognize *[Documentary Film]* as a little like drawing water for one's own field [i.e., self-serving]. Above all, his rejection of the feature film, and explanation making documentary the main path for cinema, is clearly ridiculous; even as a theory of art, it never exceeds shallow abstraction."[18]

The most scathing attack on Rotha came from Tsumura Hideo, who sarcastically wrote:

> Put a different way, Rotha's book is extremely heroic and vigorous. He praises documentary based on materialist socialism as the most valuable cinema of tomorrow. In contrast to that, it pulverizes the fiction film into dust, with writing akin to vicious gossip. The way it attacks fiction film is extremely rough with ideological tricks. I confess that this is one of the reasons I have the courage to criticize Paul Rotha.[19]

This now famous attack provoked a response from Takagiba Tsutomu, who ran Toho's Shinjuku News Film Theater and was a frequent essayist on documentary film. Takagiba humorously rewrote Tsumura's article, substituting "Tsumura" for "Rotha" to turn the attack back on the Japanese critic.[20]

However well this strategy neutralized Tsumura's critique, it did not address the key issues: that Rotha's definition of "fiction" in documentary was less than clear, and that the book was less a theory of documentary film than a specious promotion of government cultural policy. There is a grain of truth to their accusations against Rotha—his arrogance, his self-promotion of the English documentary, and faith in government sponsorship—but the critical debate that actually affected Japanese filmmaking practice was over the problem of "fiction" in documentary.

The most tempered discussion of this issue was offered by Kubota Tatsuo in *Bunka Eiga no Hohoron* (The methodology of the culture film, 1940). This was one of the more serious attempts to explore the phenomenon of the *bunka eiga*. Although he came out of production (Shochiku's Kyoto studios), Kubota was very well read. He draws on the writings of Münsterberg, Arnheim, Balazs, Eisenstein, and most other major theorists to that point. But the book is ultimately a disappointment. Kubota's aesthetic agenda centered on expunging any influence of the avant-garde from documentary, positioning the *bunka eiga* with a hard-and-fast opposition between fiction film/"sensitivity" *(kansai)* versus science film/"intellect" *(chisei)*.[21] Unfortunately, this colors his discussion of Rotha as well. Kubota had originally intended to structure his entire book around *Documentary Film*, a measure of Rotha's prestige and influence over the very conception of nonfiction filmmaking. In the end, he wisely saved the discussion of Rotha for the final chapter. After his careful discussion of the avant-garde, Kubota warns readers that although Rotha has his good points, his vague definition of "dramatization," bolstered as it is by questionable examples such as Pabst's *Kameradschaft* (1931), could lead documentary to stray too completely into the world of fiction.

This represents one typical brand of discussion that was occurring in all sectors of the Japanese documentary world. In actuality, the relatively innocent-looking debates about Rotha's conceptions of "fictionality" and "actuality" veiled struggles over documentary's function in Japanese society. The written record on this score is decidedly one-sided. Rotha proposed a nationally sponsored documentary film committed to the enlightenment and unification of the citizenry, precisely the kind of cinema necessary for a country deeply imbricated in foreign warfare. However, under the restrictive circumstances of 1930s Japan, many other important perspectives went unrecorded. This aspect of Rotha's appeal— especially his apparent sympathies for socialism—necessarily had to be concealed from the public sphere; restricted to private discussion, this body of discourse never appeared in the written record, posing a battery of problems for the historian. There are, however, traces remaining that provide access to these hidden spaces, and in the remaining sections of this chapter we will explore their furthest reaches.

Battle of the Translators

Like many other (underground) leftists in the documentary film world, Atsugi found Rotha's writing inspirational. Here was a filmmaker committed to social change, someone who saw cinema as a medium for critiquing everything from class discrimination to totalitarian political systems. Having spent the last decade immersed in Marxism and committing her life to demonstrating its relevance to filmmaking, criticism, and translation, Atsugi found a true compatriot in Paul Rotha. *Documentary Film* became the "hidden sacred book" of filmmakers like Atsugi who opposed the direction their nation and film industry were taking. Only after the war was over, however, could they reveal their views publicly.

One can feel Atsugi's intense relationship with Rotha's book by scanning her personal copies, which she donated to the National Film Center of Japan just before her death. Opening their pages provides both a thrill and a challenge to the historian. Her 1976 Miraisha version appeared brand-new and unopened. Her 1960 Misuzu copy contained only a few penciled-in notes and an inscription inside the cover: "To Takeshi, the husband I love."

Her first editions—Rotha's and her own translation—are far more intriguing. One can quickly detect a pattern in the highlighted sections. For example, in this time of stricture, she singled out the following sentence with a scratch of a pencil: "There is little within reason and little within the limits of censorship that documentary cannot bring before an audience to state an argument."[22] Although there can be no doubt why she liked such a sentence, the pages are also filled with more obscure checks, question marks, circles, and exclamation points. Strange symbols and many "M.B."'s lie mute in the margins. Bookmarks sit in curious passages—did *she* leave them there? We will never know their significance, but three marks stand out among them all for their powerful evocation of what this book meant at the height of the China War. Apparently, Atsugi took her own translation in hand and read it over the space of several weeks in 1939, because she left dates next to three paragraphs. Scratched on the pages at a time when the government was taking steps to convert all documentary into propaganda in support of the emperor's war, a time when brilliant filmmakers were subverting these efforts with clever editing, and when open resistance meant persecution (Kamei Fumio's *Fighting Soldiers* [*Tatakau heitai*, 1939] had just been suppressed, and he would be in prison within a matter of months), these three passages make Atsugi's cathexis with Rotha's text palpable. For this they are worth quoting in full, with Atsugi Taka's notes rendered in bold:

> Relative freedom of expression for the views of the documentalist [*sic*] will obviously vary with the production forces he serves and.the political system in power. In countries still maintaining a parliamentary system, discussion and projection of his beliefs within certain limits will be permitted only so long as they do not seriously oppose powerful vested interests, which most often happen to be the forces controlling production. Under an authoritarian system, freedom is permissible provided his opinions are in accord with those of the State for social and political advance, until presumably such a time shall arrive when the foundations of the State are strong enough to withstand criticism. Ultimately, of course, you will appreciate that you can neither make films on themes of your own choice, nor apply treatments to accepted themes, unless they are in sympathy with the aims of the dominant system. And in view of the mechanical and hence expensive materials of cinema, it will be foolish of the documentalist if his sympathies do not lie, or at least appear to lie, with those who can make production a possibility.[23]
> **[June 28, 1939]**

The following is a critique of the apolitical approach of Robert Flaherty, the director of *Nanook of the North* (1922):

> In every location which he has chosen there have existed social problems that demanded expression. Exploitation of native labour, the practises of the white man against the native, the landlords of Aran, these have been the vital stories, but from them Flaherty has turned away... Idyllic documentary is documentary without significant purpose. It takes romanticism as its banner. It ignores social analysis. It takes ideas instead of facts. It marks a reactionary return to the worship of the heroic, to an admiration of the barbaric, to a setting up of "The Leader."[24] **[July 6, 1939]**

Finally, there is a quote on the power of montage from Soviet filmmaker and theorist Vsevolod Pudovkin:

I found the way to build up a dialogue in which the transition of the actor from one emotional state to another...had never taken place in actuality before the camera. I shot the actor at different times, glum and then smiling, and only on my editing table did these two separate moods co-ordinate with the third—the man who made the joke.[25] [**July 20, 1939**]

Atsugi's handwritten dates—these curt pencil scratches—convert this translation from the public domain to something quite new and contradictory. They act as conduits allowing those resistant discourses retained safely in hidden spaces to leak from between the lines. But this is only half the story, because the criticism and debate surrounding Paul Rotha's *Documentary Film* are an instance of oppositional discourses being coded into public view, camouflaged to deflect the threat of reprisals. To render this complicated discourse visible, we must return to the problem of translation. On the one hand, Atsugi wove her point of view into the very fabric of her translation, both in conscious and unconscious ways. At the very same time, intellectuals from far different perspectives engaged her in a veritable battle of the translators.

In the course of researching the subject of prewar Japanese documentary for a previous book, I occasionally ran across copies of Atsugi's translation in used bookstores. Taking one of these volumes in hand, one can come to a material appreciation for the respect with which Rotha was viewed through the high quality of the printing, binding, and paper, as well as the book's beautiful slipcase adorned with elegant handmade rice paper. Every time I found a copy of the Rotha translation, I pulled it off the shelf to take a peek inside and see if it belonged to anyone I knew from my research. One of these dusty first editions contained quite a surprise: every page had detailed annotations. Between every line of the book—cover to cover—someone had diligently scrawled corrections to Atsugi's translation in pencil (Figure 9). Inside the cover, this anonymous editor wrote a message: "This is a surprising book. She can't understand English. Japanese is pretty bad. Even Ms Atsugi cannot argue with this. I don't understand how this person had the guts to translate it. This caused the chaos in this country's *bunka eiga* discourse. I'm sorry these corrections are a year late." The original owner who requested this involved translation check was unclear; outside of this message, there was only an illegible scrawl across the page. (Hereafter, I will refer to this copy of *Documentary Film* as the *teiseiban* [corrected version].)[26]

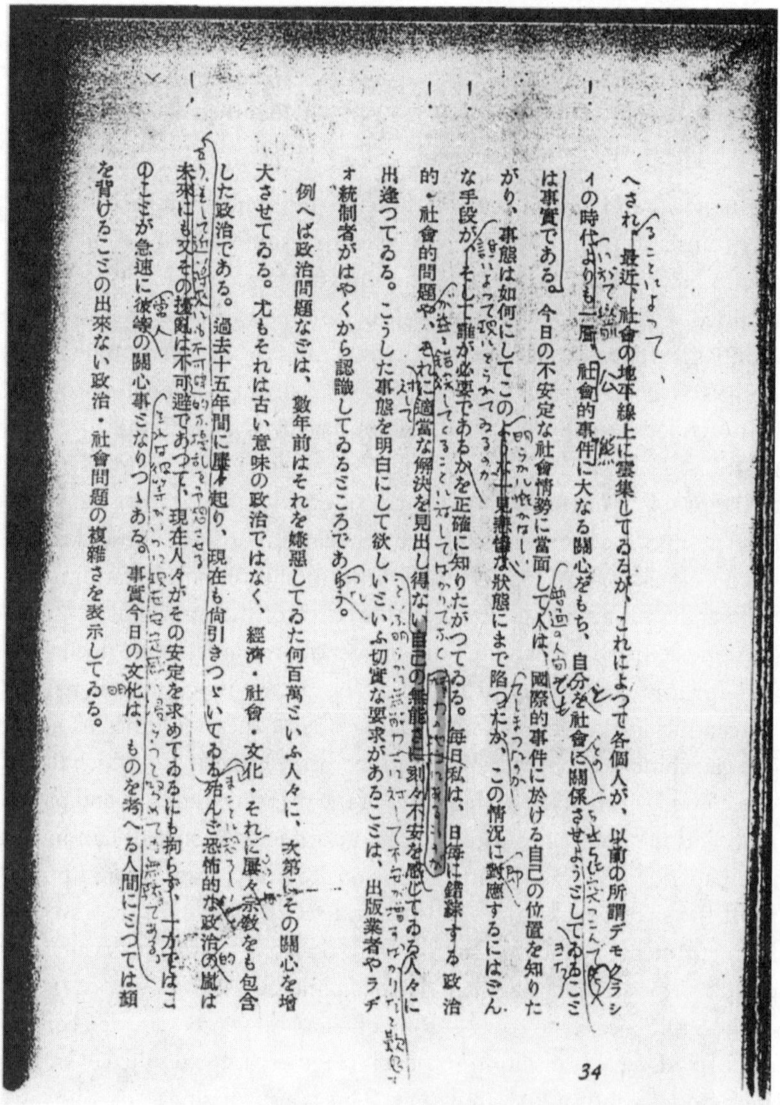

Figure 9. A page from the *teiseiban*.

The first edition of the Atsugi translation came out in September 1938, and whoever pored over Atsugi's work left us only with the message that the translation was so bad its revision took the better part of a year. Actually, the existence of this *teiseiban* slipped quietly into public view in January 1940—fourteen months after the original publication of the book—in a program passed out at Takagiba Tsutomu's Shinjuku News Film Theater. In addition to flashy advertising for the week's film slate, these pamphlets often turned gray with in-depth essays printed in tiny type. The January 18, 1940, issue contained an article by Sekino Yoshio that asserted that the controversies over Rotha spring primarily from the inexperience of the person who had translated him. Sekino wrote, "Below, let us pick out two or three parts of interest from a corrected text pretty much black with corrections."[27] He proceeded to compare passages from Atsugi's translation with corrections from the *teiseiban.* (With this in mind, the cryptic pencil slash inside the cover clearly reads "Seki" in hiragana with a long tail.) In the following months, Sekino drew on the *teiseiban* for a series of lengthy articles in which he attempted to clear up the controversy surrounding Rotha's book.[28] These also became the basis for a book titled *Eiga Kyoiku no Riron* (Theory of Film Education, 1942).[29]

The main issues for Sekino revolved around the translation of such terms as "story film" and "the dramatization of actuality." He attempted to contextualize Rotha's thoughts on documentary in terms of his development as a critic—the differences between *Film Till Now* and *Documentary Film*—as well as the vast changes in English society itself. His success in reorienting the debate is difficult to judge, although it appears to have mostly influenced Sekino's reputation as an authority on the topic. There is a good reason for this. In this series of high-profile articles, Sekino positioned himself less as a critic than as the translator. He gives a discreet nod to the help of the *teiseiban,* but the substance of his articles is unusual. Rather than provide his own interpretation of *Documentary Film,* Sekino all but retranslates the book! These articles were basically strings of extended quotes from the *teiseiban* with short passages of paraphrase inserted in between. Thanks to the corrections by Sekino's anonymous colleague, the new translations are quite good—for the most part, they are better than Ueno's or Toho's, and certainly better than Atsugi's. The *teiseiban* itself, with its rows of exclamation point annotations, remains by far the best translation. However, Sekino ultimately does not offer an actual translation as such, because significant portions of the book are paraphrased or deleted. To be more specific, they are suppressed. Here is a typical, and relatively innocuous, example from Rotha with Sekino's deletions scored through:

~~Art, like religion or morals, cannot be considered apart from the material-~~
~~ist orderings of society.~~ Hence it is surely fatal for an artist to attempt to
divorce himself from the community and retire into a private world
where he can create merely for his own pleasure or for that of a limited
minority. He is, ~~after all, as much a member of~~ the ~~common herd as a~~
~~riveter or a glass-blower,~~ and of necessity must recognize his obligations
to the community into which he is born. His peculiar powers of creation
must be used to greater purpose than mere personal satisfaction.[30]

Sekino's reading, or more properly his selective translation, evacuates
Rotha's left-leaning politics and aligns *Documentary Film* with the dominant ideology of wartime Japan. He effortlessly converts the passage
just quoted into an attack on individualism and a call for artists to serve
the mission of the national polity. Elsewhere, extremely long series of
extended quotations often skip a sentence or two in the middle when
Rotha brings in the subject of class or Marxism. The segment of Rotha's
audience to which Sekino belonged was probably enthralled with the
Englishman's high moral tone and sense of "mission."

Sekino himself was far more than a film critic. After studying art at
Tokyo University, he worked at the social education section in the Tokyo
metropolitan government. In this capacity, he promoted the use of film
for education through publications, lectures, study groups like STS,[31]
and regular Jido Eigahi (Children's Film Days).[32] In the latter stages of
World War II, Sekino worked at Nichiei as the vice president in charge
of *bunka eiga* production. Through the sum of these activities, Sekino
became a prominent theorist in the education film movement throughout the war; "theorist" in this context meant that the writer was not
in the classroom trenches where the real teaching was going on. With his
articles on the Rotha controversy, Sekino moved beyond pedagogical
issues of the educational front and claimed a position of authority over
the Rotha text, and therefore over Japanese documentary film.

The Rotha we encounter through Sekino's articles speaks of responsible citizenship and the central role of cinema in educating the nation's
populace. Sekino's Rotha heightens the stakes of these ideas by drawing
the reader's attention to the worldwide sense of crisis—that theme so
central to pre–Pearl Harbor Japan—but the English filmmaker's calls
for peaceful settlement of conflict, disarmament, and intelligent social
critique are suppressed from Sekino's blow-by-blow "translation = correction" of Rotha's book. With these themes purged from the text, one

is left with a discourse on propaganda and the necessity for state support of the documentary to the end of enlightening its citizenry. It is no wonder that Rotha was attractive to Sekino and the new leadership emerging with the Film Law. A further example of this political reinscription of Rotha is *Eiga Kokusaku no Zenshin* (The progress of national film policy), a 1940 book outlining the national film policies of all the major Western nations. The second half of this book covers the situation in Japan, and offers essays on the implications of the new Film Law for various segments of the film industry. Its chapter on the deployment of film as an instrument of state propaganda cites Rotha as the international authority, posing the English filmmaker's innovations as the proper course for a nationalized film industry.[33]

Although Sekino performed an intentional mistranslation of *Documentary Film* in a manner analogous to Atsugi before him, the differences between their texts are even more revealing. *Documentary Film* inhabited the space between publicly acceptable discourses and those that were kept hidden for fear of retaliation. The multiplicity of readings this position implies was built into all of the published translations. The following example reveals how the differences between Atsugi and Sekino play out in their translations. This is one of Rotha's numerous digs at the powers that be, followed by its extant translations (for the relevant page from the *teiseiban*, see Figure 9; I will only translate back the key phrases, which are italicized and discussed below):

ROTHA: Every day I come across persons who manifest increasing anxiety not only at the growing complexity of political and social problems, but at the patent inability of *those in power* to find adequate solutions.[34]

ATSUGI: Mainichi watashi wa, higoto ni sakuso suru seijiteki, shakaiteki mondai ya, sore ni tekito na kaiketsu o miidashi enai *jiko no munosa* ni kokkoku fuan o kanjite iru hitobito ni deatte iru.[35]

UENO: Mainichi watashi no au hitobito ga seijimondai ya shakai mondai no shinkokuka suru fukuzatsusa ni tsuite fuan o kataru bakari de wa naku, *jibunra ni tadashii kaiketsu o miidasu noryoku no nai koto* o gaitan suru no de aru.[36]

SEKINO: Taezu watashi wa, seijiteki, shakaiteki na jyaku mondai ga masumasu fukuzatsusa o mashite kuru koto ni taishite nominarazu, *toro no hitobito* ga sore e no tekito na kaiketsu o miidashi enai to iu meihaku na muryokuburi ni taishite mo, fuan ga kuwaete iku bakari da to tansaku suru hitotachi ni ikiatte iru.[37]

TEISEIBAN: Mainichi watashi wa, seijiteki, shakaiteki mondai ga masumasu sakuso shite kuru koto ni tai shite bakari de naku, *kenryoku no chii ni aru mono* ga, sore ni taishite tekito na kaiketsu o miidashi enai to iu akiraka ni munoryokusa ni taishite fuan ga masu bakari da to tansoku suru hitobito ni deatte iru.

Rotha's original text sets up a relatively straightforward contrast between, on the one hand, common people who find themselves bewildered by the complexity of the world on the verge of war, and, on the other hand, those in power who seem too incompetent to deal with the situation. Here Rotha's critical spirit comes out in force, but he is writing things that landed Japanese in prison in 1939. All of the translators seem to deal with this problem of potential censorship or reprisals in their own way; everything from vocabulary choices to mistakes reveals the ideological undergirding of their respective translations. The *teiseiban* provides the best, most straightforward, translation of the quotation's most problematic phrase, "those in power": *kenryoku no chii ni aru mono* (people in positions of [political] power). However, Sekino strays from the guidance of his *teiseiban* and substitutes this with the rather vague *toro no hitobito* (authorities, intellectuals), deflecting the criticism into ambiguous territory. His other decisions further weaken Rotha's criticism, as a rendering of this phrase back into English reveals: "but at the clear powerlessness of authorities/intellectuals in finding appropriate solutions."

Both Atsugi and Ueno completely erase "those in power" from the sentence. The effect is to create a single group of common people who feel anxiety about the world's complexity and their inability to effect change. We might assume that the translators expunged Rotha's attack on the powerful to preempt punishment by their own authorities. Without more documentation, the case of Ueno is difficult to judge; however, Atsugi produced a postwar version of *Documentary Film* when threats of reprisal were not an issue. In the 1960 translation, she significantly revises the text with the help of two young scholars, and although this sentence was completely rewritten, Atsugi retains the mistake.[38] Even the 1995 "refurbished edition" *(shinsoban)* remains unchanged. In other words, Atsugi simply did not understand the meaning in the first place.[39]

At the same time, Atsugi's word choice is still significant. Ueno's exasperated, anonymous masses are literally the people Rotha has met on the street ("jibunra ni tadashii kaiketsu o miidasu noryoku nonai koto o gaitan suru no de aru"), but the Marxist Atsugi does not shirk social responsibility and uses the much stronger language "jiko no munosa," which places the burden of history on herself and the reader—it is the difference between "their own inability" and "our own incompetence."

Atsugi's misprision circulates in a gray area between Rotha's original English text and its dim representation in Japanese—the latter reflects a conception of documentary combining Rotha's thinking with that of Atsugi's own filmmaking community of leftist filmmakers who restrict their politics to hidden spaces in the teeth of power.[40] Rotha himself said, "I came nearest to becoming a Socialist in my Documentary Book."[41] This was not lost on the filmmakers who found themselves subject to censorship and the whims of political power. Many of them had recently spent time in the "pig box" (*butabako*, or "slammer") for their filmmaking activities in Prokino. For some filmmakers, Rotha's book simply confirmed the direction they were already taking nonfiction film in the late 1930s, and knowing that someone outside of Japan thought the same way gave them a measure of confidence.[42] However, many others had a far deeper, hidden relationship to *Documentary Film*. Kuwano Shigeru worked at Domei Tsushin's film unit before becoming the section head in charge of *Nippon News* at Nihon Eigasha (Nichiei). He was probably the second person in Japan to read *Documentary Film*, having received it from Imamura Taihei, himself a Marxist critic. In a 1973 book on documentary, he left a reminiscence about his own wartime encounter with Rotha:

> This book, for me, was a shock. He was choosing his words extremely carefully, but this is clearly what Paul Rotha was saying: The duty of documentary filmmakers was to somehow replace today's rotting capitalist society and construct a new socialist society, and indicate the clear, social-scientific analysis of it (capitalist society) by the emergent classes—the proletariat and the farmers. There was no question that the so-called documentary, which started out as the news film, would become a strong weapon of the movement for social revolution. This has been evidenced by the Soviets. Even in Japan, which was under the violent oppression of a militarist government, each and every cut of the news film preserved a fragmentary "truth." Therefore, if we consciously shoot that at the location, and if we edit these scenes purposefully, the "truth" of modern-day Japanese society—the anguish of the people, the necessity of collapse because of those contradictions—we could precisely indicate this to the people of the emergent classes of Japanese society. However, even though we can do this, what are we Japanese documentary film producers—no, what am *I* doing right now?![43]

As a filmmaker working in what were basically semigovernmental agencies (Domei Tsushin and Nichiei), Kuwano was extremely limited by the form of the newsreel. He did try to include subversive moments in his films to direct spectatorial readings in directions that went against the grain. For example, he recalls inserting a funeral pyre of some fallen soldiers with melodramatic narration such as, "Even now, the soldiers' souls return to their hometowns, where wives and children quietly wait." However, this was inevitably snipped by the censors, leaving Kuwano clinging to the hope that his documentary images of the fighting retained some grain of truth.[44]

Filmmakers in the budding field of *bunka eiga* had far more latitude in coding multiple readings into their films. This is the issue running quietly behind many of the debates over the fictive qualities of nonfiction film between 1939 and 1942. Filmmakers were working out the nature of this new brand of fictionality. Rotha was, in the end, exceedingly vague on this point; Japanese filmmakers, on the other hand, were looking for prescription. Shirai Shigeru spoke of Rotha's influence on documentary production, but had he not seen six or seven of the British school films at the Education Ministry (including *Drifters* [1929] and *Night Mail* [1936]) he admitted he would have had no idea what Rotha meant by "dramatization of actuality."[45]

Certainly, the filmmakers who did not attend those screenings were handicapped in their reading of *Documentary Film* and the massive discourse it generated. Many articles discussed the definitions of Rotha's terminology and its translation,[46] but the bulk of the writing was a continuation (and vulgarization) of earlier Yuiken debates concerning the epistemology of cinema—"Documentary as art" or "Documentary as science."[47] This itself, as Ueno Kozo has suggested, was a structural continuation of earlier struggles over whether film was art; the aesthetic domain simply migrated from "Cinema as art" to "Talkie as art" to "Documentary as art."[48] However, in one of Atsugi's best articles responding to her critics, we find the best hint at the core issue:

> In order for documentary film to have a meaningful existence as art, we must correctly recognize the essential meaning of this "fiction." This is what I want to state over and over again. To this same end . . . filmmakers' efforts must be more than the turning of the camera as it has been up to today. There needs to be more care for "working" on works,

more intensity, more like throwing one's entire soul into the hardships of a novelist.

"Poetry is more philosophical than history."—Aristotle.

Today we can find the meaning of this saying if, while native born to the turbulent breath of history, we seek in documentary film the possibility of finding poetry (fiction) in the very center of that history (actuality).[49]

In the midst of the spectacular war films of the day, a new kind of documentary emerged from this group. While other filmmakers were locating their filmmaking practice at the sites of greatest power—the military, the bureaucracy—these filmmakers were endeavoring to produce a new documentary film that (indirectly) pointed to the backwardness of the nation, and to the sheer poverty and suffering in everyday life.[50] For their producers, these films were the finest examples of documentary being made. Ishimoto Tokichi set the pattern with *Snow Country*, spending nearly three years recording the fight between Yamagata villagers and their fierce winters. *Snow Country* was unusual for its long-term study, foreshadowing the Yamagata films by the most important postwar documentarist, Ogawa Shinsuke; historian Tanikawa Yoshio goes so far as to say it marked the start of Japanese documentary film.[51]

Other films include Atsumi Teruo's *People Burning Coal* (*Sumiyaku hitobito*, 1940–41) and *Village without a Doctor* (*Ishi no inai mura*, 1939). The latter, Ito Sueo's first film, shows the terrible health conditions in village Japan and the government's obvious inability to provide adequate health care for all its people. Kyogoku Takahide's *Village of Stone* (*Ishi no mura*, 1941) shows the severe manual labor at a rock quarry, and his *Field Diagnosis Boat* (*Homensen*, 1939) follows a medical group traveling the Sumida River to treat river workers. Imaizumi Yoshitama turned his camera to the rough life of train workers in *Train C57*. Ueno Kozo's *The Pearl Diver of Wagu* (*Wagu no ama*, 1941) contrasts the hardships of life for female shell divers (including steep pay inequities in comparison to men) with stunning underwater sequences that aestheticize the work itself. Atsugi's *Record of a Nursery* (*Aru hobo no kiroku*, 1942) shows the cooperative work between working mothers and nursery school teachers to raise healthy, educated children. This impressive body of work arose from the competing claims over the significance of Paul Rotha's *Documentary Film*.

Although Rotha inspired them all, these filmmakers took varying positions vis-à-vis the use of reenactment and screenwriting in documentary. What they hold in common is a striking exclusion of the war hysteria and its rhetoric and a focus on the difficult life of Japanese citizens, a socially conscious documentary that resisted the temptations of explosions and exotic locales. In this way, the filmmakers encode to various degrees the discontent usually restricted to hidden spaces into their very public media. The filmmakers perceived their efforts to be interconnected and bringing documentary to an unprecedented level of excellence. Although they never gave themselves a collective name or identity, they did consider their combined efforts to be akin to a "documentary movement."[52] Their films constitute the finest of the prewar documentary cinema, and an instance of "cultural translation" where theory and practice were finely tuned and brought into thorough interaction through the mediation of translators—even incompetent, if enthusiastic, translators.

CHAPTER THREE

Voices of the Silents

If the motion-picture screens of each country in the world were spread edge to edge across the land they would probably overlap at each international boundary line and form a cover for continuous studio activities underneath.

—*New York Times,* May 16, 1920

If Rudolph Valentino appears on the screen, then the *benshi* must become Valentino. If he does this, the female fans will become excited.

—Matsui Suisei, 1931

"Remember that dialogue doesn't photograph," read one of the rules tacked onto the door of the scenario department at Mack Sennett's old Keystone Studio.[1] This chapter refutes the commonsense assumption this maxim belies. Sennett, of course, built his reputation on the raucous Keystone Cops and the comedy of Roscoe "Fatty" Arbuckle, Mabel Normand, and Charlie Chaplin. This was the inventive comedy of the silent era with its preponderance of physical pratfalls and gags involving speeding cars, flying objects, ladders, and human bodies put in one precarious situation after another. It is no wonder tha\t he reminds his writers to keep it physical.

But Sennett's delightful rule also repackages a commonplace argument about the first thirty years or so of cinema. This was a silent medium. Stories were told through visual means. The actor's only resource was his or her body. Acting was pantomimed by default. Where language entered in, it was to be found in codified gestures. As for the resources of cinema, the emphasis was on clarifying visual access to that body through the developing "language" of narrative space—something that will be a central concern in this initial chapter on cinematic translation. Directors, cinematographers, set and lighting designers, all conformed their work to these attitudes about cinema, rendering the expressivity of the actors' bodies as legibly as possible. Of course, there were local variations, particularly in the European and Soviet avant-gardes, but there is no question that these values spread to most of the world by the 1920s. This happened to be the most logical way to communicate a complex narrative without the benefit of the actor's voice. Dialogue doesn't photograph. It was this extralinguistic legibility, according to cinema's advocates, that enabled the new art form to internationalize in ways unimaginable to the playwright or the novelist. In 1920, a critic in the *London Times* described the global character of cinema:

> The cinematograph can run thorough the whole gamut of human emotions without the use of a spoken word. It can describe the story of a Greek tragedy in so convincing a fashion that the Chinaman sheds tears, and can set forth stories like "Solome" with such barbaric splendor that the Mohamaedan and the Farsee are overcome with amazement. It discovers a comedian in America and causes an outbreak of hysteria in London. A tragedian is found in Japan and Paris is thrilled. The potentialities of such an instrument are beyond all calculation. The cinematograph might become the greatest aid in the spread of culture since the days of the Renaissance.[2]

It was in this spirit that Carl Laemmle called his new studio "Universal Pictures Corporation" in 1927, just a year before sound technologies confronted him with a gauntlet of verbiage. Lurking behind Laemmle's idealism is the cultural arrogance of Enlightenment thought and the Orientalism built into its universalism. The quote from the *London Times* is revealing in this respect. While the author celebrates the wordless internationalism of the silent cinema, his examples incorporate both a directionality and a certain instrumentalism. In this vision, the distant Chinaman breaks down in tears as he comes into contact with a source of Western civilization. Cinema also allows the West to teach the Orientals the splendor of their own cultures. Curiously, only Japanese cinema has something to offer Western cinema, but considering the context this discovery is likely fodder for the genius of filmmakers working in the metropoles of North America and Europe. The silent cinema thus ushers in a new phase in the spread of (Western) culture—enlightenment by the light of the projector.

Needless to say, all this cultural difference implies a constitutive linguistic difference as well. The triumphal internationalism of silent film culture was probably only possible because the issue of actual translation seemed so simple. Of course, there was language in the silent films that demanded translation. However, there was little controversy there. All one need do was clip out the few intertitles, translate and photograph new ones, and then reedit them in. Simple as that.

In actuality, it was hardly a straightforward matter. The rhetoric of universalism hides a quite complicated situation. Those simple intertitles served numerous functions and transformed slowly over the course of decades. Producers, distributors, exhibitors played with a variety of methods for their translation, just as they took varying stances in regard to the task of the translator. Intertitles also provided a convenient mechanism for both censorship and cultural domestication. Furthermore, the presence and performance of live lecturers in various eras and places added a further layer of complexity to both the text and its translation. This chapter will examine the cinemascape of the first decades of the twentieth century. By teasing out the specificities of film translation at this formative moment, we will discover some hints about what lies in store in the remainder of the book.

Intertitles—Translators Unbound

Seen from our temporal vantage point in the twenty-first century, there would seem to be a remarkable synchronicity accompanying the global appearance of cinema. The Lumière brothers grabbed bragging rights for the invention of the medium with their Grand Café screening on December 28, 1895, in Paris; however, there were teams in other countries with similar machines in various stages of completion. Through a combination of inventiveness, marketing savvy, and piracy, motion pictures were being shot and exhibited all over the world by the turn of the century (although it would still require many more decades to achieve saturation into the rural nooks and crannies of the world). The approach of the initial films also appears in rough sync. No matter where they were made, they tended to be the same length, use similar techniques of cinematography, and draw on similar subject matter. As Eileen Bowser notes, "In the beginning the universality of the film medium was particularly evident: the same kinds of subjects and styles appeared the world over."[3]

Over the first few years, traffic picked up and that rough synchronicity gave way to distinct transnational flows. In much of the world, the currents quickly became unidirectional, from the United States and Europe to everywhere else. There was small-scale circulation within regions or dispersed language groups—such as Eastern Europe or South and Central America—but this activity was dwarfed by Euro-American exports, and particularly the exchange traversing the Atlantic. In the first few years, Europeans found it difficult to penetrate the U.S. market, and the rampant piracy of Continental films did not help matters. However, through complex legal negotiations and partnerships with U.S. companies such as Edison, their market share increased steadily after 1904. As we will see, the films of Pathé Frères were particularly popular with American audiences, so much so that pirates like Edison and Lubin continued to sell dupes because the French company could not keep up with demand. In 1907, only a third of films in the United States were produced domestically; the rest were European, half of which were from Pathé.[4]

The balance began to tip in 1909, when foreign and domestic productions achieved rough parity. The domination of the domestic we now associate with American film culture begins here, and this process was intimately tied to changing translation practices. In 1912, 80 percent of titles in release were American; seen strictly in terms of bulk, 14 million feet of positive (in other words, exposed and developed film) were imported and 80 million feet were exported. By 1914, the latter figure was four times that.[5] American producers made their move on European markets in the wake of the war, which left European industries in ruins, and have maintained their dominant position ever since. After this, even historically prominent national cinemas were, in fact, dominated by imported product; for example, in 1924 a full 95 percent of films on Soviet screens were foreign.[6]

This steady increase in traffic was accompanied by—and sometimes in synergy with—the gradual elaboration of cinematic narrative. The story film emerged between 1903 and 1906, giving rise to the nickelodeon. Plots incrementally gained complexity, particularly in 1908 to 1909 when features extended to fifteen or twenty minutes in length. Filmmakers like Georges Méliès, Edwin S. Porter, and D. W. Griffith played with the medium, inventing crosscutting and special effects to represent mental imagery or whole other worlds. From 1912, acting in American film became more naturalistic, and filmmakers increasingly deployed close-ups and medium shots to dynamize editing and photography. It was at this point that intertitles took the form we associate them with today.

This is only the most schematic history of early cinema, although I will flesh it out as I turn to matters of translation.[7] Before that, I want to look carefully at the development of the silent film intertitle and the gradual infusion of language into both theatrical and cinematic space.

It is impossible to discuss the work of the translators without understanding the nature of the textuality they were trafficking in. As with modernity itself, change in the most modern of media was swift and uneven, making it dangerous to generalize across the temporal and spatial reaches of the "silent era." While stressing this unevenness, I will concentrate on the influential cinema of the United States, where the main features of this development are most legible. To begin with, we must back up to visual culture before the Lumières take the stage.

Of all the precursors to the motion picture, the most important from the purview of translation study was the magic lantern lecturer. There were many of these figures in the late 1800s, and some of them achieved a measure of fame, such as John Stoddard, Dwight Elmondorf, Edward S. Curtis, and Burton Holmes.[8] These men would travel with a set of slides, giving illustrated lectures or telling stories that prefigure the cinema. With the stunning success of the first motion pictures, many found integrating shorts into their lectures a natural step. Some even became directors in their own right (thanks to his films on First Nations peoples of the American West, Curtis is often identified as one of the first ethnographic filmmakers). As Charles Musser argues, these showmen were integrating the new medium into established screen practice, and so transformed it.[9]

Within a year of its invention, cinema was anything but silent. At the point of reception, exhibitors were adding live lecturers, music, and even elaborate sound effects. They also began inserting the precursor to the intertitle, magic lantern slides that would introduce each short film. The producers of the films often sold these slides, but exhibitor magazines also taught theater owners how to make their own. With their control over the aural context of the movies, the exhibitors became the arbiters of meaning. They were the facilitators of narrative, the coauthors of the shows.

Intertitles begin their shift from exhibitor to producer in 1903 with the British film *Dorothy's Dream* (dir. G. A. Smith) and Porter's *Uncle Tom's Cabin*. This was enough of an innovation for Edison to prominently feature it in its ad campaign: "In this film we have made a departure from the old method of dissolving one scene into another by inserting announcements with brief descriptions as they appear in succession."[10]

This kind of intertitle was called a "leader." It introduced either a short film or, as narratives increased in complexity, a group of shots. Although leaders enjoyed an early introduction, they remained relatively unusual in the first decade of cinema. This is probably because they simply were not that necessary. Audiences at this early moment in many parts of the world were illiterate, and lecturers often accompanied films, which were also deeply intertextual. Spectators knew the stories and this relieved filmmakers from the obligation to make their narratives self-contained and thoroughly explicated. It would only be in the next decade that film stories were told as if for the first time. Until then, a combination of leaders and lecturers cued audiences to read the film against the intertext they brought with them to the theater.

Aside from the lecturers, another aural accoutrement was performers in the auditorium. Especially from 1907 to 1909, actors stood behind the screens of the larger theaters in America and performed all the voices. There was the "Dram-o-tone," the "Actologue," and Adolph Zukor's "Humanono." Poorly capitalized theaters with this inclination used a lone actor for all the voices. An early historian of cinema complained, "[This] economic shortcut resulted in poorly prepared scripts or improvisations, repetitions of the same dialogue for different pictures, strange aural-visual combinations and the use of 'actors' with little dramatic inspiration."[11] Presumably, this integrated some degree of translation for foreign films, but this remains unclear owing to its ephemeral nature. In any case, the practice did not last long, as the quality was often poor, the cost prohibitive, and, perhaps most decisively, it was rendered redundant by the increasing sophistication of cinematic narrative.

In 1908 and 1909, filmmakers modified the leader to represent human speech, naming it the "spoken title"—dialogue photographed. In 1912, the shift of spoken titles from the beginning of scenes to the instant of the utterance becomes pronounced and Europe followed suit a couple of years later. Soon after this, intertitles also take on the function of ellipsis, acting as bridges over chunks of time the filmmakers wished to dispense with. Close-ups of written text, such as letters, telegrams, and newspaper text, came to constitute a quasi intertitle and were called "inserts." Barry Salt's sample of 1913 productions found sixty-three of 171 films with intertitles, half of which used spoken titles. This would increase year by year, while the lecturers simultaneously took their final bow and all but disappeared.

None of this was lost on the critics, who began agitating for the change. In 1912, one wrote, "It is quite natural for the writer to begin the scene with a subtitle announcing the main incident of that scene, but the proper place for the subtitle is usually at a place just preceding the incident. I have seen many films made unintelligible by this fault."[12] In 1915, the trade paper Wid's noted that intertitles had swiftly gone from an "incidental" to a central aspect of filmmaking, and cried out for quality control: "They think that most any one can write 'titles' just because in the good old days they used to write them in their spare moments... Why spend thousands on a production and then allow some poor sad mutt to injure it?"[13] In subsequent years, critics increasingly commented on the quality of writing in intertitles, granting it the kind of attention usually directed to acting and cinematography.

By the beginning of the next decade they were seen as essential tools in the construction of narrative and still filled with untapped riches. In 1921, Gertrude Allan wrote, "The sub-title is pregnant with possibilities... the chalice of expression from which the screen author should drink deeply" thanks to its "far reaching power of poetic expression."[14] In the same year, director William C. DeMille (Cecil's elder brother and an accomplished playwright) compared the intertitle to the Greek chorus of classical theater, arguing, "There is much of life that can only be expressed with the aid of words, the psychological overtones and colors, which action alone cannot portray. We will no more be able to dispense with the sub-title in the photoplay than we can eliminate action from the spoken play."[15] Taking this logic a step further, the screenwriting team of John Emerson and Anita Loos stirred great controversy when they used the pages of Photoplay to advocate using as many intertitles as possible. "Subtitles are now a convention," they wrote in response to a New York Times critique, and modern audiences are accustomed to a stoppage of action for a printed insert, instead of boring them or "telling the story with words," subtitles often have a contrary effect. Watch any movie audience and you will notice that after a good subtitle everyone sits up and eagerly looks at the screen; for a good subtitle has the effect of clarifying action that is past and at the same time throwing forward the mind of the audience to the next scene, without giving it away beforehand.[16]

Although many critics disagreed with Emerson and Loos on the proper quantity of intertitles, the conventions they described were now commonplace in cinemas the world over. Furthermore, this quote hints at the naturalizing power of convention. Accustomed as we are today with the textless sound cinema, we may find the intertitle an interruption in the flow of narrative; but audiences who knew nothing else found them a very different experience.

A final indication of the new seriousness with which intertitles were perceived is the prominence of the writers. The tasks of writing shooting scenarios and intertitles were often separate steps in the production process. From 1922, the trade papers began recognizing the authorship of intertitle writers, and quality titles were associated with names like Terry Ramsaye (better known as one of the first film historians), Ralph Spence, John Emerson, and Anita Loos. By 1925, the intertitle authors working in Hollywood became "personages" at the Hollywood studios. Their numbers were few; one contemporary estimate counted around twenty in 1927. Nine of the key players organized into an association with the charming name "The Titular Bishops"—"Nine men of assorted waistlines, accents, and origins," joked the *Times*.[17]

Among their ranks was future director Joseph Mankiewicz (*All About Eve* [1950], *Julius Caesar* [1953]), who began his film career translating intertitles for Universal Filmaktiengesellschaft (UFA) in Berlin. He and Alfred Hitchcock in London demonstrated how intertitle writing could be a stepping-stone to the upper reaches of the film world. Of course, these two had to become directors to be remembered by history, and as far as I've been able to ascertain Mankiewicz is the only silent era translator whose name we know.

Obviously, the ideology of invisibility is at play here. However, another factor is the way the visuality of the silent film historically trumps its linguistic features. This is why, when sound technology was wed to the apparatus at the end of the 1920s, many critics disparaged it as uncinematic. "The people of all nations have eyes to see, but every people has its own language," wrote Italian playwright Luigi Pirandello.[18] He was wrong, of course. Although he was willing to afford the "talkie" a musical sound track analogous to the silent film, he felt that talk itself was strictly the domain of the theater. However, the duality he strikes between silent and sound cinemas is predicated on the suppression of written text in the cinema prior to 1929.

The renowned universality of the silent star's pantomime was embedded in language. As film narratives became self-enclosed and less reliant on intertext, the crutch of that gestural semiosis at the locus of the actor's body shifted from the lecturer to the intertitle. When the conventions of the continuity system fell into place and the value of motivation kicked in, language finally became a problem. Even pantomime could not escape the readings of spectators automatically searching for verbal language in their oh-so-human ways. Audiences were lip-reading and registering English words coming from the mouths of supposedly foreign characters. Critics complained that this was "jarring," a vocabulary choice deeply connected to the values embodied by the new cinematic realism of Hollywood cinema. It was also argued that foreign characters should "speak" broken English in intertitles, unless, of course, they talk to someone in their own tongue, and then it gets complicated. When characters write notes, they argued that the best filmmakers use inserts in the foreign language and then dissolve into English.[19]

This finally brings us to the issue of translation, beginning with the nuts and bolts holding the entire enterprise together. That silent film translation involved substituting target-language intertitles for the originals is obvious, but the mechanics of the process bore down on the nature of the traffic between the cinemas of the world. It is difficult to confidently judge how the translation strategies generally developed, but we can find a hint in the records of one of the earliest studios. William N. Selig was one of the pioneers of the cinema, having started his Chicago business in 1896 by reverse engineering and ripping off the Lumière brothers' camera and then successfully repelling the legal maneuvering of the Motion Picture Patents Company. He was the first producer to make the move to Los Angeles (in 1909), and he is one of the key figures responsible for longer films, the Western, and Tom Mix. In the first decade of the new century, Selig set up distribution points abroad but prepared foreign-release prints in the United States. The foreign distributors of his films would receive a list of intertitles, which they would translate and send back to the Los Angeles studio. Selig would then produce a newly titled print for them.[20]

It appears that was not the best of strategies because it relied heavily on technicians with no linguistic expertise. In 1915, Selig's Dutch distributor raised a complaint about rampant misspellings, and asked that the studio send prints with only a frame or two of each intertitle in place; they would use that as the basis for the translation, shooting the text in a frame with the Selig trademark and inserting these new intertitles into the print.[21] This appears to have become the standard Selig practice by 1916.[22]

In the 1920s, many producers used the latter method. However, both were widely deployed. Some companies were translating their own intertitles in as many as a dozen languages, with most prepared to offer ready-made prints in three or four.[23] In the mid-1920s, Sidney Kent, vice president of Famous Players-Lasky, boasted that his company was shipping prints all over the world with intertitles in thirty-eight different languages. Furthermore, each Famous Players-Lasky film was also accompanied by fifty or so other items that required translation and printing in the target languages. Regarding these publicity materials, Kent said, "They are to the picture, like the food and ammunition of a soldier, who can't live and fight with only a gun."[24] Most conquest metaphors since the time of Saint Jerome and Horace have described the power of the target language to pillage the literary and linguistic treasures of faraway cultures. In contrast, Kent's imperium is Hollywood's global market, and his comments clearly suggest how the American studios recognized that their armies of translators guaranteed Hollywood's hegemony over world cinema.

This was, however, no guarantee of quality. Film criticism of the late silent era is filled with rants over intertitle translation. Reviews castigated producers and distributors for unforgivable misspellings, the incomplete grasp of English idioms, and the hilarious mistakes that resulted. For example, a *Variety* reviewer critiquing the Chinese film *Retaliation* (1929) compained about what might be the first instance of the "hex error":

> While to the Chinese the titles are seriously drawn, the Caucasian will
> find much humor in the literal translation to English . . . When three
> characters are simultaneously surprised there will be three separate

titles, reading in their order, "Ah!" "Yea!" "Oh!"... To complain about food in a Chinese café, so far as the pictures shows, was cause for murder. In one scene when the hero calls the wine served him "insipid," the maid sends his two cop companions into the "yonder world" by means of wine which she termed "tepid."... The choicest translation comes when after the picture has had its several big murder scenes the greatness of Wu Soan and the screen flickers this *[sic]:* "Wu Soan's career was intimately connected with his wine cup"—as his friend says to him: "Brother, you are intoxicated." Ah! Yea! Oh![25]

These problems appear to have been endemic outside the major traffic routes for production and distribution. One critic in 1929 carped, "What happens, seemingly, especially with these indies, is that a native, with a British university knowledge of English, merely transposes the literal French into literal English without cognizance of Anglo-Saxon idioms, like an American or British caption writer would be prone to fall into unconscious traps if translating literally into French."[26] Placing responsibility for the translation in the hands of the distributor or exhibitor probably ensured natural prose; however, it also subjected the film to translations the filmmakers may not have appreciated. Let us look at the example of the American film *Within Our Gates* (1919). This was produced by the great African American director Oscar Micheaux, who was largely forgotten to history before a band of scholars and archivists dug up archival materials, conducted oral interviews, and combed the world's archives for long-lost films.[27] One reason this is an interesting example is that it demonstrates how translations can facilitate time travel and salvage lost texts.

As already mentioned, the source-language texts distributors worked off of were often a mere frame or two in length. These "flash titles," as they were known, saved considerable expense by shortening the length of film stock that had to be purchased, developed, and shipped abroad. *Within Our Gates* was discovered by film scholar Scott Simmon, who helped direct its restoration. The lone print happened to be in a Spanish film archive under the title *La Negra*. Naturally, all the intertitles had been displaced by Spanish-language translations, but Simmon was delighted to discover that the Spanish distributor mistakenly left in four of Micheaux's flash titles. Working off these, Simmon was able to study Micheaux's writing style, the nature of the translation, and then translate all the Spanish titles back into English for the restoration. What concerns us here is the nature of the translation. Two of the four translations for which we have original intertitles were quite straightforward, although one of the flash titles was the beginning of an iris-in that cut off the edges of the frame (I've rendered the visible text in all caps, the rest being Simmon's best reconstructed guess):

ENGLISH: Tell-tale smoke.
SPANISH: La humareda les traiciona.

And:

ENGLISH: Years ago,
in the dePTH OF THE FORESt, but
not sO FAR THAT ONE could
helP HEARING OF A LATE afternoon
THE SOMBER ECHO of
cOW BELLS STEALING ACross
the VALLEY FROM THE GRidlestone estate...

SPANISH: En un rincón del bosque pero no tan distante que a la caída de la tarde no oyesen los mugidos del ganado de la Graja de Gridlestone.

The next two intertitles are far more revealing. The first reads:

ENGLISH: That night.
SPANISH: Aquella noche. Una partida de cartas
para desplumar una víctima.

One could roughly translate the title back into English as "That Night. A card game to fleece a victim." This suggests that the distributor was troubled by Micheaux's plain intertitle. It worried that the Spanish audience would find this juncture of the plot confusing. Perhaps the audience would find the idea of poker, and by extension its implications in the plotting, perplexing and in need of either excision or demystification. It is an approach to translation that, according to Antoine Berman, "brings everything back to its own culture, to its norms and values, and considers what is situated outside the latter—the Foreign—as negative or just about good enough to be annexed, adapted, to increase the richness of that culture."[28] As we will see, this impulse to supplement translation with explication runs through the history of cinema. It has been argued that this is a universal aspect of translation, but what ultimately interests us is the way this is rarely separable from ideological concerns. The fourth example from *Within Our Gates* is particularly suggestive of this:

ENGLISH: Yes. Gridlestone had cheated him, also,
and when he had called him to terms,
had laughed in his face, calling him "poor white trash —
and no better than a negro," whereupon he had sworn . . .
SPANISH: Sí, Gridlestone le engañó también y además le
insultó ferozmente, así es que juró vengarse.

Translated back into English this reads, "Yes, Gridlestone cheated him as well and insulted him ferociously, so he swore he would avenge himself." Here the distributor's intertitle tames the specifics of the racial insult, this in a film so deeply about race relations and lynching in the United States of America. In a second restoration project, Simmon found that another Micheaux film was subjected to a similar domestication and deflection of controversial subject matter, when *Where Are My Children?* (1916) was originally shown in Holland. The Dutch version was one of two surviving prints the restoration was based on. Its distributor had completely revised the story — about birth control and abortion — by rewriting intertitles and shuffling the order of shots in the translation process. In this case, it is possible the distributor had no choice, as censorship laws often necessitated this kind of tampering.

At the very least, these examples hint at how translators in the silent film world were considered indispensable and at the same time despised. When their work attracted comment, it was for ridicule. For film studios, their contribution was an afterthought in the business of exporting product. For distributors and exhibitors, it was a convenient camouflage for censorship and a tool to ensure a return on investment through domestication and explication. Because the vast majority of films were conceived and executed purely for entertainment value — in other words, for quick and easy profits — distributors did not think twice about their freest of free translations. On one end of the spectrum of licentiousness, there were "terse" translations that pared intertitles down to a bare minimum. This shortened the films and thus saved money. On the other end were those that "retitled for burlesque," throwing out the source-language intertitles wholesale and "freely" writing parodic ones in their place.[29]

We must consider the status of the text undergoing such free translation. That the text could be "retitled for burlesque" or translated "tersely" suggests that we are not simply dealing with an alternative conception of fidelity. One of the founding notions of poststructuralist approaches to language was that speech, with its immediacy and live presence, is privileged over writing. Jacques Derrida wrote of a phonocentrism built on a conception of communication that began with an ideal stability of meaning, something many models of translation assume in their search for secure equivalencies between languages. Curiously enough, we find an alternative phonocentrism in the silence of the silent film. Here the value of writing is discounted for the visual "speech" of the body. This phonocentrism sees the body talking through coded gesture and facial expressions and grants intertitles only the lightest of meaning. Lacking the weighty centrality that demands a sense of debt from the translator, intertitles too often suffered what most would call free translation— what some would refuse to call translation at all.

It would be a mistake to assume that this free translation simply shaved off various meanings to arrive at a simple, stable essence to be trafficked into the target language with suspicious additions and petty exclusions. One of the useful aspects of silent cinema's use of language is its very materiality. This points us to what will be a central concern in the final chapters of this book. The textuality of cinema is marked by hybridity, such that it is difficult to think of it as a univocal text. This begins with its complex interplay of written text and gestural performance, but one need not stop there. The popular notion of silent film translation, for example, sees it simply as the process of substituting curt blocks of sense with their target-language equivalents. Yet consider the language itself. It is often not colloquial speech, nor is it poetry. However, one certainly knows it when one reads it. This was obvious to Marjorie Charles Driscoll, who submitted a delightful poem to *Motion Picture Classic* some years after the coming of sound. Filled with a sweet nostalgia, it looks back at the language specific to the English silent film intertitle:

I met a very ancient man
with gray and revered head.
"It's growing dark," I said to him,
And this is what he said.

"Drifting shadows crept over the
World as suppliant Day knelt at the
threshold of Night, pleading for the
black of darkness."

I looked up at him in mild surprise,
He wept: "Ah, well-a-day!

I once wrote titles for the films,
And now I talk this way!"[30]

This is, indeed, the way people often "talked" in the first decades of cinema. However, translators did not necessarily attend to these aspects of language in their winnowing out of sense. The particular structures and stresses of their intertitle texts rarely enjoyed the rigorous engagement typical of, say, translators of poetry.

Just as crucial to the way intertitles make meaning are their visual qualities. For one thing, there is the type itself. Even the most nondescript and curt intertitles use some sort of font. Studio mogul Louis B. Mayer, for one, recognized the importance of typeface, and went so far as to commission Linotype to cut five fonts to his specification. Even today we recognize this font, and thus it is parodied in present-day films along with the requisite scratches and dust added virtually through digital filters.

This graphic text was often accompanied by illustrations. This practice probably starts at the birth of intertitles with Porter's *Uncle Tom's Cabin* (1903), which he shot between *Life of an American Fireman* (1902–3) and *The Great Train Robbery* (1903). Porter printed cards that share many conventions with the graphic design of posters, including oversized letters, curved lines of text, and various visual embellishments around the type. Furthermore, filmmakers probably began framing text with decorative borders in 1910 with Vitagraph's *Daisies*, which lined the edges of its intertitles with the flowers of the title. The same year, *Hako's Sacrifice* (1910) referenced its Japanese setting with bamboo borders.[31] The following year a few films added drawings, and by the end of the decade some filmmakers even animated their intertitles. Big-budget films often sported elaborately designed intertitles that were works of art in and of themselves. Indeed, silent filmmakers inspired by art movements like futurism brought those aesthetics and their approaches to typography to intertitle design. By the mid-teens, many intertitles took on overt narrative devices that helped establish settings and link scenes. Kristin Thompson notes a 1916 review of William S. Hart's *The Aryan* that calls attention to this development:

> The subtitles of Triangle productions have been worth attention for some time. At first they were pleasingly decorative; later they aided in interpreting the mood of the play. The text of the subtitles not only advanced the story, but when conversation was used, helped the characterization; and the skillful word pictures aided and completed the scene.[32]

Among filmmakers and titlers attuned to the complex semiotic productivity of the intertitle, the best knew that their resources were not limited to linguistic signs and figurative symbolizations. One of these titlers happens to be Alfred Hitchcock. For example, one critic recalled his initial encounter with the future director of *Psycho:* "When I first met Hitchcock he was writing and ornamenting subtitles for silent pictures. He used to announce 'Came the dawn' in black letters on a white ground, or tell us that 'Heart spoke in the hush of the evening' in white letters on a black ground."[33] Aside from the possibilities offered by tone and color, Hitchcock wrote at the time that illustrated intertitles do far more than vivify the action they are embedded in. They also help to "space episodes," recommending "appropriate symbols." This is a slightly more sophisticated version of Emerson and Loos's defense of the intertitles quoted earlier. Hitchcock is cognizant of cinema's temporal aspect, and how intertitles interact with live action in time. For him, intertitles point to the subsequent image, "spacing episodes to interpolate a pause, emphasizing the process of 'telling' and 'reading.'"[34]

This posed a problem for the people trafficking films across linguistic frontiers. These visual supplements were inextricable from the artfulness of the film and point to the protean complexity of meaning in the intertextual flow of the silent film. However, they were difficult (in other words, expensive) to reproduce. Not surprisingly, they were often the first layer of textuality stripped away in the course of translation. Filmmakers were probably concerned about this to some degree. Barry Salt finds an increase in the use of art titles in American films after World War I shut producers out of the European markets. He speculates that they were harder to "translate" for foreign-language versions, so ornamentation increased as the volume of translation decreased. This would explain why the illustrated titles decline again after the markets reopen.

This points to the economic conditions underlying film translation. We can even see the same logic the treatment of these silent films today. Some archivists involved in restoration keep antique presses that were used for printing intertitle cards. Like Simmon, they go to great lengths to replicate the original intertitles, sometimes going so far as to degrade the new photochemical image to ensure an aesthetic match to the texture of the old, stressed celluloid they are embedded in. At the same time, some video distributors simply alternate between the subtle, analog visual texture of the film and the blank, utterly black and white of

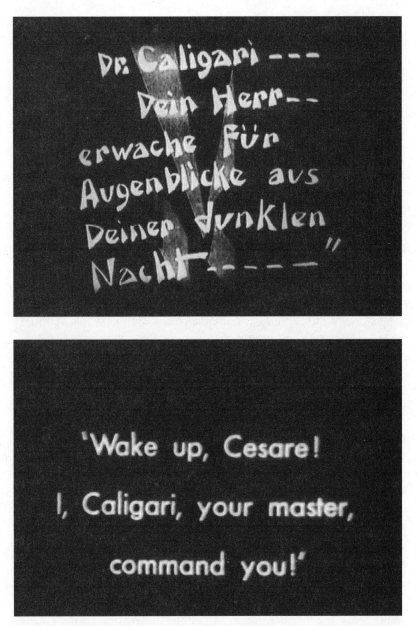

Figure 10. Intertitles from *The Cabinet of Caligari* (*Das Kabinett des Dr. Caligari*, 1920). The original intertitle scrolls downward and features expressionist typestyle and ornamentation. The English intertitle winnows down the German source text to the barest of meaning. A more accurate translation would be: "Cesare—Can you hear me? Cesare—I am calling you—I—Dr. Caligari—Your Master— Awaken for a moment from your dark night—"

digital electronic imagery and with inappropriate fonts. This is to say that bargain-rate video distributors replicate the worst practices of the past in the present.[35] We will find this simple logic of economy—that tension between art and industry—operating in postwar subtitling and dubbing as well.

One of the most fascinating schemes exhibitors and producers devised to save money was the multilingual title. This was common in border regions where several language groups overlapped and interacted. It is also yet another example of cinema's uniquely multifaceted relationship to language. For example, Cuba's inland theaters exhibited monolingual films, but the movie house on the Prado put bilingual intertitles in Spanish and English to attract a multicultural audience.[36] In regions all over the world, linguistic diversity led producers to make films with bi-, tri-, and even quadralingual intertitles (as was the case in Egypt).

Consider the case of Transylvania. Like other "margins" of the film world, the development of cinema was affected by the region's overlapping cultures and languages. Transylvania is a complicated geopolitical border zone. Moldavia and Valacchia featured the Romanian language, but there were also Hungarians who used the competing name of Erdély.[37] To make matters more confusing, to these groups must be added Germans and a fourth group called Skélezy and of Magyar extraction. Over the century of cinema, these various groups competed for both political power and linguistic hegemony, with the nation-states of Hungary and Romania staking out a shifting political border. Not surprisingly, the Germans and Skélezy are the big losers in this story. Early films were produced with Hungarian intertitles; however, when Transylvania passed from Hungarian to Romanian hands after World War I, the intertitles became bilingual with the addition of Romanian. Thus, a monolingual cinema implying domination and assimilation transforms into one marked by hybridity and contamination. As Sergio Germani suggests, the situation would seem to be crystallized in the iconic representative of Transylvania, Count Dracula.[38] Although modeled on a Romanian historical figure, his most famous incarnation in the cinema featured the Hungarian Bela Lugosi.

Alternatively, monolingual intertitles can take on a territorializing function. One of the most bafflingly diverse regions of the world is the Indian subcontinent. The typical thumbnail sketch of Indian cinema history describes a homogeneous silent cinema, centered on the remarkable films of Dhundiraj Govind Phalke, plunged into regional divisions by the babel of sound cinema, and unified only by the song-and-dance– fueled hegemony of Bombay films produced in a Hindi hybridized by a wide variety of accents and regional inflections. However, this single-sentence summary sidesteps the fact that Phalke himself was inserting intertitles in Hindi. In fact, by the late 1920s India had already become largely regionalized into twenty-eight distinct cinemas based on language difference, with the colonizer's films released untranslated in English.[39] Audiences disliked films from other provinces, probably because of the intertitles, but Hindi films were already beginning to cross linguistic borders just prior to the introduction of sound.

It must also be pointed out that bilingual intertitles did not lead to hybridized readings in any automatic sense. By extension, it cannot be assumed that the films necessarily hybridized their audiences. A useful example is the early South African epic *Die Voortrekkers* (*Winning a Continent*, 1916).[40] Shot only six years after the Union of South Africa reconstituted the region as a sovereign nation-state, this film was simultaneously homogenizing and hybridizing by design. It tells the mythic birth of the nation, and was undoubtedly inspired by the Griffith film of that title from the preceding season. The Voortrekkers, otherwise known as Boers, were Dutch farmers who moved inland to Natal from the confines of British rule at the Cape Colony. They established their own settlements, providing a central founding myth to Afrikaner nationalism. They eventually took the form of two distinct states until being annexed by Britain in 1900 during the Boer War. The film was produced by an American (I. W. Schlesinger, who had deep British business interests) and directed by a Brit (Harold Shaw). The writer, however, was a well-known champion of the Afrikaans language, Gustav Preller, who had already written a popular novelization of the Voortrekker myth. Thus, the film was meant to reconcile the two (white) communities of the new nation-state, and in that spirit Preller suppressed the anti-British sentiments of his previous writing by scapegoating Portuguese traders and black Africans.

Preller wrote his intertitles in both English and Afrikaans, making it the first film to use the new language (it wasn't until 1925 that Afrikaans became the official state language, displacing Dutch and English). Interestingly enough, this pedagogical function of the film—homogenizing the split identities within the audience under the sign of the nation—

was undermined by the bilingual titles. Differences between the Afrikaans and English texts bifurcated the audience, and the former subsequently recouped the film for Afrikaner nationalism by recourse to the intertext and resistance to the preferred reading built into the film.

Bilingual titles were not necessary for a film to "inhabit translation." As this chapter argues, the cinema was globalized from its first years. The conceptualization of a given film usually built in this reception by some foreign audiences somewhere, probably a somewhere that demanded both cultural and linguistic translation. This is to say that translation was written into the most monolingual of films. All intertitles were a source for some target language. For the producers of these texts, this has nothing to do with Benjamin's mode of intent toward Pure Language, that reverberating resource within language that invites but defies translation. Rather, it was a matter of business. Charles Musser notes that "because of their dependence on foreign markets, European producers had to take a more cautious approach to the ephemera of their local national culture than did most of their American counterparts. Imports generally avoided titles or reduced them to a bare minimum."[41] They strove to create a nonspecific popular culture, privileging genre over local storytelling, and minimizing the use of intertitles. It is generally agreed, for example, that part of Pathé's success in the United States was attributable to these factors, particularly its minimalist approach to intertitles. In other words, the internationalism of the silent film was partly a business strategy, not something inherent to the medium, and those armies of translators ultimately enabled it. As Derrida would have us ask, How are we to conceive of an autonomous original when traffic is built into its substance? Filmmaking and translating are interdependent activities and inextricable from cultures they are intertwined in. We will refine these links between cinematic narration, nation, and translation in the next section, which examines the other major mode of silent film translation: the lecturer.

Lecturers—Performing the Unbound

The live narration of moving images was a global phenomenon in the first fifteen years of the medium. In Europe and the United States, it virtually died out in the 1910s, enjoying a short-lived renaissance before all but disappearing in the 1920s. By way of contrast, screen-side lecturers remained a standard practice in Quebec and across much of Asia

"To be a lecturer you have got to have feeling."

Figure 11. Illustration for a *New York Times* article in 1920 with the headline "Survivors of a Vanishing Race in the Movie World: 'Lecturers' on the Lower East Side—Five of 'Em—Still Explain Eloquently What Is Happening on the Screen, and Regard Their Work as Art."

throughout the silent era and into the age of the talkies. At the end of the twentieth century, there were still practicing lecturers in Japan and Korea who either got their start as youths in the silent era or received training by that earlier generation.

There were also isolated postwar traditions in Southeast Asia. For example, Thai cinema in the 1960s and 1970s was a 16mm, silent film industry. Theaters were constructed with green rooms and translation booths next to the projection booths. From there one or more actors would supply the sound track live over a PA system. For outdoor showings, they would perform behind the screen. This was the standard practice for both domestic and foreign films; for the latter, they would turn the sound track down or off to make way for the translation. Apparently, this approach survived in rural areas of Thailand as late as the 1990s and is still found in Laos.[42]

Ultimately, very little is known about what exactly these silent-era narrators were up to. They attracted scarce comment in the contemporary English-language press, and came to the full attention of film scholars only recently. The exception is Japanese cinema, where they have been the subject of lively debate running from the 1910s to the present. These *benshi*, as they generally called today, wrote articles, how-to books, and autobiographies. They made recordings of their performances, which were popular enough to become a stand-alone commodity sans the accompanying film. As this suggests, they were often a bigger attraction than the films they "supplemented," leaving a wide array of ephemera usually associated with actor-centered star discourses. We also know about the *benshi* from censorship laws designed to control them, and by extension the films and their audiences. Finally, there is a small but fascinating nostalgia industry that preserves (a certain version of) silent-era narration through screenings with live performers and videos with *benshi* sound tracks[43] (Figure 12). Post-sound histories of Japanese film often disparaged the *benshi* as noncinematic. However, when some (mostly Western) scholars began reconsidering silent lecturers in Japan and elsewhere, Japanese critics recouped the *benshi*'s reputation.[44] Suddenly, the supposedly unique endurance of the *benshi* became a point of pride for Japanese historians and film fans, tainting the reconsideration with a nationalism blind to all the narrators in the rest of Asia. Nevertheless, those debates are of some interest to us, and I will reorient them around the issue of translation.

Initially, Japanese lecturers restricted their performance to introductions to the films. Called *maesetsu*, these were structurally analogous to the "leader" intertitle, except that they were longer, aural, and quite elaborate. In the 1910s, roughly about the time spoken titles become conventionalized, the *benshi* began extending their performances into the film itself. The style of their delivery was called *kowairo* and was closely linked to the singsong vocalizations of kabuki and precinematic forms of storytelling. Imagine a film screened with kabuki-like music and narration. A group of *benshi* would usually take turns, imitating the actors, reading intertitles, and generally embellishing the action.

This was also how foreign films were exhibited, so there was no need to translate and replace intertitles. In the course of the 1910s, *kowairo* was replaced by less song-like vocalizations, more colloquial speech, and Western music for foreign films. Scripts for these films began to accompany prints to Japan starting in 1907, and translated dialogue scripts for *benshi* became the norm after 1915. At the same time, *benshi* sorted themselves out through professionalization and specialization (Figure 14). Foreign film *benshi* were generally better educated, as their job required them to understand much about modern life in faraway places. Obviously, it helped to know something about foreign history, religions, and customs, and the ability to read intertitles and postproduction scripts was certainly a plus.

Of course, that does not necessarily mean they were careful interlocutors and translators. Film lore has it that characters in American films were usually named Mary, Jack, and Robert (who was always the villain).[45] Furthermore, film critics often complained about misprision. As an example, "He is the Kipling of the movie world" was rendered "He sells movie tickets" because Kipling sounds like *kippu uru* (selling tickets).[46] Or there was the *benshi* that turned an intertitle as simple as "Rocking chair" into "Rock chair" *(iwa no isu).*[47] As Jeffrey Dym points out, some misprision probably had something to do with censorship legislation, which understandably focused great energy on the *benshi's* activities. This example from D. W. Griffith's *Orphans of the Storm* (1921) hints at government intervention or industry self-patrolling:

ENGLISH: The lesson—The French Revolution RIGHTLY overthrew a BAD government.
JAPANESE TRANSLATION: The lesson to be learned from this movie is that the French political strife was caused by a tradition of bad governing and the consequences of this were worse.[48]

These examples simply evidence either the specter of censorship or the impoverishment of the translations. The latter cannot necessarily be blamed on a dearth of decent translators. After all, this was precisely the

Figure 12. Lecturers survived the talkies era in Japan and other parts of Asia.
Sawato Midori is a professional *benshi* in Japan and one of the leading authorities
on lecturers in Japanese film history. She carries on the tradition by training
young disciples, some of whom are voice actors in the dubbing industry.
Photograph courtesy of Matsuda Eigasha.

period when most major literary and philosophical works from the West
enjoyed their first publication in Japanese translation. Rather, this con-
firms the lowly status of film and the doubly low status of film translation. As I argued in the introduction and chapter 2, misprision interests
us primarily to the extent that it can be characterized by productivity.
What is of great interest here is the way lecturers' improvisational and
individualized performances interact with the free-form conception of
translation we discovered in the treatment of the intertitle.

Thanks to the *benshi*'s vast popularity, we have performances from quite a few of the more important *benshi* preserved on phonograph discs. Better yet, some *benshi* made multiple recordings of the performances on which their reputations were made. One of these is Satomi Yoshiro's three recordings of the 1921 *Camille,* starring Alla Nazimova in the title role and Rudolph Valentino. Benshi historian Jeffrey Dym painstakingly transcribed and translated the climatic scene of the film from each disc.[49] Run in parallel columns, we can study the improvisational particularity of the *benshi*'s translation in Figure 12, a sample extracted from Dym's chart. I have added a fourth column on the far left containing the original intertitles.

The first thing we notice about these performances is the way bits and pieces are identical, suggesting that Satomi worked off a common script and seamlessly integrated that text into his flow of verbiage. Second, he can, as in the middle column, completely ignore the intertitles on an apparent whim (the amount of "silence" varied from period to period, *benshi* to *benshi,* and performance to performance). He completely ignores a set of intertitles (numbers 94–99) while embellishing another, returning to rough sync with the intertitles at number 100. In the last sequence, Satomi vividly demonstrates how *benshi* played off the image. Around intertitle 101 one can easily perform a "reverse translation" back to the image, even without having seen the film. This only hints at how the *benshi*'s performance vivifies the experience of the film. It is a brand of intermedial explication splitting the translator's debt between typographic and gestural texts.

The actual translations here are strikingly similar to those we found in intertitles. Especially combined with the *benshi*'s intermedial explication of the action, they add up to a novel form of what John Catford evocatively called "unbound translation."[50] In a fundamental sense, we may trace this back to Cicero, but it is most closely associated with Dryden. In his 1680 preface to his translation of Ovid's *Epistles,* Dryden wrote of translation as imitation. He is using the term paradoxically to mean something quite opposite to its everyday sense—to stray from the source language text too liberally. He suggests that imitation is "where the translator (if now he has not lost that name) assumes the liberty, not only to vary from the words and sense, but to forsake them both as he sees occasion; and taking only some general hints from the original, to run division on the groundwork, as he pleases."[51] Forsaking the text, the *benshi*'s

Original Intertitles	Yoshiro's 1st Recording	Yoshiro's 2nd Recording	Yoshiro's 3rd Recording
100 "Do not weep, Gaston, the world will lose nothing. I was a useless ornament—a plaything—a momentary aurora."	"Even if I die, it will be no loss to the people of the world. I was a useless ornament, a toy, nothing more than pale, ephemeral, phosphorescent glow. If I die like this, I will have not the littlest regret. In this lonely life of mine, I am thankful to you for making such happy times, and I will never forget what you did for me."	"But within this lonely lifetime, you gave me some happy times. I will never forget your kindness. I have already confessed about what I did sometime ago in my last letter to you. It seems that people consider everything a woman like myself says as a lie."	"As a woman, I was a useless decoration, a boring toy, nothing more than a pale, ephemeral, phosphorescent glow. If I die like this, I will have not the smallest regret. In this lonely life of mine, I am thankful to you for making such happy times, and I will never forget what you did for me."
101 "Armand."	"As I have been writing, breathing has become even more difficult. Armand, please return to my side just one more time, I can't wait any longer. I've begun to cough, red blood is coming out. No, I am happy. I'm really happy. While the pen was moving, many creditors had jostled together by her side."	"As I have been writing, breathing has become even more difficult. Armand, please return to my side just one more time. No one is looking after me, yet by my side many creditors have gathered."	"As I have been writing, breathing has become even more difficult. Armand, please return to my side just one more time. While the pen was moving, many creditors had jostled together by her side."

Figure 13. A sample of the translation/transcription by *benshi* historian Jeffrey Dym of three of Satomi Yoshiro's recordings of the climatic scene from *Camille* (1921).

translation is acutely additive, grafted onto a cinematic text supposedly complete in and of itself. Thanks to its liveness, it was both protean and uniquely particular. Every performance was a discrete event, subject to play, serendipity, and the *benshi*'s state of inebriation on a given evening. The same film was sometimes radically different from *benshi* to *benshi*. Outside of the capital, the performances were even delivered in dialect. Most radically, the more powerful *benshi* could reedit films to suit their peculiar needs. The stance of the *benshi* vis-à-vis film could be explanatory, pedagogical, translational, competitive, combative, or all of the above. Dryden helps us see the reason why the unbound translation of the *benshi* is so scandalous when he writes, "To state it fairly; imitation of an author is the most advantageous way for a translator to show himself, but the greatest wrong which can be done to the memory and reputation of the dead."[52] Indeed, it was common for spectators to base their movie selections on who was providing the live narration rather than on the film itself. This is why a movement of intellectuals did its best to destroy the institution of the *benshi* in the 1910s and 1920s. This reaction was intimately tied to innovations in cinematic narration, developments that spelled the demise of the lecturer's position in the West.

As we have seen, filmmakers stepped up the intricacy of their films after 1907, moving them from a string of static tableaux to use more and varied shots, spoken titles, and lengthier stories. In reaction to this increase in complexity, there was a renewed, if short-lived, demand for lecturers in the West.[53] In smaller theaters, exhibitors met this demand by taking the stage themselves or putting their wives or projectionists to work. Marcus Loew created a "company of Ciceros" to ply the countryside. A writer from the late silent era attributed Loew's decision to fire his Ciceros to money—the lecturers thought their pay was too low and Loew felt they were too expensive. However, the author also speculates that another reason was that films were not the "finished product" they are "now" in 1920.[54]

This writer refers to the major feature in the transformation of narrative, from what has been called a "cinema of attractions" to the self-contained diegetic world of the continuity system. The latter conception of cinematic textuality was based on a new kind of realism that closed the world of the story off from the space of the audience, demanding narrative motivation for everything on-screen.[55] This put the lecturer in a paradoxical position. As Tom Gunning explains:

The lecturer could supply such values only as a supplement, an additional aid, rather than as an inherent organic unity. A lecturer's commentary undermines an experience of the screen as the site of a coherent imaginary world in which narrative action took place ... The narrator system could not afford a discontinuous presentation which might undermine film's illusionism. Such a practice would be totally at odds with the cinema of narrative integration, which maintained the film's illusion through a strong diegetic realism and an empathetic narrative.[56]

Ironically, the lecturer helped guide audiences through the increasingly elaborate films being shown in the nickelodeons after 1907, but that very elaboration involved a segregation of the story world from the world and, as Miriam Hansen argues, the presence of a human voice inhibited closure of the fictional world.[57] Scholars such as Gunning argued that the "narrator system works as a sort of interiorized film lecturer."[58] In other words, the lecturer served as a pivot around which cinema turned from an open text of dispersed attraction to a closed narration system that absorbed the lecturer's own role. The pivot became internalized and the lecturers found themselves unemployed or selling tickets in the box office. As we will see, only where they did double duty as translators did the lecturers survive into the late silent era.

The situation in Asia was quite different, though not completely disconnected from the movements afoot in other parts of the world. The same innovations that spelled doom for lecturers in North America caught the collective eyeballs of Japanese intellectuals who began noticing the stylistic and narrative differences between domestic and foreign films. Rather than the diegetic illusionism and closure of the latest Hollywood offerings, Japanese films were too open and dependent on the intertext audiences brought to the theater. Reasoning that it was the *benshi's* fault, these critics initiated the Pure Film Movement and strove for the elimination of lecturers, just as in the West. When this proved impossible, they worked to change the task of the *benshi*. Arguing that the *benshi* must align their performance to the site of enunciation within the filmic text, the reformers stopped calling them *katsuben* or *benshi* (orators) and switched to *setsumeisha* (explainers). Their Pure Film Movement fought the imitation and the rhetorical excesses of the *setsumeisha,* asking for unmarked speech and a self-effacement before the text. Aaron Gerow writes:

The *benshi* forfeited his own subjectivity and became identified with the subjectivity of the film, such that, as Gonda [Yasunosuke] explained at the end of his own short teleological history of the *benshi,* "there is no explanation outside of the film and no film outside of the explanation." In Gonda's vision, the *benshi* "must become the film itself."[59]

Put in a manner familiar to translators, the *benshi* found themselves becoming invisible. Curiously, this occasions what might be the film world's first deployment of translation as metaphor in 1921. Referring to the terminology used to restrict the role of the Japanese lecturer, reformer Takeda Kokatsu argued:

> People in society derided them as *benshi,* or called them *katsuben,* failing to treat them as equal human beings. At the same time, they attacked the moving pictures. Those reverberations have produced results today and the word *benshi* has disappeared and under the name *setsumeisha* [explainer], they have come to explain films. Yet the word *setsumeisha* is definitely not appropriate . . . More than that, it should be better to boldly rename them *honyakusha* [translators].[60]

Elaborating on this metaphor was Musobei, a *benshi* who wrote one of the more influential books on the arts of the *setsumei.* He asserted: "Translation must be faithful to each word and line of the original work, but a word-for-word translation will just not express the artistic taste permeating the original. The only thing that will bring that to the surface is originality as a translation."[61] That translation is a new site of textual enunciation that displaces and can overwhelm the original is no great surprise to students of translation. What is ultimately wonderful about *benshi*—and so frustrating to the reformers trying to keep their cinema pure—is that they demonstrate the inextricable interdependency of original and translation by their mere presence in the theater. However, the reformer's arguments held a powerful attraction and continue to inform postwar historians of the *benshi* to the present day. For example, Jeffrey Dym takes the movement's side: "When *kowairo* benshi were in harmony with each other and the movie, the illusion generated was magical. However, when *kowairo* benshi were not in harmony, the impression given was undoubtedly similar to the one a contemporary viewer garners from a poorly dubbed 1960s or 1970s martial arts film."[62]

This comment should give us pause, as it cuts straight to a central conundrum of this volume. As Aaron Gerow suggests, the *benshi* served as a supplement that helped define what he was appending, in this case a *visual* form of narrative art supposedly sufficient unto itself. This move simultaneously requires a suppression of the supplement itself, an impulse felt on either side of the Pacific Ocean. Inspired by the metaphoric leap taken by Takeda, Musobei, and Dym, we could see subtitles functioning in the same way. The supplementary subtitle *helps define an original,* one that we enjoy uniquely unfettered access to on the screen and sound track. Unlike the domestic film, the foreign film demands the supplement. Thus, the values driving our desires for unmediated access to the closed-off world of the diegesis deal with this necessity by shuttling subtitles to the edge of the screen and rendering them as obsequiously nondescript as possible. It is on these same grounds that the detractors of dubbing stage their attacks in defense of a despoiled original made painfully visible through aural supplementarity.

Little of this helps explain why the *benshi* accompanied silent films until the mid-1930s, while their American colleagues so swiftly disappeared. Most theories point to the *benshi*'s unionizing, their star system, and the sheer pleasures they offered in the theaters. However, this is where Gerow makes his most significant contribution to the history of the film lecturers. First, he points out how Western scholars like Hansen and Gunning (as well as *benshi* scholars like Burch, Anderson, and Dym) see the lecturer as necessarily separate and antonymic to the closed text of the continuity system.[63] Gerow demonstrates how reformers reconceptualized the lecturer's role and centered it as a point of enunciation within the diegesis. His research also reveals how the elites, in and outside of government, considered the *benshi* indispensable for controlling meaning. Thanks to the *benshi*'s identification with the univocity of the narrative, they could bring potentially "dangerous" texts under control. Musobei, for example, wrote: "The true attitude *benshi* must take is to offer an explanation that will satisfy and make people of all classes understand. They know that reeling off difficult words or phrases will in most cases not bring the film to life but will, on the contrary, mix in other meanings and kill the film. Also, to them, separating themselves from the film when explaining the mixing in their own impressions should be avoided at all costs."[64] The *benshi* thus divests the powers of interpretation from the audience, in effect becoming the exemplary spectator that individuals were asked to follow.

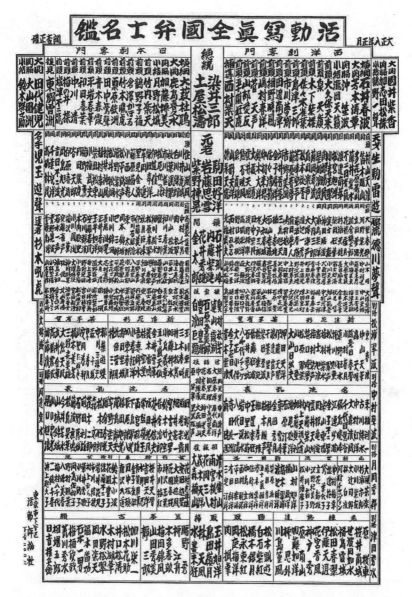

Figure 14. *Banzuke* for *benshi* in 1918. *Banzuke* are used to rank sumo wrestlers, kabuki actors, and other entertainers, and so express the relative popularity of Japanese lecturers (with the names of the best written in larger print). The left and right halves separate the specialists for domestic versus foreign films. Courtesy of Matsuda Eigasha.

We can find a similar dynamic back at the metropoles of the film world. Long after lecturers vanished from most American theaters, they remained in ethnic communities where one of their roles was translator. As usual, the most spectacular example is New York City, which had twenty-six-odd language communities where lecturers continued to ply their trade in the 1920s. Here is a description of the movie theater space in 1926 on Manhattan's Lower East Side:

> Not learning "the President's English" is one of a number of disadvan-
> tages faced by the immigrant: An inability to decipher motion picture
> sub-titles [intertitles][65] is one of these, although that handicap is over-
> come, in certain quarters of the city, by considerable impresarios. In a
> movie house of modest pretensions on Forsythe Street, for example, the
> purport of the clarifying paragraphs is divulged to the audience through
> an interpreter and a megaphone. He translates the descriptive passage
> and conversation of the characters into the throaty patois of the locality.
> His is not the stereotyped manner of the court interpreter. He breathes
> life—including love, hate and intermediate emotions—into his lines.
> Translations are as free as the great outdoors. When the text of the young
> district attorney's defiance of his powerful political mentor burdens the
> screen, the megaphone endeavors earnestly, if not successfully, to employ
> the combined eloquence of Patrick Henry, Cicero, and Corse Payton. The
> interpreter voices a villain's threats with such ebullient bitterness that it
> often seems slightly unfair to even the most vicious screen character.[66]

As with the *benshi,* the nature of the American lecturer's role changed over time (although not in identical ways). One reason so many histori-ans have been interested in the linkages between developments in cine-matic narrative and the fate of the lecturers has to do with the scene of the theater at this formative moment. Miriam Hansen influentially argued that waves of immigrants found the nickelodeon an alternative public sphere where they could negotiate their relationship to moder-nity and the new mass consumer culture. As a novel art form based on photographic reproduction and offering new modes of perception, film became industrialized in the context of these cycles of consumption and commodification. The nickelodeons offered a shared space where these immigrant spectators could negotiate their place in it all. They were hybridized spaces, where even the "domestic" film underwent trans-lation. For example, a writer in the 1920s wrote, "In the old days there were Jewish lecturers who told the story of the picture in graphic language interspersed with Yiddish, something on this order: 'From behind, the man—he steps up to the lady and grabs her pocketbook. "Ganef! Robber! Help! Ganef!" she screams.'"[67]

Then, at the same time that lecturers die out elsewhere, the narrators of the immigrant communities take on new roles in line with the homogenizing forces taking over the cinema. Their performances became less hybridized, and commentators admired the way lecturers taught immigrants "the President's English" and thus "Americanized" their audiences. In 1920, a *New York Times* correspondent ended a piece on the immigrant lecturers by relating a conversation with one of the old hybridizing lecturers who was now forced to sell tickets:

> When I broached lecturing to Gerdel, one of those who told the tales partly in Yiddish, he grew dreamy and his thin, wiry figure relaxed as much as the box office of his little movie theater would permit.
>
> "Those were the good old days," he said, "ubber now, the people won't even listen to you for a half minute. Everybody wants English now. Maybe when the greenhorns come to this country again I'll go back to that way of lecturing. Is it true not a single one can come from Europe for five, six, seven years?"
>
> Gerdel sighed.
>
> "My English ain't good enough."
>
> He sighed again as he pushed two admission coupons through the niche in the window. Once an artist, always an artist![68]

The pedagogical function, to use Homi Bhabha's phrase, that forces an assimilation of people into the nation-state and its consumer culture, came to the fore just as cinema's new diegetic illusionism represented the social reality in powerfully new ways. It brought its audiences into a relationship with a (national) domestic to identify with, one in opposition to a panoply of foreign others, both rivals and subordinates. This cinematic contact with the foreign was facilitated every step of the way by those armies of translators, ironically enabling the "birth" of homogenized national cinemas enunciating a univocal national character. Richard Abel's groundbreaking research on French film in the United States emphasizes the overlooked importance of first Méliès and then Pathé Frères in the establishment of "American cinema."[69] Their experiments in narrative were vastly influential in spurring the shift from attractions to the story film. When the market solidified with the nickelodeons and required a steady, reliable stream of high-quality product, Pathé was there and more reliable than American producers. Without Pathé, Abel argues, the striking expansion between 1906 and 1910 would not have played out as it did. After this, a combination of government controls and domestic competition from indies such as Lasky, Universal, and Famous Players forced Pathé to assimilate to the homogeneous consumer culture along with the immigrant audiences. It ended up making westerns in New Jersey. Thus, the "American cinema" was paradoxically founded on foreign films in translation.

Similarly, Gerow critiques the typical historiography that locates the "birth of Japanese cinema" with the reforms of the Pure Film Movement. Historians espousing that view constituted the mainstream view until very recently, and argued that what came before was uncinematic and "unpure." It was only when filmmakers dispensed with the theatrical codes of kabuki, and *benshi* turned from *kowairo* to *setsumei,* that cinema became cinematic. It was when filmmakers and lecturers subscribed to the basic values of Hollywood realism and its internalized narrator that cinema in Japan became "Japanese cinema." Thus, Gerow demonstrates that, through translation both linguistic and metaphoric, Japanese cinema is paradoxically founded on its own negation.

These dynamics of assimilation, accommodation, and negotiation, combined with the force of linguistic nationalism, could be devastating to cinema industries smaller than those in Japan and the United States. The new mass medium provoked a situation with interesting parallels to the initial emergence of print culture, where printers were forced to choose the language they published in. Market forces predictably held sway, and linguistic diversity was slowly winnowed down as minority languages were forced to accommodate to the print language or die out. One can find similar dynamics in the film world. For example, in interwar Poland filmmakers and distributors could exhibit prints with bilingual or trilingual intertitles (mainly Polish, Yiddish, and German), depending on the region. However, when sound arrived producers were forced to make a choice, and they naturally began shooting films for their largest market, the Polish speakers. Yiddish cinema effectively ground to a halt in Europe, and would not revive for seven years. Films in German, Russian, Ukrainian, and Lithuanian could only be imported from across the political borders of the nation-state.[70] As we will see in the next chapter, sound amplified the regionalization and territorialization of cinema, thanks to a new univocity of the text after the expulsion of both lecturers and written text from the cinema.

CHAPTER FOUR

Babel—the Sequel
The Talkies

For Hollywood, at least, silence should be golden on the silver screen.
How, otherwise, is it to maintain its practical world monopoly? A
picture made in Los Angeles can be comprehended in Tibet. But
how about a picture which depends for its exposition not entirely on
pantomime but on dialogue expressed in 100% American? Japanese
cinemas employ commentators to explain silent films to their slant-
eyed patrons. Will they now need to employ interpreters?
>   —John MacCormac, 1928

As a result of the fine work Selnick has done with the talkie I have
just finished, millions of Chinamen are going to make the astonishing
discovery that I speak excellent Chinese.
>   —Douglas Fairbanks Jr., 1929

When sound films hit the theaters in the late 1920s, they were greeted
with everything from glee to panic in film industries across the globe.
The trade papers and books from the talkie era make for amusing reading
as one gets a palpable sense of the chaos. Sound rendered the silent-era
translation methods meaningless, and it was difficult to imagine how
one could translate the barrage of verbiage emanating from the theater
speakers. Studio executives everywhere honestly thought this would be
the end of international cinema, the moment that bound cinema to a
multitude of disconnected domestic spheres. "Thanks to the talkie," wrote
Japan's Takeyama Masanobu, "the internationality of cinema has vanished."[1] Hollywood found the situation alarming while its competitors

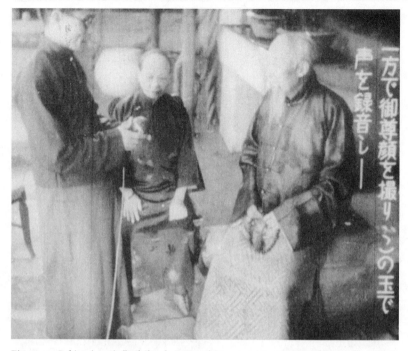

Figure 15. *Peking* (1938): "While photographing your countenance, they will record your voice with this ball."/"Today, thanks to Councilor Tanaka's introduction, the cameramen from our allied nation . . ." *Peking* was a Japanese film by Kamei Fumio shot in the city after the Japanese began their occupation; it was probably Japan's first documentary talkie. This scene exemplifies the way early Japanese subtitles accounted for the composition of the photography. When the man on the left speaks, his subtitles appear on the opposite side of the frame, and vice versa.

found it potentially liberating. Whether this was a loss or not depended on one's perspective, but the erosion of silent film's "internationality" quickly became a convenient pivot around which sound versus silent debates raged.

While the technicians had invented novel methods for combining sound and image, the problem of translation was an afterthought. As we have seen, the silent film's linguistic elements could be easily disengaged from the image, and then excised or replaced with intertitles in the target language. With synced sound, however, there was now an interpenetration of body and language. There was no way to disconnect the two. It was a serious predicament.

Sound posed a vexing problem for many film studios throughout the world, which depended on foreign distribution for a significant part of

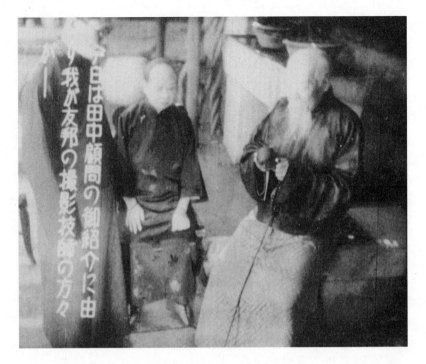

their income. The predicament was particularly acute for the American film industry, which had come to dominate nearly every market in the world by the 1930s. This dominance was fueled by Hollywood's power, its ability to produce and distribute films at a level of polish foreign filmmakers could only dream of. This also made it vulnerable.

Initially, critics envisioned the end of international distribution, except for old-style silent films and musicals because they could be enjoyed without the benefit of translation. A reader of the Japanese journal *Kinema Junpo* complained in 1929: "I am thrilled with the way the appearance of the talkie has allowed me to hear the voices of screen lovers, but I think the dialogue talkie will probably meet its end as a passing fancy."[2] This reception pleased those in the film industries outside of Hollywood. In 1931, Ishimaki Yoshio, one of the few film commentators who published industrial criticism in Japan, summed up pages of data-driven analysis of the global film system with the following optimistic conclusion: "Until now the differences between national languages were, more than anything, the most reliable barrier for countries being invaded by American films . . . What secures the safety of one's own national cinema is not censorship, nor is it quotas. It is the difference between languages."[3]

Ishimaki's analysis was circumspect, as his research showed how colonial powers had a distinct advantage over national languages with limited geographic scope. In contrast, the editor of *La Cinématographie Française* believed, overly enthusiastically, that the Hollywood industry was now something other than a threat to the nation's film industry:

> Numerous are the territories where the French language is spoken and employed, or where it is utilized as the preferred second language [his examples are Belgium, Switzerland, North Africa, Egypt and the Near East] . . . The coming of the "talkies" is all for the good of the French industry, for now film production can be covered, with considerable profit, within the country itself; in addition to which there is a certain sure *[sic]* foreign market. Competition from outside is no longer to be feared.[4]

Back in Hollywood, trade papers like the *Hollywood Filmograph* called the alarm over the swift changes taking place in market demand:

> But their present cry is for talking-pictures in their own Spanish tongue . . . if the American producer cannot supply the insistent demand for a Spanish talking pictures *[sic]* there is grave danger that this market will be lost within a very short time to the American producer. Should no pictures come forward from America within a reasonably short time, the South Americans will make their own pictures.[5]

The introduction of sound promised an opportunity to wrench domestic markets away from Hollywood. At the same time, it injected a dynamic of competition into transnational efforts to create blocks in the face of Hollywood hegemony over market share, the most significant being Film Europe.[6] Obviously, since Hollywood came to dominate nearly every country in the world, these were ephemeral dreams. As early as 1928 a French film magazine predicted subtitling, dubbing, and even the DVD when it suggested, "In the future, regardless of the expense, Hollywood businessmen will probably market a sound film with multilingual interpretation."[7] Indeed, it was only a matter of months before strategies to resolve the language problem proliferated.

Much has been made of Hollywood's innovative attempts to overcome the obstacles that sound posed to business in non-English-speaking countries. However, current histories concentrate nearly exclusively on the multilanguage version: teaching stars new languages and making identical foreign-language versions with different actors on the same set.[8] Surprisingly enough, subtitles and dubbing—the greatest innovations and ultimate solutions to the language problem—are something of a gap in movie history. This chapter will chart out the global transition to sound cinema from the perspective of the translator, looking for hints at what the future held in store at this key moment in the history of film translation.

Lanterns and Lecturers—The Dawn of the Talkies

Until recently, film historians and pedagogues often restricted their treatment of the conversion to sound to the debates over the artlessness of the talkie.[9] Because of the bulkiness and noisiness of the new equipment, the film cameras were constrained in their movements and often relegated to soundproof booths. Actors were forced to hover around hidden microphones, whose range was quite limited. Just when the silent film reached the apex of its artfulness, the talkie reduced the cinema to clunky, static filming filled with stilted performances. This moment was actually quite short, and creative filmmakers and dedicated technicians quickly surmounted the challenges the new equipment posed. What historians rarely consider is the particular inflection language issues gave to the debates. Although they almost always cite the work of Rudolf Arnheim, that obstinate critic of the talking film, they overlook his 1929 essay titled "Sound Film Confusion" in which he discussed his frustration with early attempts at translation:

> We are already caught in the midst of a babel of tongues. Erich Pommer wants to mix languages when he makes his next UFA film. This will also force him to judge his actors not only by way of artistic measures, but also those of the Berlitz school . . . Those with no linguistic geniuses among their actors must either sell talking films as silent abroad, in which case the dialogue scenes are shortened and replaced with laborious inter-titles (a process which is already beginning to raise general protest), or they must shoot the same film twice, as a talkie and as a silent. Both processes are only possible when the film is a piece of industrial waste for the masses and not art. For a work of art is not a shirt with removable sleeves.[10]

Arnheim hoped that such frustration would repel spectators from the talkie and turn them back to the glorious silent film. He was not alone in this hope. Echoing Arnheim on the other side of the planet, Japanese essayist and film policy maven Tachibana Takahiro assessed the cacophonous chaos of the moment and forecasted the doom of the foreign film:

In certain theatres foreign talkies are simply shown without any accompaniment, and in others with Japanese translations of the dialogue shown on the side of the picture itself. It is, however, obvious that here the appeal is limited only to those who have a fair command of the spoken foreign language. It would thus appear that if the talkie is going to take the place of the silent picture altogether, then the position of foreign films in the Japanese market will inevitably be less favorable. The musical talkie will of course always have an appeal, but the plain talkie-talkie will undoubtedly decline in popularity as the novelty wears off, and as Japanese made talkies increase in number and quality. This indeed is the sense in which the future may be visualized. Sooner or later the Japanese made talkie must develop, and with its development the scope for foreign films will be limited to silent films and such talkies as contain musical features. On the other hand, the foreign style Japanese picture, whether talkie or silent, will tend more and more to offset the pictorial reproductions of the stories of old.[11]

Unbeknownst to Tachibana, translators were searching for strategies to transport the unwieldy sound apparatus across the language barrier and, as both Arnheim and Tachibana indicate, the first attempts on the cusp of the sound era often resulted in strange hybrids. Initially, one common practice was to strip the sound track off a sound film, insert intertitles, and release it as a silent film. In many parts of the world, exhibitors would simply show the sound films untranslated and offer detailed synopses in theater programs. In the United States, exhibitors probably did this to satisfy European quotas without expending precious capital on the competition's product or eating into their own domestic market.[12] Much of the world reached this point of confusion with rough synchronicity, whether they had live narrators or not. In 1932, Erich Pommer, the orchestrator of Weimar cinema in Germany, observed:

Paradoxical as it may sound the international talking film is an accomplished fact. During the first year of the new medium neither the experts nor the public believed this to be possible. It was thought that the internationality of silence could not be adequately replaced by the national limitation of language. The spoken word appeared to become an insurmountable barrier. It was considered that the end of the international film had arrived and, at the same time, the end of the film as the incomparable medium of culture and propaganda that it had been.[13]

Pommer is writing in the past tense because of the proliferation in translation strategies at the time of his writing in 1932. In his impressive history of the period, Donald Crafton argues that few producers worried seriously about the loss of foreign markets because of the talkies. He also provides statistics that suggest that there was little impact on foreign receipts. However, looking at other sources, the picture would not seem to be so clear-cut.

Behind the rather hyperbolic panic expressed in some of the preceding quotations are reams of dusty ledgers around the world, filled with figures ending in many, many zeros. Few forms of translation are predicated on business transactions as massive as those of the cinema. For those used to thinking about translation in the print media, the scale is difficult to appreciate. One way to recognize the stakes is to spend some time wading in the statistics behind the transition to sound.

In 1930, a commentator in the *Harvard Business Review* noted: "There are few American industries that are more dependent on foreign markets than the motion pictures industry; and there are still fewer industries in which American dominance of world markets has in the past been more dramatic and more complete."[14] In 1927, just months before the coming of sound, the U.S. Bureau of Foreign and Domestic Commerce estimated that nearly 75 percent of the world's screen time was occupied by American films, and that 30 percent of the gross revenues from all sources on American films came from outside the country.[15] At about the same time, a Japanese critic known for industrial analysis cited similar figures, that the U.S. film industry brought in roughly 25 percent of its receipts from foreign countries (5 percent of which came from the United Kingdom and Australia).[16] This indicates the scale of the potential losses, combined with the contemporary estimates that the cost for conversion itself was anywhere from $250 million to twice that.[17] Although Crafton's figures indicate little change in foreign income, a financial journal published by the *New York Times* recorded an abrupt drop in Hollywood's foreign receipts—by about 50 percent after 1928.[18]

Furthermore, there is no shortage of public pronouncements of concern. Or, seen from the flip side, there were even commentators who harbored chauvinistic dreams of their own language spreading across the globe. Speaking at the Academy for Motion Pictures Arts and Sciences, director William C. DeMille pronounced: "In as much as the introduction of American films into Europe has resulted in Europeans wearing American hats and shoes and almost everything else, so we may be sure that in a couple of generations from now, all Europeans will be speaking English so that they may continue to see and understand American films."[19]

DeMille wasn't the only American entertaining such imperial fantasies. In a speech back at the film world's metropole, Fox Theaters' Harold B. Franklin imagined a very different scenario in which he envisioned a "universal understanding" and "cosmic peace" once the talkies forced a homogenization of major languages. When the final barriers break down, he said, films will be produced in a single tongue: "What that language will be, and which civilization will so dominate the world as to dictate its syllables, no man can say. There is no doubt in my own mind that its course of accomplishment will be such as to reiterate the age-old theory of the survival of the fittest."[20] I think we can guess which language Franklin was betting on.

The point is not that the concerns about the foreign markets were minimal, but that translation strategies swiftly proliferated, and so it was not long before producers knew they were safe. There was simply no time for those concerns to build to a level of hysteria. As Crafton points out, the simple novelty of the new technology was bringing in audiences at this early date, and exhibitors could also hedge their bets by showing sound films as silent films by inserting a few choice inter-titles. Although it was unclear which translation approach would win, a handful of methods achieved wide currency in the first few years of sound.

In parts of the world lacking the economy of scale to support trans-lation, exhibitors simply projected the original prints without modi-fication. For example, in 1931, Warner First National's general manager for the Orient toured his Asian markets and found this tendency in Southeast Asia. He reported that in Java they were projecting German and Dutch films with no translation, along with the occasional Ameri-can film. However, only the ones with more music than dialogue were making money.[21] Obviously, this was hardly satisfactory to the studios, whose domestic audience was already expecting all-talkies. Foreign audiences were equally eager, but they also wanted to know what char-acters were saying. As Marie Dressler pointed out on the heels of a European tour with the "audible" *Anna Christie* (1930), "The statement by Will Hays that a mother's smile is the same in any language is not so good as it was, because nowadays people want to understand what the mother says when she smiles."[22] To meet this desire for understanding, and by extension the primary pleasure of cinematic immersion implied by Dressler's comment, a wide variety of movements were afoot.

Some screenwriters experimented with narrative structure. They concentrated dialogue into easily translated chunks, or dispensed with it as much as possible; Hollywood's famous action cinema is probably this experiment's legacy. *Sous les Toits de Paris* (1930) was an attempt to make films that could communicate past the intermediary figure of the translator. Its advertisement in the Japanese press boldly declares, "From France, the country of art and poetry, the brilliant René Clair has discovered the road to tomorrow for the world's talkies. Don't talk about the talkies without seeing this international talkie, which the infamous Chaplin, who hates the talkies, loved and doffed his hat to."[23]

Other writers relegated speech to nondiegetic narrators, which could be easily rerecorded into any language without any regard for sync. A variation of this is the revue film, which proliferated in the talkie era. Revue films were introductions to the studio players and were largely song-and-dance numbers strung together by a narrator. Paramount attempted to create foreign versions of *Paramount on Parade* (1930) and *Happy Days* (1930) by flying in celebrity narrators from Germany (Egon von Jordan), France (Maurice Chevalier), Spain (Rosita Moreno), Sweden, and Japan. It added intertitles for Czech, Dutch, Polish, Hungarian, Danish, and Serbian. The Japanese talent it imported was none other than the popular *benshi* Matsui Suisei. He must have made quite an impression, as the *Times* went so far as to describe Matsui's visit to New York: "He is so small that Paramount had to manufacture all his costumes, his size being less than any in their vast wardrobe; he says, 'Yes, I think so' in answer to almost any question; he is very much the urbanite—having been made sad by the amount of grass in Hollywood and homesick for his native hearth."[24] A review from the time praised his witty performance,[25] but the Japanese advertisements pulled out all the stops: "With this single film our Suisei will become a world-renowned star and at the same time Suisei will make this film unique in the world as something only Japanese can enjoy."[26] Unpacking this quote, we can see a complex articulation of Japan's place in the world, where the *benshi*'s presence in Hollywood both proffers particularity and creates a place for Japan in the international order of world cinema. It is as if Matsui translates in two directions.

There were many other equally elaborate experiments. In 1930, something called the "Dunning Process" took background shots photographed in Hollywood and combined them with actors anywhere in the world.[27] Using a variety of tints, it was essentially an early version of the blue screen traveling matte made famous by post–Star Wars special effects. Carroll Dunning made a demo with *Beau Ideal* (1931) in German, Spanish, French, and Swedish, but it never caught on.[28] Some American studios were producing shorts executed in the target language, testing them on various immigrant communities. Lasky (Paramount) and Meyer (MGM) considered selling detailed scripts to European producers, or simply sending them films to replicate scene for scene. There were even French-language films shot in France with French stories—essentially French films!—which were actually produced through the Hollywood infrastructure and capital. Finally, there were polyglot films. The most famous is Pabst's *Kamaradschaft* (1931), but my favorite is Duvivier's *Allo Berlin! Ici Paris* (1931), which stages a long-distance, multilingual love story over the phone lines.

Although it is somewhat difficult to fathom, the first sound films in East Asia were presented by *benshi*. A foreign visitor in 1931 described the situation he found in the theaters:

> *Benshi* are as indispensable as ever; only, in relation to the "talkie," they must sandwich their words between an exasperating jumble of mechanical foreign-language dialogue and sound effects, a task that cannot but make the whole ensuing struggle (for that, indeed, it is) seem farcical. The *benshi*-plus-silent-film combination was beautifully suited to Japanese needs and temperament. With the advent of sound films the unpopularity of American pictures for a time threatened to become almost as emphatic as once had been their popularity. But this feeling was in no measure due to the fact that an anti-American sentiment had arisen. On the contrary, it was the simple reaction of a public chagrined at not being able to comprehend something that in the past had brought it genuine pleasure.[29]

A visiting sound engineer from Hollywood put it in more antagonistic, if confidently arrogant, terms after watching a *benshi* shouting his interpretation over a screening of *The Redskin* (1928): "It gave the impression of *benshi* vs. ERPI [the General Electric sound system] . . . [The *benshi*] was getting rather angry, according to the manager, who explained one day that if we did not favor him he might start a general strike."[30] There are indications that Japanese audiences shared this exasperation with the *benshi* translators as well. Tachibana Takahiro's description of the same scene is worth quoting at length:

[The *benshi*] explains the difficult points in a complicated intrigue, reminds the spectators of what has gone before, and generally indicates who's who and what's what to those to whom such things might not be obvious. Moreover, in the tensest moments of a drama, he will impersonate the figures on the screen, and, with considerable *ventriloquial* skill, will be successively the murdering villain, the wailing mother and the awe-struck child. For the foreign pictures he does all these things with equal skill, and incidentally he translates the printed captions, so that the language difficulty never presents any insurmountable problems. With the introduction of the foreign talkies he has attempted to carry on in the best traditions of his craft, with results that can be perhaps better imagined than described. The unfortunate spectator's ears are assailed on the one side by the strident accents of a foreign tongue, and on the other by the gallantly explanatory *benshi* forever doing his best. It is Man versus the Machine, and the result pandemonium, or as a foreign friend once described it to me in parody of Mr. Kipling's lines, "The *benshi* brawls / But the talkie squalls / and it weareth the *benshi* down." Thus it can be seen that the *benshi* who was a great asset to the foreign silent film is hardly that to the talkie.[31]

Audiences were probably sharing these feelings. The *benshi* struggled to deal with the problem in a variety of ways. They reserved their trans-lations and explanations for moments of silence on the sound track. Some used what came to be called *kirisetsu,* or "cut-in explanations"; they would cue the projectionists to turn down or cut off the sound when they wanted to interject a bit of translation. Some apparently were power-ful enough to have volume controls installed in their podiums. In 1934, they even started using microphones to put themselves on even ground with the electronic amplification of the sound tracks.[32]

Where there were *benshi* in other parts of East Asia, notably the Japa-nese colonies of Korea and Taiwan, translation was conducted in the same haphazard manner. A charming enactment of this can be found in *A Borrowed Life* (Duo-Sang, 1994), a Taiwanese film by Wu Nien-Jen. One scene set in a Taiwanese theater shows a Chinese-language *benshi* translating over a Japanese sound track; to the film's dialogue, he adds advertising asides and occasional announcements to individual audience members. This film was set in the immediate post–World War II era, hinting at the way this mode of translation represented an economical holdover from the talkie era.

This example from the 1940s is exceptional. Despite Tachibana's pre-diction that the *benshi* would enjoy a never-ending role as translator,

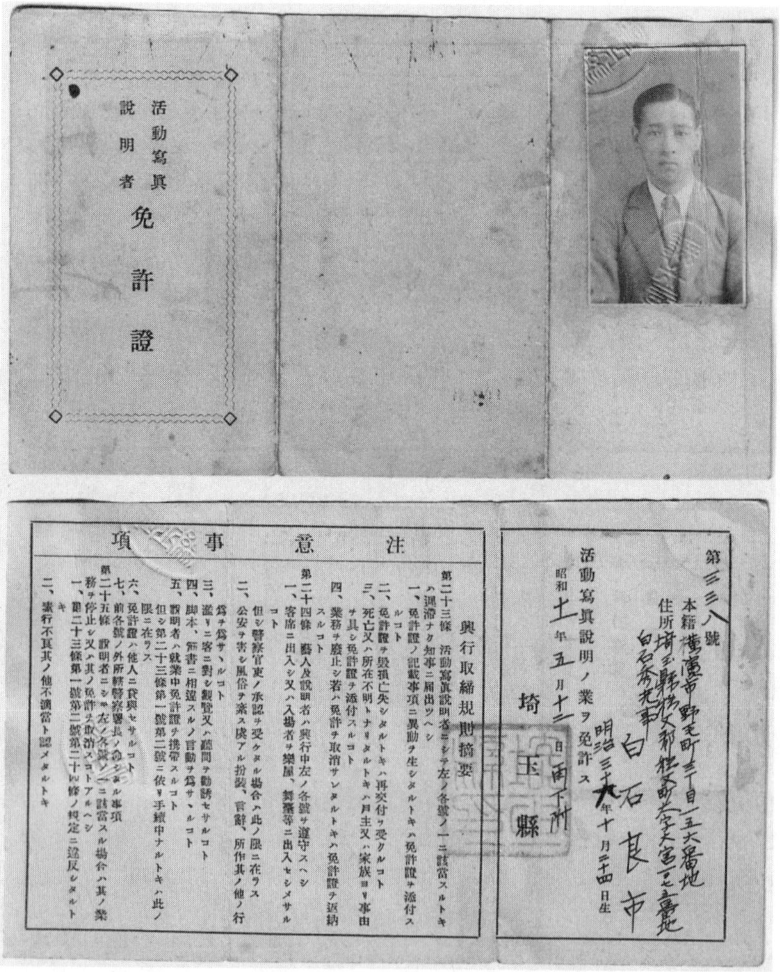

Figure 16. A *benshi* license from 1936. With their uncommon power over the interpretation and translation of films, *benshi* came under the intense scrutiny of both critics and the state, which tried to control texts (and thus spectators) by regulating the performances of *benshi*. Judging from what this license proscribes, there were problems with *benshi* deviating from the approved script as well as backstage monkey business with spectators. Courtesy of Matsuda Eigasha.

Japanese distributors followed their foreign counterparts and immediately began to adopt new strategies for translation. Critics were panning the talkies and it was unclear whether they would ultimately become economically viable, but some theater chains were already firing all their *benshi*. Others hedged their bets by showing a given film with subtitles or side-titles, and then once again with a *benshi*. Many commentators felt torn. Kitagawa Fuyuhiko reported a little experiment where he saw Pabst's *Kameradschaft* (1931) twice on the same day, once with *benshi* and again with side-titles; despite his frustration with the cacophonous struggle between the *benshi* and the sound track, he felt that the *benshi* helped him discover aspects of the film that the titled version kept hidden (although he admitted that he had no idea if that information was translated from the script or simply the product of the *benshi's* fertile imagination).[33]

In late 1929, the famed *benshi* Matsui Suisei predicted that the next year or two would be rough and decisive, and called for an all-out struggle against the transition to sound. If the *benshi* failed to do so, he imagined they would only be working for foreign talkies.[34] He argued that it was the *benshi's* setsumei that gave the foreign talkie its flavor. In his struggle to survive, he wrote many articles and made highly visible attempts to train young people for this new role as "foreign talkie *benshi*."[35]

Matsui was correct that 1931 would be rough, but little did he know that the threat would come from other quarters. Early in the year, *Tokyo Asahi* newspaper's headlines asked, "What's going to happen in the film world this autumn?"[36] It appeared that most foreign films would now be released in Japanese versions of one sort or another. Obei Film Company (RKO and Pathé), Warner Brothers, and Universal were committed to the intertitled versions, and Paramount, MGM, and United Artists were making noise about a new titling system that superimposed the text on the image. Universal and Fox went to far as to announce bilingual subtitles, so that students of English could better use the films for language practice.[37] One newspaper in Tokyo reported that cuts in *benshi* ranks at the top Tokyo movie houses were reverberating down the theatrical food chain.[38] Unemployed *benshi* would move off to the countryside, where their verbal skills were still the preferred method of translation. However, these same theaters were eyeing the successes of the urban theaters and putting their orders in for the new projectors as a panoply of translation methods emerged. About this time, the Hollywood trade paper *Variety* reported, "All foreign picture managers [in Japan] . . . have reached different conclusions as to the solution which at the moment is the leading trade question. Most are in the air and stalling while they wonder if the potentialities of foreign markets are worth the cost."[39]

Back in Europe, distributors showed *The Jazz Singer* (1927) with a second screen placed just to the right of the moving picture screen. Upon this they projected slides of translated text using a magic lantern. Europeans swiftly moved on to other experiments, most notably the subtitle, which this strategy prefigures. However, for several years the magic lantern became the standard method in some parts of the world, such as China.[40] Curiously, Japanese visitors to the continent brought home stories about the Chinese method. Not long after, the American director for Paramount in Tokyo traveled to Shanghai to acquire one of the Chinese magic lanterns. He found it poorly constructed and hopelessly inconvenient. Thus, with the help of a staff member, they dismantled it, reverse engineered it, and Paramount started exporting them back to China.[41] They sold the machines to theaters across Japan as well, even to theaters without sound equipment. Paramount's MacIntyre told one film journalist, "In the theaters where they aren't being used as intertitle projectors to threaten the *benshi,* they become a wonderful publicity machine to project advertisements in the lobby."[42] These side-titles, as they came to be known, were eventually eclipsed by other methods. Spectators found the image too dim, and they disliked having to ping-pong back and forth between the two screens.

A variation of this method was to periodically insert silent-style intertitles to explain what was happening in the film. The first example in Japan was Frank Capra's *Donovan Affair* (1929), which was billed as the first "Japanese Intertitle Talkie" *(hobun jimaku sonyu tokii)* when it hit theaters in September 1929. Tokyo's Shochikuza Theater published a pamphlet that tried to convince its audiences that this new technology of translation was the answer to the language problem: "This eight-reel adaptation of the stage play... is a sound film of great interest for the way it revolutionizes the rough, hard-to-understand talkie thanks to the Japanese intertitles throughout."[43] However, the shakiness of this confidence is belied by the fact that the theater occasionally turned the sound off, brought in a *benshi,* and showed the Capra film as a silent film.

Shortly after this, Warner Brothers adopted this method for the Japanese market, dubbing it the "X-Version" (a delicious term of obscure origins) and using it until the early 1930s. One of the most beloved *benshi* and spirited agitators against the sound-film "invasion" was Tokugawa Musei, who made a stir when he jumped ship and accepted MGM's invitation to do the translations for its X-Versions.[44] His first attempt was Greta Garbo's *Anna Christie* (English: 1930/German: 1931), and it was roundly criticized upon release. Asking whether Musei was a good translator did not occur to his critics; rather, they felt he ruined the films by bringing a *benshi*'s sensibility to the translation. This basically meant deploying inappropriately florid language in the intertitles.[45] Some theaters in Japan presented what they called "foreign version talkies" *(gaikokuban tokii)*, which involved the insertion of intertitles in dialogue-heavy sequences, but then turning off the sound and adding music and/or *benshi* for the rest of the film.[46] Considering all these variations, one could say that the X-Version is the true intermediary method between silent and sound cinema. This transitional quality of the X-Version, as I will argue in my chapter on subtitling, ran far deeper and lasted much longer than this ephemeral experiment. The rest of this chapter will examine the three translation strategies that finally gained traction in the first years of the 1930s: multilanguage versions, dubbing, and subtitling.

Multilanguage Versions

For a brief moment, it appeared that the solution to the language problem was the multilanguage version (MLV, or sometimes known as LVs), the mode of translation that has attracted the most attention from film historians (far more than subtitling and dubbing combined).[47] Erich Pommer called the MLV "The Esperanto of the talking screen."[48] They were essentially carbon copies of the same film, only in different languages. For example, after director Tod Browning finished up a day of shooting for *Dracula* (1931) with Bela Lugosi and Helen Chandler, the cast and crew all evacuated the set; then a new director, George Melford, entered with actors Carlos Villarias and Lupita Tovar to shoot the same scenes in Spanish (Figure 17); they worked through the night, finishing in time for the English cast to take the stage in the morning. Both movies sprang from the same script, but demonstrate how the MLVs ended up relatively autonomous texts.[49] Most people familiar with the Spanish *Dracula* prefer its luscious photography and racy atmosphere to the "standard" Lugosi version.

The first MLV was *Atlantic*, shot at London's Elstree Studios in November 1929. By New Year's, the studio was shooting films in English, German, and French. The American majors United Artists and Warner Brothers followed its lead in London. Some of the most famous directors in world cinema made MLVs. Hitchcock's *Blackmail* (1929) was shot in English and German. Pabst's *Threepenny Opera* (1931) was made in Berlin in German and French. Von Sternberg's *Blue Angel* (1930) was both a

Figure 17. *Dracula* was shot simultaneously in English and Spanish on the same set. Most people familiar with the Spanish version prefer its luscious photography and racy atmosphere to the so-called standard Lugosi version. MLVs confound the conventional opposition of source versus target in translation.

German and an English film, and it used the same actors. To motivate and justify the English in *Blue Angel*'s German setting, Emil Jannings's class was converted into an English as a second language course. Jannings and Marlene Dietrich were among a select group of polyglot actors for the MLVs, including Anna May Wong, Lilian Harvey, Brigitte Helm, Adolphe Menjou, Claudette Colbert, Maurice Chevalier, and Greta Garbo.

Donald Crafton cites Jacques Feyder's German version of *Anna Christie* as the most famous MLV, especially for the transformation Greta Garbo underwent in the title role. The American actors were replaced by Theo Shall, Hans Junkerman, and Salka Stevermann, but the aspect that made the difference was the treatment of Garbo herself. Her German was better than her English, she wore sexier costumes, and her character's sexual past was made more explicit than in Clarence Brown's English version. This was not lost on contemporary commentators such as Mordaunt Hall, who wrote in the *Times*, "Her presence is if anything more striking in this current work than in the English version."[50] This difference in representations of sexuality appears to have been common; aside from the example of *Dracula*, *Blue Angel*'s German version also had a racier cabaret show and lyrics, and dialogue.

However, focusing on these spectacular examples by major directors deflects attention from the sheer volume of MLVs and their industrial importance at the coming of sound. The 1931 *Kinematograph Year Book* noted: "The problem of 'foreign versions' is still a vexed one. The solution has not yet been found. In some instances, the foreign market is supplied with the American dialogue versions, plus subtitles in the language of the country of release. In others, the picture is 'dubbed' by having the lip-movement of the Hollywood folk matched up with lines spoken in a foreign language. But the belief that the 'foreign language problem' will be solved only by producing special versions, with players imported from Europe to Hollywood, is growing, and the result is that several of the big studios on the Coast are bringing actors and actresses from abroad. The additional expense entailed is, of course, great, but America's stake in the foreign market is something that cannot be dispensed with."[51] In much of Europe, up to fourteen versions were made of a given film, and in most cases a different director produced each of them. In Germany between 1929 and 1931, 22 percent of 251 features were MLVs (mostly from UA); between 1931 and 1932, 20 percent were subbed, 10 percent dubbed, and 70 percent were MLVs. Joinville produced a hundred features in fourteen languages in one year.[52] They peak in July 1930 when 75 percent of foreign-language versions would be produced in Europe in remaining months of that year. There was even at least one intralingual MLV, *The Last of Mrs. Cheyney* (1929), in which American actors reshot their scenes affecting British accents.[53] One of the memes circulating in Los Angeles at the time was the idea that the MLV would be a way to combat the charge that Hollywood was invading the world. Upon Paramount's move to Joinville, Jesse Lasky announced, "You can readily see that the Americanization of the world's movie screen will no longer be true. Instead, we will soon serve each country with talking films in its native tongue and by its own actors."[54]

Asian producers did not jump on this particular bandwagon, although some did express designs on the potential market. Kondo Haruo, the general secretary of the International Cinema Association in Japan, stated that it was the group's plan "to foster production of films with Japanese stories and played by Japanese actors who will speak English, the plays so presented as to be interesting to American or English audiences. It will have the important result of explaining Japanese life to the outside world, just as your films have shown us your national life."[55] This quote suggests that race played a role in the MLV. Kondo's rhetoric of national character was probably a default position. Where the MLV was a localization that tended to erase evidence of foreignness, the visual difference of these Asian actors made it impossible for their films to be anything but marked. This was an era in which the cultural products from the non-West were denigrated, unless they were displays of traditional arts and/or stereotype. Thus, *while statistics reveal the inequality of languages in translation flows, the visual properties of cinema added yet another factor making resistance difficult.* Entering a foreign market was no easy thing for producers outside of North America and Europe.

Despite the energy being thrown into MLVs, they all but cease by 1932. The initial inability of studios to settle on a method and the sudden failure of MLVs has something to do with the quandary of all capitalist industries. Ginette Vincendeau first articulated this in her oft-cited "Hollywood Babel." She states that it was a symptom of the constant tension between the necessity for standardization to increase profitability, on the one hand, and, on the other, the need for differentiation to ensure the renewal of demand. MLVs were, on the whole, too standardized to satisfy the cultural diversity of their target audience, but too expensively differentiated to be profitable.[56]

Vincendeau sees this in terms of capitalist rationalization partly because she is writing industrial history, but she is also self-conscious about the need to consider culture. Our starting point for this consideration can be the observation that the spectrum of degrees of foreignness neatly corresponds to cost. Subtitles are by far the least expensive route, but they flood the film with what Lawrence Venuti has called the remainder.[57] On the other end of the spectrum, MLVs were terribly expensive attempts to thoroughly domesticate films for a given linguistic territory. At the same time, even within the MLV there is a spectrum of differentiation, with MGM basing its operation in Hollywood and using immigrant talent (resulting in a slight retention of foreign odor), while Paramount and others relocated to places like Joinville where local actors and directors could cater more intimately to target culture and language.[58]

This spectrum of options from subtitling to MLVs corresponds rather neatly to Schleiermacher's famous dictum: "Either the translator leaves the writer alone as much as possible and moves the reader to the writer, or he leaves the reader alone as much as possible and moves the writer to the reader."[59] Without discounting the economic factors entering into the transition period's chaos, we can see how the relationship to the foreign ultimately weighs in with more force than economic rationalization. Where dubbing succeeded, it mediated between these two poles. It hid the foreign origination of films to a certain degree, basically turning it into a text of mixed birth and allowing the American studios to continue exporting their product. As Richard Maltby and Ruth Vassey observe, "The bifurcation of sound and image localized the act of consumption, not Hollywood's act of production."[60] Or, as translator Robert Paquin slyly put it, "There are dubbing countries and subbing countries, and there is one country that does remakes."[61] In the early 1930s, each linguistic territory across the globe shook out in favor of dubbing or subbing. In contrast to Japan, the larger European markets (places where domestic films put up strong competition to Hollywood) tended to prefer dubbing. In fact, it was in deference to this phenomenon that Hollywood began exploring dubbing in earnest.

Figure 18. *The Great Dictator* (1940). Chaplin speaks! In subtitling countries, people hear him say, "In this world there's room for everyone, and the good earth is rich and can provide for everyone." The Japanese reads: "There is a richness in the world that can care for all humanity." Dubbing deprived many audiences of hearing Chaplin talk in his own voice, but perhaps they heard a better translation.

Dubbing

Sound technology pushed the noses of Hollywood executives into the obstinate whims of nationalism wherever it went, forcing it to accommodate fetishistic relationships to domestic language and taste. The best evidence of the nationalism factor is all the riots that occurred when foreign tongues emanated from behind the silver screen. In 1929, *Variety* reported that hostility was growing: "Without exception every time an American talker has been flashed on the screen in Paris it has got the razz and what a razz!"[62] At the Moulin Rouge, *Fox Movietone Follies of 1929* caused riots, "with the mob tearing up carpets and seats and demolishing everything breakable about the place."[63] Other trade papers contained similar disturbing reports about Milan, Budapest, and Prague: "The very fact of hearing the much-resented German . . . caused havoc to the point of street demonstrations and physical destruction of the interiors of several movie theaters in Prague in the fall of 1930."[64] This was one impetus for German filmmakers to send French-language versions of their films to Eastern Europe and the Balkans. There were also riots against German subtitles in Poland in 1929, as well as in Nice, France, where audiences ripped out seats at a screening of *Les Innocents de Paris* (1929).[65] As Adolphe Menjou points out, these sentiments were wrapped up with frustrations over the ad hoc quality of the available translation methods:

> [With dubbing] such faking would be detected and resented imme-
> diately... Closeups would be out of the question. They tried putting
> subtitles in French at the bottom of American talking pictures. What has
> been the result? The film is blurred and streaky. The audience cannot
> read subtitles and flow the action of the picture at the same time. And to
> their further distraction, the actors are chattering away in English. Justi-
> fiable irritation is soon demonstrated by the whistling and jeering that
> European audiences indulge in freely when they are not pleased.[66]

Even slight foreign accents could provoke complaint, something Men-jou himself was not immune from. Of the Paramount MLVs produced in the United States before Joinville became its production center, a *Variety* critic writes, "The trouble is that Frenchmen now want their films, where French dialogue is spoken, without any foreign accent whatso-ever. Menjou's French is very good, but his accent is nevertheless felt at times. The daughter who plays the Corbett daughter... is obviously American, and speaks as one. The time is over when French patrons are ready to put up with a foreign accent if the talker is in French, and pro-ducing talkers in America with anything but an all-French cast will soon become a hazardous business so far as distribution here is concerned."[67] In Germany, critics were complaining about Lillian Harvey's accent. Portuguese-language MLVs recorded in Los Angeles drew on Brazilian talent, which the Portuguese themselves resented.[68] Accent became a handicap. This kind of criticism could explain Paramount's decision to start producing films for the European market in Joinville.

One of Hollywood's most perplexing accent problems was for Span-ish, which enjoyed enormous markets spread across several continents. One of the largest was conveniently located a few hours from Holly-wood. Some of the first Spanish MLVs drew on talent from across the border in Mexico and parts beyond. Critics in the Hollywood trade papers detested MLVs "engendered with a conglomeration of dialect, Spanish enunciation that ranges from the Greek manner to the Mexi-can... Regardless of the dialect a foreigner speaks, when he must listen to his mother tongue from the stage, screen, or platform, it's got to be the original and undefiled . . . There's only one plain, unadulterated Castilian. Any other rumples the national pride somewhere. The Argentinean won't go for the Mexican, and the Mexican won't go for the Yucatan."[69]

Paramount opted to please the European audience, certainly a business decision as much as a cultural inclination. They started using actors from Spain, putting thespian Ernesto Vilches into starring roles. *Variety*'s Spanish critic praised the studio for hiring Vilches for *Cascarrabias*, the Spanish MLV for Cukor's *Grumpy* (1933), hoping this spelled the end of the cacophony of accents: "Little by little American producers are learning to avoid the pitfalls into which they fell when making their initial foreign versions—talkies, that is. We must be thankful that Mexicans and Central Americans no longer offend our ears, however lucid their offering may be in their own countries."[70] Of course, this same development was greeted with chagrin in Latin America, where spectators complained about Hollywood dubbings in Castilian Spanish.[71]

Vilches actually starred in one MLV that demonstrates a creative application of accents. Jacques Feyder directed at least three versions of *If the Emperor Only Knew* (*Si l'empereur savait ça*, 1930), a Ferenc Molnár comedy set in the Austrian court. It was popularized in Spanish-speaking areas through a play starring Vilches. In the Spanish MLV, Feyder uses what the reviewer for *Variety* called "polite Spanish" for the court scenes and a variety of dialects for scenes set elsewhere, a technique the reviewer admired.[72] By way of contrast, the French version used an all-French cast to avoid any unwanted accents that might impact its reception there.[73]

There were also instances where nationalist disgust with foreign accents in MLVs dealt with marked language through camp appropriation and loving denigration. For example, Laurel and Hardy made MLVs of their own films in several languages, reading cue cards to deliver lines in languages they had never studied. Audiences found this either disturbing or amusing or both. This reading protocol for their MLVs eventually became codified in dubbings of their subsequent films into Italian. Initially, producers decided to use Italian Americans so they could record the new sound track domestically in New York City. However, these immigrant nonactors had already lost their ability to produce "flawless" Italian. This provided audiences in the home country a peculiar brand of amusement, one structurally analogous to Laurel and Hardy's own attempts at pronouncing Italian from cue cards for their first talkies. This proved so pleasurable that, when the dubbing was moved to Italy to take advantage of favorable quota laws, they cast comics Alberto Sordi and Mauro Zambuto and had them mimic the strong American accents of Laurel and Hardy and the immigrant voice actors. All the other voice actors used the dialect of Italian preferred by Mussolini's government.[74] Laurel and Hardy received comparable treatment in at least two other languages. When MGM dubbed their *Night Owls* (1930), it used "freak French" that was modeled after a "clowned Spanish version in 'trick pigeon *[sic]* Spanish.'"

These campy dubbings are exceptional, probably because they were comedies and thus released from many strictures of the continuity style. In other genres where accent or regional issues were problematic, studios and distributors quickly discovered that dubbing could generally accommodate the whims of chauvinistic audiences and for far less money than the MLV. The best evidence for this comes from the fascist countries of Franco's Spain, Hitler's Germany, and Mussolini's Italy, where the hostility to foreign languages and the desire to envelop the nation in a standardized speech manifested itself in the legislation of dubbing. The language of the Italian decree promulgated by Mussolini provides a strong sense for the sentiments underlying these legal strategies:

> Foreign language cinema cannot become a useful tool of linguistic culture, but on the contrary, functions as a pernicious vehicle. It encourages the propagation of sung expressions and artificial pronunciation. Its affected phrases disfigure our language's spontaneous maturation and development. It contradicts our mode of expression, our attention, in a word, our national traditions.[75]

Some Italians recognized that translation was every bit as important as the substitution of foreign language and the elimination of untoward accents. In 1936, critic Raffaello Patuelli wrote, "Immersed in the atmosphere of the original film, the translator lost not only his feeling for the Italian language but also for our customs, for our way of life. He forgot that, whenever possible, the naturalization of the film depends on his judgments."[76] With its ability to insulate audiences from the grating sound of foreign languages and accents, there is no question that dubbing was attractive to those with nationalist sentiments. By extension, this aspect of dubbing was clearly on the minds of foreign distributors looking to crack those markets. It was one reason behind certain industries' decision to choose dubbing over other methods, but the situation was probably too fluid and complex for nationalism to be the determining factor. By looking at the history behind the technology's development and implementation, we can see that many unpredictable forces bore down on dubbing after the initial experiments.

Dubbing was already possible in 1928, but the technology was crude and there were no conventions for its use. The inventor of what was probably the first dubbing equipment, the Vivigraph, conjured up the following process:[77] First, he imagined, American actors would have to learn the languages of the four or five major markets for Hollywood films so that they could perform their lines in each language. It did not matter if the actors did not speak the language fluently, as they could simply commit to rote memory the lines of languages they didn't know and cue cards could be placed on the set to help them if necessary. Accent was also beside the point because everything would be shot silent, and native speakers in the postproduction process would dub a translated sound track. This was thought to be the only possible method to achieve the synchronization of lips and voice. This technique was briefly adopted for translation into English for Czech and German films, such as Kurt Bernardt's *The Last Company* (1930), but it was swiftly dropped as technologies and conventions evolved, and as the powers of economy put pressures on translation practices.[78]

The original equipment for dubbing featured only one sound track, meaning that the basic elements of film sound—voice, music, effects—were conglomerated and inextricable from each other. With the invention of the multitrack Moviola in 1930, the synchronization of separate tracks became possible. However, this technical resolution did not mitigate the initial controversy over the practice. Scholars such as Kristin Thompson and Martine Danan have charted this history for the European case in some detail. Paramount and United Artists initially renounced dubbing. The latter, which was also distributing RKO's films in Europe, had conducted a market test of *Rio Rita* (1929) in Spanish, German, and French and had been scared off by the hostile reaction.[79] Paramount's general manager declared dubbing unsatisfactory as early as 1929, but soon Paramount would find it unavoidable.[80] Other early dubbings endured similarly dicey receptions. In reaction to the dubbing of Lothar Mendes's 1929 *Dangerous Curves,* one Polish critic described the approach as "making the same impression as a fake, pasted-on beard."[81] These were purely functional translations; much to the consternation of audiences, no attempt was made to construct elaborate mixes or even create sound perspective, so all dialogue was at the same volume no matter the spatial relationship of sources on the sound track.[82]

That did not prevent a number of the American studios from deciding to try dubbing for the European market starting in August 1930. It was far cheaper than MLVs and had the added attraction of enabling the majors to cash in on Hollywood star power from the silent era. Columbia set up shop in France in an attempt to achieve authentic accents while MGM remained in Hollywood for financial reasons, drawing on immigrant talent. The first "successfully concealed dubbing job" was probably *Derelict*, a Paramount production executed in Joinville using the new Moviolas and premiering in Paris in March 1931.[83] Its success probably convinced the studios to construct sound tracks utilizing three tracks with dubbing in mind. Around this time, the Hollywood studios had thrown their energies into the MLV and dubbing all but disappeared; however, the economics of the MLV proved untenable just as dubbing technologies advanced sufficiently for a reevaluation of the process. By November 1931, it was clear that the latter could minimize cost, and thus risk, and ultimately bring home the most profit.[84] The quality of the dubbing increased steadily, and soon all the studios except for MGM had dubbing studios set up in the major linguistic markets of Europe, including Spain, Germany, France, and Italy. By 1932, dubbing was the norm in France. Germany adopted it wholesale by 1933.[85]

On the other side of the world, Fox took out full-page advertisements in the Japanese film magazines in the summer of 1931. Against the photograph of the Fox back lotshot from above, it superimposed an enormous question mark—a diacritical mark foreign to the Japanese language—and the following legend:

Fox was the first to introduce talkies to Japan. Since that time, Fox has presented any number of new kinds of talkies, overcome the difficulties of understanding the voices of the talkie, and we've now arrived at the era when all films are talkies. However, thedifference in languages remains the fatal shortcoming. Fox was moved by the enthusiastic voices of its fans, and in the near future will present a wonderful plan. We can't tell you what it is now, but I can promise it is a plan that will thoroughly satisfy you fans. Please look forward to it.[86]

Fox's big surprise was Japan's first dubbed film. Japan lagged behind Europe in this respect because of economic reasons. The process was expensive, and there were too few sound theaters for economy of scale to slide it into projected profitability. However, as the advertisement suggests, Fox was committed to making dubbing the translation mode of choice. In his public forecast for 1932, the Fox representative in Tokyo explained that attendance for foreign film theaters had dropped since the novelty of the sound film wore off, so theaters started greeting this decline with a variety of strategies: turning the sound off and showing the films with *benshi*, lowering ticket prices, or the still experimental X-Version and subtitling systems. Despite these developments, he argued that the talkie still suffered a built-in "distance from the masses," and dubbing was Fox's answer to the problem.[87] Fox's first release, on January 11, 1932, was Raoul Walsh's *The Man Who Came Back* (1931), which *Kinema Junpo* celebrated as a "Japanese version in the finest sense."[88] Most reports were lukewarm. Adachi Chu wrote, "*The Man Who Came Back* Japanese version—if you sit down and think about it, the idea is incredibly absurd. Foreigners, Farrell and Gaynor, speaking Japanese. First you have to get rid of that unnaturalness. It's only tolerable because it's that kind of melodrama."[89]

While calling the experiment a mild success, the critics also mentioned certain unusual problems. Fox had undertaken the dubbing back in Los Angeles. It had hired a professor at the University of Southern California, Nakazawa Ken, to direct local performers whose primary qualification for their work was their innate language ability. These immigrants plucked out of the Little Tokyo community were not only nonactors, but they were all from Hiroshima and spoke in a thick dialect roughened by years of living abroad. People complained bitterly about this unwitting use of nonstandard Japanese, and shortly thereafter the method that became standard operating procedure in Japan was the "superimposed (sub)title" *(supa inpozu-ban)*—the "sub" in parentheses because it was not always at the bottom of the frame.

Japanese distributors shunned dubbing until the postwar period. Even a cursory look at the dictionaries of film terms finds that they list dubbing as simply the transfer of sound from one to another medium, for example, from film to wax disk. Film dictionaries give no mention of the technique's use for translation before the 1960s.[90] As Shimizu

Shunji suggests, the shock most audiences felt upon hearing Gloria Gaynor speak in Hiroshima dialect may have been a deciding factor in the standardization of subtitling in Japan.[91] Had Fox conducted its initial dubbings in Japan, this might have been a very different history.

Subtitling

The other method that emerged triumphant in "Babel—The Sequel" was subtitling. Happily, the people who subtitled the first films, and in so doing wrote the rules and conventions of subtitling, have committed their memories to print. Herman Weinberg was the first translator in the world to use subtitles; he is probably their inventor, starting with the German operetta *Zwei Herzen im Dreiviertel-Takt* (*Two Hearts in Waltz Time*, 1930) by Géza von Bolváry.[92] In the course of his career, he claimed to have titled more than four hundred films, including those in Sicilian, Japanese, Swedish, Hindustani, Spanish, Brazilian, Greek, Finnish, Yugoslavian *(sic!)*, Czech, Hungarian—obviously, he was a believer in knowing the target language better than the source language. (Surprisingly enough, this is not so unusual. In his 1989 profile, Okaeda Shinji claims more than a thousand titles to his credit, including *Citizen Kane* [1941], *Star Wars* [1977], and films in French, German, Italian, Russian, and Spanish.[93] Needless to say, one must wonder about quality in the face of such enthusiastic boasting over quantity.) Here Weinberg explains, in his own way, the experimentation that led to the codification of the practice:

Someone with nothing better to do one day discovered the principle of the photo-electric cell which made it possible to transmit soundwaves into light waves and vice-versa, and which now made it possible for movies to talk. But when the films I was working with talked it was in French and German. What do we do now? Full screen titles was the first answer, stopping the action and giving the audience a brief synopsis of what they were going to see in the next ten minutes. Ten minutes later, another full screen synopsis. This was not only silly but annoying as those in the audience who could understand the language could laugh at the jokes in between the full screen titles while those who couldn't (and they constituted the majority, by far) sat there glum, doubly irritated by the laughter of the linguists in the house. Obviously something had to be done to placate the customers before they started asking for their money back. Then someone discovered the existence of a mechanism called a "Moviola."[94] ... It had a counter which enabled you to measure every piece of dialogue because it, too, was now equipped with that magical photo-electric cell so that you could now measure not only the length of every scene but that of every line of dialogue. And from these measurements we were able, by the trial and error method . . . to determine what we were doing and why. Whew! And when I say "we" I mean me, as no one knew any more than anyone else did about it and I seemed to be the only one willing to go ahead with the actual writing and make something out of it. At the beginning, I was very cautious and superimposed hardly more than 25 or 30 titles to a ten-minute reel . . . Then I'd go into the theatre during a showing to watch the audiences' faces, to see how they reacted to the titles. I'd wondered if they were going to drop their heads slightly to read the titles at the bottom of the screen and then raise them again after they read the titles (like watching a tennis match and moving your head from left to right and back again) but I needn't have worried on this score; they didn't drop their heads, they merely dropped their eyes, I noticed. This emboldened me to insert more titles, when warranted, of course, and bit by bit more and more of the original dialogue got translated until at the end of my work in this field I was putting in anywhere from 100 to 150 titles a reel . . . tho', I must repeat, only when the dialogue was good enough to warrant it.[95]

Within a year or two of the talkie's public appearance, the major studios brought translators to New York to subtitle the latest films. The initial languages were French, Dutch, and German, but soon they began subtitling other languages as well. It is likely each linguistic context underwent a process roughly analogous to that of Japan. In late 1930, Paramount sent Tamura Yukihiko to New York to conduct the first translation with film subtitles in Japanese. The film was von Sternberg's *Morocco*. Tamura was editor of Japan's most venerated film magazine, *Kinema Junpo*, and he sent his readers a diary about his experiences.[96] As the Japanese film community awaited the fruits of his labor, Tamura reported his encounter with a set of novel problems:

First of all, the initial dilemma we encountered was whether to use vertical or horizontal lines. For this, I performed various experiments. In the case of vertical lines, three-and-a-half feet of film were required to read one line with twelve characters. However, we found that if we printed the same line horizontally it would be impossible to read without five or more feet. Besides the decision to print vertically, we had to decide to put the subtitle on the right or left side. It was impossible to settle on a position. We'd put them on the right to avoid covering something on the left and vice versa [Figure 19]. So we watched previews and investigated

Figure 19. *Morocco* was the first film subtitled in Japan. Its success relative to all the other experiments led to the standardization of subtitles in Japan. Note how the subtitles switch from side to side in respect to the mise-en-scène.

the problem scene by scene . . . About thirty cards per reel was the limit. We were careful to avoid showing the embarrassing sight of titles from one scene running over into the next.[97]

The next problem was finding someone capable of calligraphy who could draw the titles to be photographed. Tamura put an advertisement in a local Japanese-language paper, but the fifteen or so applicants were all unemployed and looking for whatever work they could find. He gave them writing tests and was horrified at the results. He finally found someone just as the translation was complete. Another predicament was that his translation of a given line tended to take longer to read than the temporal duration of the utterance. At least that was his impression, having never done this before. A final challenge was deciding how much of the film to translate. He suspected that too many subtitles would distract viewers from the image and leave them frustrated; too few and they would be unable to understand the story. He watched European versions and counted more than four hundred subtitles per film. Tamura felt this was far too many, and his first attempt resulted in 234 subtitles. After viewing a test, he felt even this was excessive.

When *Morocco* finally had its release, it caused a sensation throughout Japan. It gave the critics one more translation method to debate, and there were also the inevitable complaints. Koizumi Yasushi thought the subtitles were ugly, and asked Paramount to use more beautiful characters.[98] The celebrated essayist Furukawa Roppa complemented Tamura on his "dialogue selection" and lucid translation, which he thought was "kind to the audience"; at the same time, he felt the Chinese character choices and title positioning needed work. When subtitles cover someone's hands or face, it "kills the beauty and wrecks the feelings," he argued.[99] Some commentators disliked the large size of the titles, or the way they appeared all over the screen. Kitagawa Tetsuo estimated that at least a third of the subtitles for *Over the Hill* (1931) disappeared before he had a chance to read them.[100] Other complaints, some of which continue to be a problem today, included misprision, the use of modern-sounding language for period films, overly long subtitles, text rendered illegible by white images, and difficult Chinese characters.[101]

Not surprisingly, the *benshi* weighed in with heavy criticism. Tokugawa Musei, one of the most beloved *benshi,* was always quick to criticize methods that did not include *setsumei* and joked, "Eh, you start waiting and wondering which side the title will appear on, and it's not long before you feel like placing bets on it."[102] Regarding Tamura's work, he wrote, "I saw *Morocco* and thought it was OK. This is one model for the talkie industry, but I don't believe it would be good if everyone used this method for all talkies"; he goes on to plead, "if you only gave us volume controls it would be fine."[103] Yamano Ichiro notes that *Morocco* may have played two weeks without *setsumei* but Paramount's second effort, *Tom Sawyer,* left people so confused that, except for Horakuza Theater in central Tokyo, the distributors turned down the sound and brought in a *benshi. Morocco* worked, Yamano said, because von Sternberg made a masterpiece. "What if we were to imagine those Japanese subtitles on an insipid film?" he asks. "On an insipid film where a single reel amounts to two people talking? What would it be like with those huge Japanese characters flashing—*pokari pokari*—like that?"[104]

Despite these kinds of protestations, the subtitle had taken hold. That summer Universal Japan undertook a survey of audiences to determine preferences for translation methods. It found that a preponderance of theatergoers preferred subtitling over other methods.[105] It was even popular enough that United Artists rereleased the hit MLV *Hell's Angels* (1930) in a subtitled version.

MGM's first subs encountered unexpected technical problems in Japan. For example, it performed the translation and shot the subtitle sub-negative in Tokyo, sending it back to Los Angeles for final printing. The consequent lack of control meant that when the film was eventually screened in Tokyo the subtitles were out of sync. Paramount started out making its subtitles in Hollywood, but it sent Tamura Yukihiko back to Japan in May 1933. Paramount then conducted the entire subtitling process in Japan. The press reported Tamura's homecoming at Yokohama's port as a revolutionary moment in Japanese film history.[106] Paramount's decision marks the end of the talkies experiment and the beginning of the new era (as long as we ignore the fact that Japanese filmmakers continued to make *benshi*-narrated silent films until 1936).[107] The approach it forged remains the standard operating procedure to the present day.

Along with dubbing, this new technology of translation is what enabled Hollywood to avoid any interruption in its dominance of the international film market. We have seen how one of the prevalent discourses surrounding the new sound cinema was its supposed "anti-international-ism." Critics rued the extralinguistic universality of the silent cinema, emphasizing the way sound accentuates the national character of films. What I will highlight in the subsequent chapters is the manner in which this unexpected awareness of the source culture through the insertion of the source language = sound is precisely the quality that both subtitlers and dubbers came to suppress.

CHAPTER FIVE

For an Abusive Subtitling

Original language is always best, like breast milk, and twice as convenient in a crowded cinema.
—Joe Joseph, "Here Comes That Synching Feeling"

A Corrupt Practice

Ever since the subtitle's invention in that chaotic babel of the talkies era, translators confronted the violent reduction demanded by the apparatus by developing and maintaining a method of translation that conspires to hide its work—along with its ideological assumptions—from its own reader-spectators. In this sense, we may, in a sincerely playful spirit, think of them as *corrupt*. They accept a vision of translation that violently appropriates the source text, and in the process of converting speech into writing within the time and space limits of the subtitle, they conform the original to the rules, regulations, idioms, and frame of reference of the target language and its culture. It is a practice of translation that smoothes over its textual violence and domesticates all otherness while it pretends to bring the audience to an experience of the foreign. The peculiar challenges posed by subtitles and the violence they necessitate are a matter of course; they are variations of the difficulties in any translation, and in this sense are analogous to the problems confronted by the translator of poetry. It is the subtitler's response to those challenges that is corrupt. Subtitlers say they promote learning and facilitate enjoyable meetings with other cultures, bringing the sense behind actors' speech acts to the viewers through their skillful rendering at the edges of the screen.[1] In fact, they conspire to hide their repeated acts of violence through codified rules and a tradition of suppression. It is this practice that is corrupt—feigning completeness in their own violent world. One of the few attempts at theorizing the subtitle, by Trinh T. Minh-ha, touches on these issues, although is ultimately unsatisfying:

> The duration of the subtitles, for example, is very ideological. I think that if, in most translated films, the subtitles usually stay on as long as they technically can—often much longer than the time needed even for a slow reader—it's because translation is conceived here as part of the operation of suture that defines the classical cinematic apparatus and the technological effort it deploys to naturalize a dominant, hierarchically unified worldview. The success of the mainstream film relies precisely on how well it can hide [its articulated artifices] in what it wishes to show. Therefore, the attempt is always to protect the unity of the subject; here to collapse, in subtitling, the activities of reading, hearing, and seeing into one single activity, as if they were all the same. What you read is what you hear, and what you hear is more often than not, what you see.[2]

We can accept Trinh's gloss to the extent that we recognize how, in this mode of translation, all forms of difference are suppressed and troublesome texts are fitted into the most conservative of frameworks.

Take the example of sexual difference. In Japanese, gender is clearly marked linguistically, and subtitles dramatize difference through stereo-types of the way men or women *should* speak. In subtitles this is accom-plished primarily through sentence-final particles. For example, the male ending *zo* has a hard, assertive sound, while female speech is softened by particles like *wa* and *no*. As with any corruption, habits are hard to break and behavior is ruled by convention. At the beginning of the Japanese-subtitled version of *RoboCop* (1987), for example, the female and male cops meet each other just after the female officer beats a rowdy criminal into submission. After this display of no-nonsense brutality, the new partners are introduced to each other, they get into a squad car, and drive away. The action is innocuous enough, but the dialogue in-volves an intense play for power that's entirely linguistic:

FEMALE OFFICER: I better drive until you know your way around.
MALE OFFICER: I usually drive when I'm breaking in a new partner.

In Japan this was subtitled in the following manner:

FEMALE: *Watashi ga unten suru wa.* (I will drive.)
MALE: *Kimi ni wa makaseraren.* (I can't leave it to you.)

Not only is this conversation reduced to its barest, literal meaning, but the power dynamic is changed from a struggle over knowledge to a simple domination. The woman's soft sentence-final particle *wa* contrasts with the male officer's curt verb ending; the difference strongly suggests that he occupies a superior position (a position cemented by deployment of the second-person pronoun *kimi*, which one uses only with subordinates). The woman's subtitle would have been much stronger with a different particle, such as *yo*. This particle is associated with patriarchal power and is typically used by middle-aged women when they want to speak forcefully. Indeed, it is difficult to imagine this aggressive female cop actually using *wa* in any context. Without their accompanying image, the lines read like a gangster talking to his moll. The translator took great liberties, matching the barren substance of the target language with the image but evacuating the power play.[3]

We may be able to understand the basic, underlying logic of corruption by turning to what would appear to be its most extreme manifestation: dubbing. The journal *Velvet Light Trap* published what amounts to an apology for the practice of dubbing. Its author, Antje Ascheid, argues for dubbing as an exchange of one voice for another that produces a new text free of the constraints on the translator because there is no debt to an original. This allows the translator to bring the reader (read *consumer*) a readily digestible package that easily supplants any ideological baggage carried by the original film. Although the author describes subtitles as purist and elitist, he argues that the dubbed sound track is liberating: mass audiences will not resist the foreign film because the dubber can resist the ideological underpinnings that link film to geopolitical struggles. Strange, then, that this is the essay's conclusion:

> Dubbing . . . mostly succeeds in effacing the fact of the film text's foreign origin; or, rather, it gives its new audience the chance to disavow what they really know, hence opening an avenue for cultural ventriloquism through voice postsynchronization. In doing so, the dubbed film appears as a radically new product rather than a transformed old one, a single text rather than a double one. Like a Japanese game computer, a Taiwanese shirt, or a German car, products that have been constructed to fit consumer desires in an international marketplace through the reduction of their cultural specificities, the to-be-dubbed film original initially fulfills an important criterion with which most other international commodities also comply: it foregrounds its function, ceasing to be a "foreign" film in order to become just a film . . . In the international marketplace the film

original thus functions as a transnational decultured product; it becomes
the raw material that is to be reinscribed into the different cultural contexts of the consumer nations through the use of dubbing.[4]

Just a film indeed. Aside from an insufficient theorization of translation itself, this suspicious essay reduces the foreign tongue to nothing
more than a "cultural disadvantage" where dubbing is perceived as "a
strategy of empowerment." This is a fine example of a valorization of
postmodern play being co-opted by capital. The "exchange" facilitated
by the "to-be-dubbed film" is simply of the capitalist variety: money
for pleasure. This is the logic of corruption in its dubbed version, the
one practiced by distributors for whom translation serves little more
than surplus value. Today's subtitles participate in it to an unfortunate
degree; any translator who wishes to think otherwise is blind.

These forms of corruption could be critiqued from the ideology of
fidelity, which invokes the authority of the original and portrays it as an
endangered purity or origin. This would reveal how subtitlers are reluc-
tant to discuss the issue of fidelity, as it would expose their violence and
make them appear incompetent. We could also extend the domain of
this purity under siege to the terrain of the screen itself, like the Japanese cinematographer who decries ugly, superimposed subtitles for
despoiling the image and separating spectators from the beauty of the
original.[5] Indeed, any measure of fidelity is a standard the apparatus itself
will not permit. However, even though the term "corrupt" threatens to
pose the original as territory unspoiled by subjectivity, there are theoretical reasons for steering clear of such easy binaries to take a quite
different tack. The first step is to simply expose the act of translation,
release it from its space of suppression, and understand what subtitling
actually is and how it came to its corrupt condition.

The Apparatus of Translation

The practice of subtitling has been even more obscured than the translation of written, printed texts. Indeed, most people probably have never
thought of subtitling *as translation*. There is no question that English-
language criticism about foreign cinema has taken the mediation of subtitles entirely for granted. Outside of the writing aimed at professional
translators and the academic audiences of translation studies, virtually
nothing has been written about them. Indeed, the translators themselves,
along with their technicians, filmmakers, writers, censors, and the pro-

ducers who hire them all, go to great lengths to suppress any acknowledgment of their conspiracy. It has been noted more than once that the
unlucky translator is an author but not The Author, that her translation
is a work but not The Work. But even this dynamic is absent from both
popular and scholarly discourses on the cinema. This absence speaks
doubly of the dominance of the image and the utter suppression of the
subtitler's central role in enabling a film's border crossing.

To transport the subtitle from its space of obscurity and uncover the
root of its corruption, we must consider what is specific to it as a particular mode of translation. This includes its material conditions and its
historical contingency. In subtitling, a massive apparatus necessitates a
violent translation of the source text. The film's utterances are segmented by time; natural breaks in speech are marked for the temporal
borders of the subtitle. The translator determines the length of each
unit of translation down to the frame, that is, down to a twenty-fourth
of a second. This is called spotting, the result of which is the spotting
list of timed segments available for translation. This is a crucially important step, and it is often doled out to a specialist. I know from experience, for example, that I tend to spot titles too short, so prefer to leave
this step to those with a better sense of timing than I. John Minchinton,
one of the most experienced spotters in Britain, asserts, "The spotter's
ultimate aim is to sympathise with the grammar of the film, and form a
whole with the author's work going beyond the translation of the dialogue."[6] Spotting involves creating an interface between the particular
structures of a given target language and the rhythms of both speech
and editing.

As the translation proceeds, the translator takes chunks of meaning
and refits them into newly abstracted blocks of space and time. Relatively simple utterances pose few problems. However, when the original
text features grammatical or aesthetic complexity, or a density of meaning,
this can be quite a challenge. Furthermore, the temporal blocks subtitlers
work with are far from homogeneous blanks. They strive to match the
timing of the subtitle with the sound and motion of the source text. A
humorous line, for example, must be arranged to meet its audiovisual
punctuation. As subtitler Henri Béhar puts it, "Subtitling is like playing
3-D Scrabble in two languages."[7]

Once accomplished, the translation moves through the hands of
countless technicians, some of whom think nothing of "adjusting" a

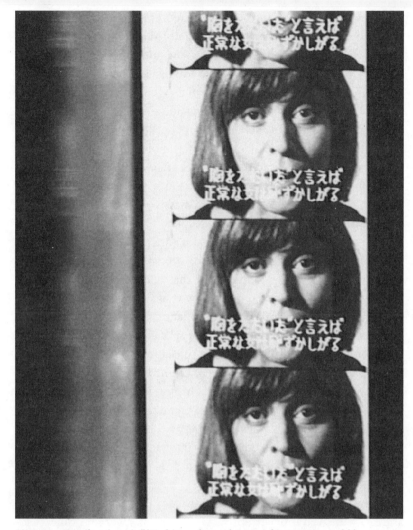

Figure 20. *Privilege* (1990): " 'He hit my breast.' A straight woman would be embarrassed." An anonymous, corrupt technician changed the translation of "straight" to *seijo na hito,* or "normal person." The translator had chosen *hetero,* an ideologically neutral term.

subtitle here or there for their own capricious or technical reasons. This can lead to the kind of embarrassing mistakes that make translators cringe (for an excellent example, see Figure 20). Finally, the translation is grafted onto the original text in one of three ways (in the case of film). The initial method was to photograph cards with the subtitle text, sandwich this filmstrip with the negative, and optically print the subtitles onto the image as a third filmstrip, literally a third track[8] (Figures 15, 18, 19, 21, 23). The next major method was to coat the film with wax, assemble printing press–like clichés for each subtitle, press these into the wax down to the film itself, and bathe the print in an acid that would eat the subtitle out of the very tissue of the image (a process invented in 1937;[9] Figures 3, 20). Originally, they used a small metal seal, heated with electricity and applied briefly upon every frame to burn the emulsion off. This resulted in fairly good quality, especially with rough edges visible against white backgrounds, but it was expensive and slow. It was abandoned unevenly across the world, although it is still in use in poorly capitalized industries (and, ironically enough, Japan). The most common method at the turn of the twenty-first century was to burn the letters into the celluloid with computer-driven lasers. This enabled translators to eliminate the expensive and accident-prone assemblage of clichés while taking advantage of the editing powers of word processing and database software. Unfortunately, the major weakness of the current laser systems is that they burn the film so cleanly that white images render them invisible. Perhaps the only other significant technological innovation was using colored subtitles so they were legible over white images. The first instance of this was *Tora! Tora! Tora!* (1970), which used filters to render its optical subtitles yellow.[10] This required significant expense, so it wasn't until the age of video that the use of colored subtitles became widespread.

In a resurrection of the principle represented by the magic lantern strategy of the talkies era, the Italian company Softtitler introduced a projection system in 1984. It was correctable, and meant that a single print could be used for multiple languages. Just before this, a French company developed a system that simply projected subtitles off a reel of film to help its filmmakers get into international film festivals. By the 1990s, new systems accomplished this with small computers, fiber-optic cable, and LED displays at the edge of the screen. After the turn of the century, a new projection system stored up to forty sets of subtitles on an optical disc. One can only guess where it will go from there, as photochemical film gives way to digital projection.

Beyond the difficulties posed by this complicated process, the translator confronts an array of challenges that seem to lead down the path of corruption. The space and time available for translation are decided by the apparatus itself; this may be analogous to the challenge posed by poetry, but is actually a different problem. In film, the machine runs at a constant speed and mindlessly unspools its translation at an unchanging rate. The translator must condense his translation in the physical space of the frame and the temporal length of the utterance. The reader cannot stop and dwell on an interesting line; as the reader scans the text, the machine instantly obliterates it. There are protocols for this condensation, but they differ depending on the translator and the apparatus. The number of spaces available for text depends on the format of the film (16mm, 35mm), the lens (1:33, 1:85, CinemaScope), and the subtitling method itself. The translator then determines how many letters or characters are legible in the second or two or three available to each title. It is often said that actors talk twice as fast as spectators can read, but this is hardly a useful starting point for the work of translation. Donald Richie, for example, allows for about one word per foot, or a two-line title per twelve feet.[11] Japanese subtitlers are fond of citing the rule "Four characters per second."[12] Toda Natsuko explains how this rule was arrived at: the first subtitlers had to determine how fast the typical Japanese could read, so they showed a film to a Shinbashi geisha (!) and came up with three to four characters per second with a thirteen-character line.[13] Over the years, they reduced the line to ten to prevent sloppy projectionists from cutting off the characters at the edges, but soon the four-characters-per-second rule was clad in iron. (By way of contrast, subtitles in other languages can be two to three times as long, depending on the format, aperture, and a number of other factors.) Actually, this history is far more nuanced than this representation of it. And today, in the era of computer-assisted subtitling, the ideal number of characters is determined by the abstract curve of a logarithm embedded in the software. In any case, against this matrix of time and space, the translator submits the original text to a violent reduction that most readers consider inept—if they dodge the translator's feints and pause to think about it at all.

The Japanese language seems ready-made for subtitling: for one thing, Japanese does not waste precious space on gaps between words, and can even break a line in mid-word. *Kanji* (Chinese characters) express the maximum amount of meaning in a minimum of syllables; neologisms and abbreviations are easily accomplished through the creative combination of characters. Even better, Japanese often leaves out the subject, direct object, or other parts of speech, saving much-needed space. Because this forces speakers to be aware of context, the language itself prepares its readers to seek out what subtitles leave unsaid. Finally, in addition to italics, Japanese has the enviable ability to be inscribed both horizontally and vertically, a resource whose abusive potential is provocative. Finding the source language a richer linguistic world than one's own target language is probably a universal—and frustrating— experience for translators, but we must not let this impression lead toward an essentialist relationship to translation and its tools. A far more powerful ground for developing a translation attuned to its time is a thorough historicization, especially one that takes into account multiple national contexts. To avoid this is to flirt with the dangers demonstrated by the nationalist chauvinism of postwar Japanese subtitlers.

The subtitle has never been entirely ignored in Japan. Since at least the 1930s, *en-face* scenarios of foreign films have been published on a routine basis. However, the bulk of these contain complete translations of the films, and this speaks more for the Japanese film world's appreciation of the art of scenario writing than of subtitling per se. At the same time, there are schools devoted to training translators, and the name of the subtitler is always included as a credit in the Japanese prints of foreign films (at least in much of the postwar era). In fact, a number of these translators have achieved reputations among general audiences. Some subtitlers even have fans! The most famous—Shimizu Shunji, Okaeda Shinji, Kamishima Kimi, and Toda Natsuko—have published autobiographies, how-to books, and textbooks that use subtitles to teach English conversation.[14]

Although many of history's most famous essays on translation have emerged in the course of practice, these authors' writings on "the art of subtitling" are deeply disappointing. Their conception of translation is regrettably simplistic. For example, the Russian cinematic adaptation and subsequent Japanese translation of *Hamlet* (1964) naturally raise the issue of the authority of the original text; oblivious to this kind of issue, Toda Natsuko—by far the most popular subtitler in Japan—uses the film only to suggest what a pity it would have been if dubbing had erased the main actor's beautiful, velvety voice.[15] Her mentor Shimizu Shunji similarly describes his subtitles for Olivier's *Othello* (1965). Noting that the great actor's performance was more theatrical than cinematic,

Figure 21. Kitano Takeshi's *Getting Any?* (*Minna yatte iru ka,* 1995). Subtitler Toda Natsuko is so famous that there are jokes about her. Every time the sex-obsessed hero meets his Iraqi workmates, they say only "Merbani." This single word is accompanied by lengthy and surreal subtitles that always end with a credit to Toda. This one reads: "Let's cooperate to protect the warthog and the Japanese crested ibis from their impending extinction. Translation/Toda Natsuko."

he made much of his going to the unusual length of listening to a tape recording of the sound track while translating.[16] Now, for most translators, Shakespeare's words provide their most daunting task, a test case for the most basic, pressing theoretical issues in translation. This does not occur to Shimizu or Toda. In both cases, the actor and his voice replace Shakespeare as the sources to which the translator owes a debt. By way of contrast, Canadian translator Robert Paquin describes his dubbing of Julia Taymor's *Titus* (1999) in the essay "In the Footsteps of Giants."[17] He walks us through the process of researching extant French translations, determining the nature of Taynor's own adaptation of the English, deciding on a variation of the French alexandrine as an analogue to Shakepeare's blank verse, and negotiating the stresses of his chosen poetic form with the stresses of the original script's labials and the actors' body language.

In comparison, the Japanese authors' approach is especially impoverished, as is their understanding of film history; they have done little or no research into the past or present conditions of their field, but they never hesitate to explain or analyze it. In his "Philosophy of Subtitling," Okaeda Shinji bases his aesthetics of cinema on a naive equation of silent and sound film narration. He unproblematically compares the narrative function of silent-era intertitles to that of sound subtitles in the 1980s to support his aesthetics of cinema: the less words a film has, the better.[18] He does not begin to consider the vast ontological and semiotic differences between silent and sound cinema. For example, he does not even mention the crucial role of the *benshi*. This is a typical example of how simplistic is the conception of cinema with which corrupt subtitlers operate.

Furthermore, their understanding of the relationship of subtitlers to the world film industry and its politics is particularly inadequate. Toda reduces "America's standard practice of dubbing" to the fact that it is a nation of immigrants, a comment that feels uncannily similar to statements over which a number of ministers have resigned in recent years. Certainly, an adequate explanation would have to deal with a complex overdetermination of forces: the emergence of English as a lingua franca of international business and politics; the world domination of Hollywood, its location within U.S. borders, and its near total domination of the home market; and an education system that places no value on foreign-language study. Furthermore, although mass-market films may be dubbed, it is incorrect to say that this is standard practice. The actual market for foreign films has historically demanded subtitles, and this has also become true of mainstream releases for foreign films as of the 1980s.

Toda's brand of radical reduction is complemented by tedious gloating over the Japanese language, the sensitivity of Japanese spectators, and the special skills required of the translator of films. Toda: "Japanese people's special tendency to want to see the original created a unique subtitle nation *[yuniiku na jimakukoku]*; here, we are happy that every Japanese can read, an extremely special condition anywhere in the world."[19] Okaeda: "Japanese people's intention *[shiko]* toward the original is strong ... (and one of the reasons) subtitles are the mainstream ... Considering this, subtitles are immortal. We could say, 'Japan: Nation of the Subtitle Culture.'"[20] Subtitling is not in a repressed condition in Japan; rather, it is overvalued through the idealization of the Japanese language and its own practice of translation of the foreign. Common sense might dictate that dubbing would be the translation method of choice for fervent nationalists (see, for example, the work of Martine Danan); however, the Japanese case suggests how subtitling may also find itself subject to cultural and national chauvinism. In Japan, both the usual methods of repressing the subtitler and Japan's unusual fetishization of the subtitle achieve an identical effect in the end. They deflect or disavow the erasure of difference and the inequality of languages that the act of translation always threatens to expose.

A Submerged History

Recalling our investigation into the invention of subtitling in the preceding chapter, the first-person accounts by the pioneers of film translation would appear to suggest that the conventions of subtitling have changed little since their invention. This is to say that the rules and regulations that govern the production of subtitles (exclusive of those related to the apparatus itself) were set during the age of the Hollywood studio system. One might think this explains why subtitles look and function the way they do. However, it must also be stressed that while the subtitling apparatus itself has changed little, the practice of subtitlers has, and the changes themselves are closely tied to the ideological context at the moment of translation. Likewise, any theorization of subtitles must be considered against its historical moment, which points to the weakness of Trinh's analysis of subtitling. Her understanding of a subtitling buttressing a unified subject position and the implicit call for an oppositional avant-garde is anchored too deeply in 1970s suture theory. Although I share her concerns over the ideological dimension of subtitling, I steer away from such essentialized arguments and toward a theorization grounded in a strong historical contextualization.

Let us focus on the example of Japanese subtitling and its historical development. A close consideration of early translations suggests that there are crucial differences between prewar and present subtitling conventions. Unfortunately, virtually all of the foreign films distributed in Japan before World War II were destroyed in the National Film Center fire in the 1970s.[21] Other prewar prints of foreign films are extremely rare, and should they exist, they would be equally difficult to view. There is, however, a way around this problem.

When a film was imported into Japan, the Home Ministry required the submission of a *ken'etsu daihon* (censorship scenario).[22] *Ken'etsu daihon* typically included a complete translation of every utterance and a description of nearly every sound effect. It also included an *en-face* listing of the film's subtitles. Only three copies were made: the official copy that received the Home Ministry seal, one for studio use, and one for preservation at the ministry (with the establishment of the Film Law of 1939, two more copies were created for the Home Ministry's Information Bureau and the Ministry of Education). In any case, it should not be surprising that only a handful of these precious scenarios are extant.

Shimizu Shunji acquired the *ken'etsu daihon* of *Morocco*. His analysis is predictably superficial, but provides a useful starting point for exploring the real history of Japanese subtitles. Shimizu counts 297 subtitles in Tamura's version. Tamura's original translation used only 234, but after seeing a test print, he felt the extra sixty-three titles were necessary.[23] Throughout his books, Shimizu often notes that before the war, subtitlers used somewhere between a half and a third of the subtitles used today. This appears to be a widespread practice. The first British film to be subtitled was *Kameradschaft* in January 1932, and it had only seventy to eighty subtitles; later in the same year, *Mädchen in Uniform* (1931) used 230.[24] Also recall the testimony by Herman Weinberg at the beginning of this chapter. With the *ken'etsu daihon* of *Morocco* in hand, Shimizu attempts to find the difference. First, he parses the scenario according to today's standards and decides that his own count would come to 492. Then he counts Kikuji Hiroshi's postwar subbing of the film, which uses 491. Finally, he compares Kikuji's and Tamura's actual translations, and concludes that outside of a few old *kanji*, excessively long subtitles, and Tamura's choice not to translate Dietrich's songs, there is no significant difference.

I find this a rather startling conclusion. Putting the actual translation of words aside for the moment, the difference between 297 and 492 strongly suggests that we are dealing with two very dissimilar conceptions of translation. Shimizu was pursuing the wrong questions. Rather than wondering about the phrasing of individual titles, he should have been asking, "If Tamura chose to subtitle only half of the utterances, then what exactly was he translating? *What was the object of translation?*"

I have found the *ken'etsu daihon* for King Vidor's *The Champ* (1931), which contains Shimizu Chiyota's subtitles, which were praised by reviews at the time for "supporting the feel of the film."[25] Consistent with Shimizu Shunji's writing, roughly half of the film's utterances went untranslated. Only 328 of the film's 869 lines received titles.[26] Upon closer examination, the first thing one notices is that the translation pares down the film primarily to narrative movement. This means that certain characters whom the translator deemed insignificant are virtually (or even completely) written out of the film because their lines go unsubtitled. For example, not only are the lines of Jackie Coogan's half sister mostly untranslated, but Shimizu ignored all references to her. The film never firmly establishes their relationship, so for viewers of the subtitled version she is simply a cute little girl who shows up every once in a while, says something incomprehensible, and then disappears. Her excision from the film via subtitles marks the film with a patriarchal reading of the film placed *between* text and reader/spectator.

Another crucial criterion for selection appears to be thematic. *The Champ* is well known as an early response to the social effects of the Great Depression. The film's characterization revolves around a woman who divorced her poor husband (the boxer) for a rich man; the mother wants to remove their son from the Champ's custody to save the child from the "poor environment." However, Shimizu's translation tends to leave out verbal references to the class discourse of the film. Virtually the only subtitles that retain it point to visual markers of class that the audiences would not have missed, such as the difference between the Champ's flophouse apartment and the mother's luxurious hotel. Significantly, even class differences in speech itself—inflection, vocabulary, grammar, and the like—are largely unreflected in the style of the subtitles. We can find the real effects of Shimizu's selective translation in a special section devoted to Ozu's *Passing Fancy* (*Dekigokoro*, 1933) in *STS*, one of Japan's earliest film-theory journals. At the time, this film was often compared to *The Champ* for its narrative centered on an intense father-son relationship, and apparently Ozu based the script on Vidor's film. In his *STS* article, Mura Chio attempts a structural comparison of the two films' scripts to investigate the differences between sound and silent film scenario writing. One of his conclusions: "In terms of storytelling, [Francis] Marion's firm, text-heavy scenario style and Vidor's direct, solid directorial method precisely show us the instinctual love of father and child. However, they do not in any way describe the world that lower-middle-class people inhabit."[27] This suggests that the translator regards speech primarily as a vehicle for narrative propulsion, not expression as such, and that many of the choices regarding what to retain as relevant have quite serious ideological implications. However, the most important criterion is also the least obvious.

Figure 22. *The Champ* (1931): if only 328 of the film's 869 lines received subtitles, what precisely was the object of translation?

The Champ has (at least) three moments of melodramatic excess that are fascinating for their translation. By "excess" I mean elements such as mise-en-scène, sound, acting, and writing, which are heightened to complement emotional distress. These scenes are the horse race where Jackie Coogan's horse stumbles just as it is about to win, the jail scene where Wallace Beery rejects Jackie and tells him to go to his mother, and the prize fight at the end. Shimizu's translation sets up each scene—and then simply stops. For example, the narrative tension of the horse race comes primarily from the announcer's call. Without his description of Coogan's come-from-behind bid for first place, it is impossible to tell which horse is in which position. There are no subtitles providing this information. The heartbreaking jail scene—by far the most memorable moment of the film—begins with a quiet dialogue between the Champ and his trainer Sponge. Of their nine lines, all but two are translated (and these were easy to guess by context). When the Champ's son Dink arrives, the melodrama gradually intensifies while the subtitle count drops steeply. From here until the moment Dink leaves the jail crushed by his father's explosive rejection, only nine of twenty-four lines are translated! Near the end, when the two scream at each other and the Champ violently strikes his son through the prison bars, the subtitles stop. This breaks the most cherished rules of today's corrupt subtitlers who—in a seemingly natural way—assign meaning to every utterance as a matter of course.

The example of *The Champ* is not an isolated fluke, as evidenced by a similar scene from *The Man Who Knew Too Much* (1934). Alfred Hitchcock is admired as one of the first filmmakers to make creative use of sound. He set the climax of this film in Royal Albert Hall, where a political assassination is to take place during a concert. Such a crowded public setting for a killing seems dubious; however, the assassins plan to use a fortissimo crash of cymbals to drown out the rifle's crack. Hitchcock sets this up in a previous scene featuring ringleader Abbot (Peter Lorre) and the killer, Ramon. The mastermind explains the plan to his doltish assassin, playing a record of the scheduled performance. As crescendo leads to cymbal crash, Abbott indicates the precise moment when Ramon should pull the trigger. Here is the delightful dialogue (which the Japanese subtitles rendered in a dull, straightforward manner):

ABBOTT, THE RINGLEADER: A record of the delightful piece which they are playing at the Albert Hall tonight.

RAMON, THE ASSASSIN: Charming. What of it?
ABBOTT: Oh yes, I forgot. Music is less in your line than marksmanship. If you listen, my dear Ramon, I will show you the exact moment at which you can shoot.

At this point, the Japanese subtitles suddenly stop altogether as the actors turn their attention to the sound coming from a record player. The next two lines are wonderfully sinister, *and they go entirely untranslated:*

ABBOTT: Now listen carefully—there!—you see at such a moment your shot can't be heard—I think the composer would have appreciated that—no one will know.
RAMON: Except for one [pointing at his head].[28]

This returns us to our original question: If not the meaning of every line, what exactly was the object of translation? On the one hand, these translators were ignoring the parts of speech that contribute to expression and simply translating the narrative meaning behind the words. They generally use a translation strategy that strips the lines of dialogue to their barest, most basic function of moving the plot (granted, as they interpret it). On the other hand, for moments when the speech act itself was contributing to the overall expression of the film's emotional impact, *they chose not to translate.* Implicit in their decision was the assumption that the grain of the voice was more important than the meanings being articulated.

In fact, other reports concerning prewar subtitling practices suggest a variety of *graphic* tactics that also exhibit a translation strategy focused on the materiality of language. In *M* (1931) there is a scene in which a boy hawks newspapers; as the camera nears the boy, his voice gets louder on the sound track. At the same time, the Japanese subtitles translating the boy's voice grow correspondingly larger and larger, providing a graphic representation of the increasing volume.[29] Furthermore, Japanese subtitlers routinely placed their titles in different areas of the scene depending on the cinematographer's composition (Figures 15, 19). It was thought that the position of the words should complement mise-en-scène and movement. At the same time, there are indications that subtitle positioning depended on narrative as well. One story from critic Yodogawa Nagaharu describes a dreamy Hollywood love scene where the subtitles appeared between the two lovers.[30] Of course!

The conception of translation in the talkie period circulated between two poles, between a hermeneutic search for, and transmission of, meaning, and a curious foregrounding of the material qualities of language (or a choice not to translate underpinned by the same values). The reason for this indeterminacy lies in the historical moment. We can detect as much from an article about the subtitling of *Morocco* that Tamura published ten days before the film's public release: "This time, there was the fear that with too few subtitles, the meaning would not come through. At least, I thought that it was necessary to use the same number of titles as silent movies. Spanish and Portuguese subtitles used far too many subtitles, more than four hundred subtitles for one film. However, because Japanese audiences are sensitive to the feelings of films, I believed it was unnecessary to attach more than thirty subtitles per reel."[31] This is an approach to translation that relies on a conception of cinema grounded in the silent era.[32] In the jail scene in *The Champ*, the subtitles initially correspond to the narrative mode of the talkie as it set up the premise for the confrontation between father and son; then it shifted back to silent cinema for the melodramatic finish.

Although this seems to be a likely explanation, we must return to the silent era to adequately understand the specificities of this national cinema context and its historical moment. One might say that the *benshi* was the first form of dubbing in the prehistory of the talkie. As we discovered in chapter 3, reformers of the Pure Film movement sought to modernize Japanese cinema by renovating the role of the *benshi* and revising the standard use of intertitles. The *benshi*, they felt, should avoid flowery elocution for everyday speech, and stick closely to the filmmaker's plotting instead of their independent elaborations of the narrative. In other words, they hoped the *benshi* would become invisible, much like the corrupt subtitles of later decades. In the end, the *benshi* proved more powerful and popular, setting the stage for the unusual subtitles of the talkie era in Japan. We can attribute the two styles of pre-subtitle *benshi* translation—paraphrase versus line-by-line—to these very discursive tensions designed by the Pure Film movement. The same reformers called for the elimination of intertitles, because film was essentially a visual medium. This could also help explain why so few subtitles were used in 1930s Japan as compared to today. These are probably precedents contributing to an overdetermination of forces bearing down on Japan's first subtitles.

And one of these factors could be the relationship to the other. Before the standardization of subtitling and dubbing, when a variety of

experimental methods were being tested and audiences complained about
not being able to follow the films' plots, some commentators in Japan
argued that that was just fine. Producer Mori Iwao suggested that, unlike
language, human feelings can be communicated—such as sadness or
anger—and as long as feelings were legible one did not necessarily need
to understand every word. Likewise, the Nobel-winning novelist Kawa-
bata Yasunari is said to have argued that it was not necessary to understand the language and dialogue of a film; it was enough to understand
atmosphere, that not understanding meaning was precisely what was
good about the foreign talkie.[33]

By the end of the decade, the shift to the postwar emphasis on narrative meaning becomes detectable. *Ken'etsu daihon* begin tagging every
utterance for translation, sending subtitle counts to numbers we recognize today. In 1938, Twentieth Century–Fox's *Wings of the Morning* features a climactic horse race not unlike the one in *The Champ*. However,
this time the translator did his best to faithfully subtitle the announcer's
brisk call of the race, which, of course, amounted to little more than the
order of the horses.

In a 1939 article titled "The Impoverished Japanese of Spoken Titles,"
Ota Tatsuo criticizes contemporary subtitles and calls on translators to
work toward a new Japanese language for film translation. He uses tropes
for translation strategies that have circulated throughout the history of
translation theory:

> Understanding [a film] means not intellectually, but perfectly matching
> the feelings, as if one with the same atmosphere, and soaking through to
> the inside of the hearts of the Japanese masses. Thus we must stop the
> spoken titles that are messengers brought from a foreign language; spoken
> titles should be messengers from a meeting with Japanese language.
> In other words, they are not translations of foreign language, but they
> must create in Japanese the things that are trying to be expressed in the
> foreign language.[34]

To this end, Ota calls for the end of direct translation of foreign words
and the creation of a new Japanese language specifically for film translation. Subtitlers must stop relying on the advice of experts hired from
university literature departments and write subtitles that speak directly
to the soul of the masses. To this end, subtitlers must recognize the limits
of *kanji* and restrict their usage of characters to a level attuned to the
masses, which he determines is somewhere at or below the elementary

school graduate's level. Subtitlers must strive to be like the *benshi,* which is to say become one with the fabric of the film so they may speak directly to their audience in the deepest sense (again a conception of the *benshi* consistent with the reformers of the Pure Film movement). Above all, their subtitles should not be direct translations of foreign words, but strive for a perfect match with the Japanese soul.

This last assertion is crucial because it expresses the shift, and its historical moment, most clearly. Ota is calling for a subtitling practice that completely dominates the foreign. As with the Romans poets' relationship to Greek literature and early Christian translators' relationship to the Hebrew and Greek Bibles, he hopes to enrich his own language in the process of appropriation. Saint Jerome stated the premise of this kind of translation most directly: "The translator did not attend to the drowsy letter..., but by right of victory carried the sense captive into his own language."[35] The issue of translation cuts straight through to the relationship of self and other. Ota's essay, written at a time when Japan was penetrating deep into China and contemplating a colonization of Asia, reveals a totalitarian wish for a subtitle that erases difference and incorporates foreign meaning into a perfected, harmonized mass readership. It is a theory of translation tailored to Japan's geopolitical aspirations. Ota's vision of a meaning-oriented translation would evolve into the codes of corruption in the postwar period, a style of translation that effaces its violent, mediating presence by hiding in the margins of the frame and discreetly translating every utterance on the sound track.

Although Ota calls for a new writing and a new language, he still defends most of the prewar conventions, such as the number and placement of titles. However, an example from the other side of the globe may teach us that conventions themselves can be changed most easily at particular moments in history when the rules governing practices are in flux. Jean Eustache's *The Mother and the Whore* (*La Maman et la putain,* 1973) is a central post-1968 film made in the wake of the French New Wave. This film movement was centered on breaking cinematic conventions and indulging in those things only cinema is capable of—it was essentially abusive filmmaking. This liberated Eustache's translator to deal with the problem of the subtitle's violence with the kind of experimentation that works only at that kind of moment in film history. Throughout

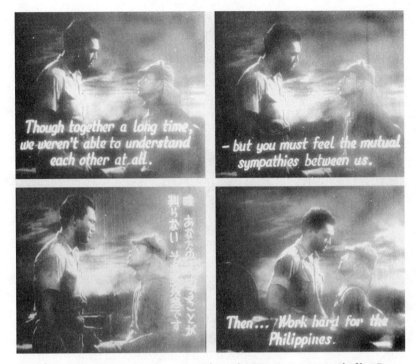

Figure 23. In this dreamy sayonara scene from the Japanese propaganda film *Dawn of Freedom* (*Ano hata o ute*, 1942), a Japanese soldier bids good-bye to his Filipino friend before departing for Corregidor. The Filipino responds, "Tadashi, I have no idea what you are saying. It's such a pity." The bilingual titles indicate a bifurcated audience, but the content reveals a colonial incorporation fantasy. The conception underlying this approach to subtitling belies a totalitarian wish for a subtitle that erases difference and incorporates foreign meaning into a perfected, harmonized mass readership. It is a theory of translation tailored to Japan's geopolitical aspirations—and later to the desires of distributors striving for the largest market possible.

this clever film, the transparency of the subtitles would be interrupted with the bracketed note: *[Untranslatable French Pun]*. This provides a cogent example of the flexibility of subtitling that is engaged in the cinematic practice of its time. The very conception of this subtitle was possible only because the French New Wave filmmakers were systematically attacking every convention of cinema. The freedom to experiment with textual knots of impossibility, however, can make the untranslatable French pun translatable. We must not reject impossibility, but embrace it. Moments of untranslatability—a nearly constant condition

for the subtitler—are times for *celebration,* for not only are they privileged encounters with the foreign, but they are also opportunities for
translators to ply the highest skills of their craft. They are moments crying for abuse.

The Abusive Turn

There is a potential and emerging subtitling practice that accounts for
the unavoidable limits in time and space of the subtitle, a practice that
does not feign completeness, that does not hide its presence through
restrictive rules. We must reconsider our own historical moment and
work toward a subtitling that engages today's sensibilities with a violence
that is not corrupt, but abusive.

The notion of an abusive translation was originally proposed by
Philip E. Lewis in "The Measure of Translation Effects," an essay he wrote
in French and translated into English himself.[36] To analyze another
critic's translation of Derrida's essay "La mythologie blanche," Lewis
delineates the differences between the French and English languages,
arguing that "translation, when it occurs, has to move whatever meanings it captures from the original into a framework that tends to impose
a different set of discursive relations and a different construction of reality."[37] The dissimilarity between languages creates differences that
simply cannot be overcome, inevitably compromising the activity of
translation. This is further compounded by the tendency for translation
of essayistic texts to concentrate on meaning to the exclusion of texture
and materiality. As both writer and translator of this essay, Lewis dis-
covers a freedom to diverge from the original text unavailable to the typical translator. It is from this position that he proposes a new approach,
"that of the strong, forceful translation that values experimentation,
tampers with usage, seeks to match the polyvalencies or plurivocities or
expressive stresses of the original by producing its own."[38] This is to locate the strength of a translation in its abuses. Where an original text
strains language through textual knots dense with signification, the
translation performs analogous violence against the target language.
Corrupt subtitlers disavow the violence of the subtitle while abusive
translators revel in it.

Put more concretely, the abusive subtitler uses textual and graphic
abuse—that is, experimentation with language and its grammatical,

's going on guys?

Qu'est-ce qui se passe?

Figure 24. *Man on Fire* (2004), set in Mexico City, has subtitles that float in cinematic space. Tony Scott uses a wonderfully abusive translation that tampers with mise-en-scène, typography, movement, and even focus. Here a passerby (left) walks in the foreground, gradually obscuring both the speaker *and his subtitle*. In stark contrast, the DVD's corrupt French subtitle is artlessly attached to the image surface.

morphological, and visual qualities—to bring the fact of translation from its position of obscurity, to critique the imperial politics that ground corrupt practices while ultimately leading the viewer to the foreign original being reproduced in the darkness of the theater. This original is not an origin threatened by contamination, but a locus of the individual and the international that can potentially turn the film into an *experience of translation.*

To sketch out the character of abusive subtitling and establish some sense for how it fits into the context of its own history, I propose to divide sound-film history into three epochs of translation, the last of which is only just emerging. The history of translation discourse is full of tripartite formulas to describe different modes of translation, from Dryden to Novalis and Goethe to Jacobsen. The epochs I suggest may be seen as historical phases through which cinema has passed, but they also surpass this synchronic structure and appear simultaneously. The potential for this simultaneity will be particularly important for an understanding of abusive subtitling. Roughly sketched, the three epochs of translation may be described in the following manner.

The first kind of translation occurs in the talkie era. It uses a straightforward prose to introduce the pleasures of foreign texts. The language of the subtitles themselves exhibits a functionality clearly designed to communicate the power of the foreign original as efficiently as possible.

In this respect, the first era of subtitles brings the foreign text to the spectators on their own domestic terms. At the same time, the translator remains fully cognizant of the material dimensions of language—both its graphic and its aural qualities. It may be that this is a conception of cinematic translation anchored firmly to that transition into amplified aurality. However, although there can be no question of its historical specificity in this instance, we still must resist restricting a given mode of translation *as a possibility* in any period of cinema.

In the second epoch of cinematic translation, the translator pretends to move toward the foreign, dwell there, and bring its wonders to the waiting crowds. This era is replete with rules designed to guarantee a translation's quality, but what this regulation actually accomplishes is an appropriation of the source text and its thorough domestication. The rules also enforce a territorialization and professionalization of translation, producing stars and experts and excluding all alternatives. This mode of translation, which I have contemptuously called corrupt, conforms the foreign to the framework of the target language and its cultural codes. All that cannot be explained within the severe limits of the regulation subtitle gets excised or reduced to domestic meanings that are often irrelevant or inappropriate. These subtitlers claim to bring their readers/spectators to a pleasurable experience of the foreign, but in fact their impoverished translations keep audiences ignorant of the conspiracy and the riches that remain hidden from the cinematic experience.

The final part of this triptych brings us to the abusive. For this epoch of translation, I wish to borrow a phrase from Goethe, both for the power of its image and to specify what abusive subtitling is not. In the third stage of Goethe's own periodization of translation, "the goal of the translation is to achieve perfect identity with the original, so that the one does not exist instead of the other but in the other's place."[39] Here the translator identifies strongly with the source text and the culture in which it was produced, so much so that he cedes the particular powers of his own culture to accomplish a translation that invites the reader-spectator to a novel and rich experience of the foreign. Of course, Goethe's conception of translation is deeply tied to Romantic notions that seek to define the self through its various others—another form of domestication. However, abusive subtitling avoids this kind of erasure of difference, seeking to intensify the interaction between the reader and the foreign. This translation does not present a foreign divested of otherness, but strives to translate from and within the place of the other by an inventive approach to language use and a willingness to bend the rules, both linguistic and cinematic.

As we have seen, the key differences between the translation of printed texts and the subtitling of moving-image media are that the cinema adds the human voice to the equation and is propped up by an apparatus that *requires* a violent translation which in turn exhibits many of the traits Philip Lewis calls abusive. Even the subtitles for the most nondescript, realist film tamper with language usage and freely ignore or change much of the source text; however, corrupt subtitlers suppress the fact of this violence necessitated by the apparatus, while the abusive translator enjoys foregrounding it, heightening its impact, and testing its limits and possibilities. To the extent that Lewis's abusive translation demonstrates a new articulation of fidelity in its will to play with convention, his model is attractive to the subtitler of the emergent third epoch. This theorization will prove particularly attractive in an age where the experience of the foreign is valued, and where abuse helps inject a palpable sense of the foreign.

In the Derridean approach to translation theorized by Lewis, abuse is directed at both language and its metaphysical assumptions. Although this is a component of the abusive subtitle, the objects and ends of abuse do not amount to a mere resurrection of 1970s film theory and its valorization of experimentation in combating the evils of Hollywood realism with a deconstructive or Brechtian avant-garde.[40] The problems with such a position have since been argued on many fronts: its Eurocentrism, its elitism, and its inability to account for popular reading modes. Still, we may consider the critiques of poststructuralist film theory the segue between the second and third epochs of subtitling.

Because we are interested in the domesticating tendencies of the conventional subtitling practices of the second epoch, we may position abusive subtitling as a critique of dominant ideology. However, it does not amount to a simple experimentation designed to block ideological interpellation through distantiation techniques. Faced with the losses inevitable in all translation, the abusive subtitler assumes a respectful stance vis-à-vis the original text, tampering with both language and the subtitling apparatus itself in order to release what Lawrence Venuti has called the "remainder," textual and cinematic effects that exceed the creation of a narrative-focused equivalence and work only in the receiving culture.[41] It is a new notion of fidelity attentive to the various aural and visual qualities of language in motion pictures, this in addition to the linguistic and literary styles of screenwriting.

Let us look at a number of concrete examples that suggest that corrupt subtitling practices are obsolete and the time for abuse is ripe.[42] Donald Richie, who has subtitled some of the most famous Japanese films, is the translator of Kurosawa's *Throne of Blood* (*Kumo no sujo*, 1957) and *Ran* (1985), two of the most abusive translations ever undertaken in the second epoch (with the possible exception of the Situationist René Viénet's appropriations of kung-fu films in post-1968 France or the dubbing of Woody Allen's *What's Up, Tiger Lily?*, 1966).[43] With the coming of talkies, Japanese samurai films found it necessary to codify a version of what pre-Meiji Japanese language should sound like. They ended up with a samurai version of Jacobean English, which has remained a central feature of the genre up to the present. This poses an interesting dilemma for the subtitler, who is well aware of the generic importance of this specialized language—one can hardly imagine a period film without it (indeed, to replace it with "standard Japanese" would probably be perceived as daringly experimental). However, there is no way to bring this important element of the genre to a foreign spectator without breaking the laws of corruption, which is exactly what Richie attempted. Of his *Ran* subtitles he writes: "Carried away by all the pageantry I relaxed my guard and thought to intrude a bit of period color of my own ... I left out the occasional prepositions in a way common to formal court English. Something like 'I want you to go,' I foolishly rendered as 'I would with you go.' Not incorrect but, in dialogue titles, completely inappropriate."[44] Obviously regretting his experiment, Richie finally exemplifies the sensibility of corruption when he calls for a "scrupulously anonymous kind of English." He continues: "I feel that the translation should be invisible ... Any oddity, any term too heightened, as well as any mistake, calls attention to this written dialogue. I won't even use exclamation points. The language should enter the ear as the image enters the eye."[45] I couldn't disagree more. Actually, these subtitles were quite wonderful for the way they released certain effects into English that correspond to the generically tortured Japanese of the film itself, but both films were ultimately released in prints with extremely anonymous translations. Richie self-censors his smart impulse to abuse the text.[46]

Rob Young confronted similar issues with Yamamoto Masashi's *Tenamonya Connection* (*Tenamonya konekushon,* 1991), which celebrates Osaka's culture and dialect. This film is subtitled *Fools Cross Borders (Aho wa kyokai o koeru),* and in the course of its ninety-odd minutes it crisscrosses between Tokyo, Hong Kong, and Osaka, blurring the boundaries between Hong Kong/Tokyo, fiction/documentary, Hong Kong comedy/ Japanese comedy, male/female, and even inside movie/outside theater. Young takes this rowdy playfulness as license to experiment ever so slightly. He manipulates his English in a manner analogous to Richie, filling his text with excessive contractions, slang, and nonstandard dialects of English where the scenario deploys an analogous fast-and-loose approach to speech, or where it celebrates linguistic markers of class and regional difference. Another tactic he uses comes far closer to the spirit of abusiveness. Obscene expressions like *konchikusho!* and *konoyaro!* are translated *!%&-$#!@!!*

We can learn several things from Young's example. First, this is not the kind of censorship we expect of corrupt subtitles, which often leave "foul" language untranslated. Granted, it would have been far more abusive to actually use obscenities in English, but to do so would risk damaging the film's chances at international distribution. As we have seen, the censors lurk at every stage of film production and distribution. So Young runs the gauntlet of censors by experimenting with language in ways that are analogous to the linguistic playfulness of the original scenario and its verbalization. Second, faced with the seemingly untranslatable, the abusive subtitler may seek to produce polyvalencies and knots of signification that may not coincide precisely with the problem in the source text. Not all of Young's subtitles using nonstandard grammar have a one-to-one correspondence with similar utterances on the sound track. Nevertheless, his approach cues the spectator to the elaborate playfulness of the dialogue that would have been completely erased by corrupt titles. Third, despite his instinctual abusiveness, Young, like Richie before him, also restricts himself to the time/space/graphic limits of the standard subtitle. Attuned to his historical moment in the third epoch, Young hints at the possibilities; but a truly abusive subtitling would have been as wild as the original film. It would have brought the spectator exceedingly close to the film. This would appear radical from the perspective of the second era, but surely anyone who lives in the emerging third era can feel the problems with convention.

There are more daring and thrilling examples of the emerging abusive subtitle elsewhere, places where capital does not enforce the rules and regulations of corruption. In the spring of 1993, Professor Laurel Rodd of the University of Colorado assigned her Japanese translation class the task of translating subtitles for the opening of Itami Juzo's *A Taxing Woman Returns* (*Marusa no onna 2*, 1987). This short sequence includes strings of *kango* (Chinese words) and snatches of classical Japanese. The students quickly learned to appreciate the difficulties facing the translator of films, but their intuitive solutions to confronting the practical issues had little to do with the corrupt rules of the second epoch's subtitlers. They regretted their "inability" to experiment by putting subtitles in different colors and in different parts of the frame. In fact, their exercise was hypothetical and nothing was preventing them from indulging in the most outrageous innovation (the new technologies of video that link the apparatus with computers can easily manipulate the material aspects of the subtitle through colors, fonts, sizes, and animation). The tools are in place, but the professionals, like Rodd's students, check themselves, held back as they are by the inertia of convention and the ideology of corruption.

Actually, this has not restrained one group of translators from whom we may learn much. In fact, this book was inspired by their work. In the past few years, a massive fandom has developed around Japanese animation (anime) throughout the world. A substantial portion of the fan activity concentrates on translation. Scripts are posted on Internet newsgroups and circulated among clubs and individuals. Fan hackers write software for the Amiga and other computer platforms, software that enables them to take the subtitling apparatus into their own hands. Groups collaborate on not-for-profit subtitled versions of their favorite anime. Working outside of the mainstream translation industry, lacking any formal training, these fans have produced abusive subtitles *quite by instinct*. In scenes with overlapping dialogue, they use different-colored subtitles. Confronted with untranslatable words, they introduce the foreign word into the English language with a definition that sometimes fills the screen. Footnotes! Some tapes include small-type definitions and cultural explanations that are illegible on the fly (here we find a com-

Figure 25. The Japanese television game show *Namare-tei* (*Accent Station*, 2005) makes creative and hilarious use of Japan's linguistic diversity, as well as all the abusive potential of televisual text. Nearly every utterance is colorfully subtitled, and many of the titles are animated. The host (upper left) uses "standard" (Tokyo) Japanese to introduce singer Megumi, who is billed as the "representative from Okuyama Prefecture." Megumi (upper right) is then challenged to take a phrase in Okuyama dialect and translate it into standard Japanese. The phrase and its translation are rendered in subtitles at the bottom of the frame. As Megumi translates off the cuff, a new subtitle wipes across the frame with a running transliteration. Every time she slips and includes a term or phoneme from Okuyama dialect, a buzzer sounds, the characters grow in size, and she is penalized (six times so far). The other Tokyo-born hosts try to correct her (lower left; note the long lines connoting an offscreen voice for the left-hand subtitle). Unable to produce the standard pronunciation, she growls in Okuyama dialect, "Oh, whatever! It doesn't matter!" (lower right).

pletely new viewing protocol made possible by video, where the viewer halts the apparatus's mindless march and reads subtitles at leisure). They use different fonts, sizes, and colors to correspond to material aspects of language, from voice to dialect to written text within the frame. And they freely insert their "sub"-titles all over the screen. It is as if history folds back on itself and we find a resurgence of the subtitling practice of the talkie era, but the underlying differences put the two worlds apart.

People confronting the idea of abusive subtitles often concentrate on the spectacular example of anime fandom to the exclusion of all other possibilities. Abusiveness is not only or exclusively graphic. More than

likely, the translator will direct her abusiveness to other aspects of subtitling, from its set of standard conventions to language itself. Perhaps
the first rule to go should be the logarithmic straitjacket of the space-
time equation. Why should all audiences be subjected to the reading ability of a Shinbashi Geisha or elementary school student? Surely Godard's
La Chinoise (1967) demands a semiotic density an order or two above
Harry Potter and the Sorcerer's Stone (2001). That monolingual closed-
caption subtitles for the hard of hearing can transcribe the most intense barrage of words in televisual flow suggests the unreasonableness
of this most basic rule of corrupt subtitling.

By way of contrast, there are times when refusing to translate is more
abusive. Robert Bresson may be one of the earliest examples of this,
excluding the practices we have uncovered in the talkies era. Where
most subtitlers would have used a thousand titles for one of his films,
the French director wanted only seven hundred or so.[47] Another fascinating example is Robert Gardner's *Forest of Bliss* (1986), the first ethnographic film to purposefully exclude subtitles. In its particular reception
context, where the ethnographic documentary renders other cultures
transparent to a scientific gaze, the filmmaker's decision not to translate
was quite radical and brought spectators into a new kind of relation with
the film's subjects. Similarly, Hopi filmmaker Victor Masayesva protects
sacred knowledge recorded in his *Siskyavi: A Place of Chasms* (1991) by
dropping the subtitles, preventing eavesdropping and appropriation by
outsiders. As Laura Marks points out, he "defies the viewer's conventional expectation that the image is a window onto a culture."[48]

There are other ways translators can creatively refigure the window
metaphor. In my abusive translation of Sato Makoto's *Memories of Agano*
(*Aga ni ikiru*, 2004), I adopted a strategy of the fragment. Sato's film
was a sequel to a documentary he made on old people suffering from
Niigata Minamata Disease (mercury poisoning). Because of the political
imperative—protesting this horrifying case of industrial malfeasance
and the government's inept and heartless handling of the matter—Sato
opted to include intralingual subtitles in Japanese because the people of
rural Niigata speak a dialect difficult for outsiders to understand. Without
Japanese subtitles, most Japanese spectators are completely lost. However, for his more experimental sequel the director wanted spectators to
appreciate other aspects of these people's humanity. Long shots of

fields, of light playing on old walls, and people singing songs direct the viewers to the setting in which they live and die. Most important, Sato wanted spectators to pay less attention to *what* people said than *how* they said it. Therefore, for the sequel he did not include Japanese subtitles. Spectators' understanding varied depending on where they came from, but the vast majority are forced to guess what people are saying from the context and the few words they are able to pick out.

How is one to translate a film that *domestic* viewers cannot completely comprehend? Standard subtitles would make every utterance—and the people themselves—appear transparent in their self-evident meaning. It would transform the documentary into an entirely new film, a thoroughly legible translation with little resemblance to the obscure original. I solved this problem by translating people's lines in fragments (Figure 26). Where utterances were highly legible, the subtitles were no different than in any other film; however, when it was difficult to understand what people were saying, my subtitles attempted to replicate the experience of an urban Japanese spectator by using sentence fragments, single words, and even my own asides in brackets. By including a translator's preface describing the problem, as one might do with a book, I prepared spectators to expect something strange and to read the subtitles with an open mind. The director said, only half-jokingly, that he thinks the abusive translation of *Memories of Agano* is better than the original.

Audiences of the third epoch find these examples of abusive subtitles fascinating and deeply pleasurable. The example of anime fandom especially reveals the distance between the often-elitist valorizations of anti-Hollywood experimentation and the abusive subtitle. Both may be canny on ideological problems, both may innovatively break convention, but the latter attempts to engage readers' sensibilities with the same sensibilities with which the readers engage their texts. Just as the spectator approaches films from faraway places to enjoy an experience of the foreign, the abusive translator attempts to locate his or her subtitles in the place of the other. Rather than smothering the film under the regulations of the corrupt subtitle, rather than smoothing the rough edges of foreignness, rather than convening everything into easily consumable meaning, the abusive subtitles always direct spectators back to the original text. Abusive subtitles circulate between the foreign and the familiar, the known and the unknown. Were we speaking of the translation

Figure 26. *Memories of Agano* (2004). This lengthy utterance in dialect had only two bits of information legible to urban Tokyo audiences. The spotting for this subtitle contained two long sections of unintelligible "jibberish," so this abusive subtitle uses long strings of ellipses to force the reader to scan the line with a rhythm analogous to a Tokyo person's understanding of the speech.

of printed texts, the third epoch would most likely be filled with inter-linear books (among other, more stylistically innovative tactics). And is this not a characteristic of the foreign film's structure? The subtitled mov-ing image is a constellated figure; both the original and the translation are simultaneously available, as if they were *en face*. Most important, viewers work off the original text whether they understand its language or not. Although corrupt subtitles work strongly against this reading practice, abusive subtitles encourage it.

The time is ripe for abuse, if only because we are in an age where moving-image literacy includes the ability to manage complex text/image relations (consider Figures 5, 24, 25). Audiences bring those talents to the foreign film, but they go entirely unused. Indeed, what once was radical experimentation is now the stuff of Hollywood cinema, MTV and pop-up video, commercials, sitcoms, and the nightly news. Complex image/text relationships are a normalized textuality from everyday experience (exceedingly so in Japan). From this perspective, corrupt subtitling is actually archaic. Thus, "abuse" is directed at convention, even at spectators and their expectations. And when abusive subtitling becomes normalized, we will think of other terms—or simply drop the adjective. It is likely that abusive translations will begin with animation, comedies, the art film, and the documentary—texts that are themselves transgressive or essayistic—but there is nothing holding us back from subjecting the most nonviolent films to abuse. The only other choice is corruption.

CHAPTER SIX

Loving Dubbing

The Translator as Ventriloquist

If we were living in the twelfth century... the practitioners of
dubbing would be burnt in the marketplace for heresy. Dubbing is
equivalent to a belief in the duality of the soul.

—Jean Renoir[1]

When it comes to dubbing, most of us are like the angry couple in Jean-
Luc Godard's *Weekend* (1967) speeding along on their road trip to Joinville—a carefully chosen destination, as the home of Paramount's dubbing studios since the talkie era. The closer they drive toward what is
nicknamed "Babel-sur-Seine," the conduit through which Hollywood
invaded Europe, the deeper they descend into barbarism and cannibal-
ism.[2] *Weekend* came to America subtitled, and its opening scene hints at
one of the potential virtues of that barbarous form of translation called
dubbing. The female lead sits on a table in a sexy nightgown, discoursing
on past sexual encounters. Much to the audience's dismay, background
noises, sound effects, and strange music swell in and out, forcing spectators to struggle to focus on her erotic storytelling. Godard is making a
point about aural voyeurism, but the subtitles, ironically enough, render
her language crystal clear. Much as I hate to admit it, I secretly long for
dubbing every time I see this film, and wonder if Godard would forgive
me—perhaps even sympathize with me.

The starting point for this chapter was a talk I gave at the turn of the
millennium at Tokyo's Meijigakuin University. I presented the idea of
abusive film translation, arguing for the natural superiority of subtitling.

Figure 27. *Dead of Night* (1945). With its affinities to ventriloquism, dubbing has been called "the Schizophrenic Stunt of Disembodied Performances... grafted voices hemstitched onto other actors' faces."

During the question-and-answer period, film scholar Yomota Inuhiko taunted me by insisting that he preferred dubbing over subbing. Against all common sense, Yomota insisted that dubbing was better, at least for some films, and so I took this as a challenge. This is my attempt to come to love what I call the ventriloquist's art: dubbing. And, being highly cognizant of the fact that most of the movies on ventriloquism feature terrifying, insane dummies, I'll attempt to keep things civilized.

This chapter attempts to push the translator to the foreground while simultaneously reconsidering my gut-level hatred of dubbing. It is easy to find confirmation of these strong feelings. For example, this is the method of choice for films aimed at children, corroborating my sneaking suspicion that dubbing infantilizes us, and thus is dangerous, to be avoided. However, at the same time we may find it difficult to ignore that fact that many major national cinema contexts clearly prefer dubbing, including Germany, Italy, and Hong Kong, all countries where even the domestic films are dubbed.

Clearly, a more subtle consideration of this form of translation is in order, starting with its history. As I argued in previous chapters, the relatively quick resolution of translation problems into two modes, sub/dub, has led historians to treat them as a foregone conclusion and the end of the story. The acceptance of subtitling and dubbing as the natural end of the talkie era's babel has left the issue of translation largely untouched, except for the work of a relatively small, international band of technicians, linguists, and translators producing taxonomies and how-to texts. In the following pages, I will examine the complicated history of dubbing to raise several of the basic issues it provokes, as well as to denaturalize it so that it appears conventionalized—a received form and not something inevitable or impervious to intervention. Then, by analyzing precisely how dubbing works, perhaps we can come to not just accept it, but love it.

Dubbing became one of two winning strategies after several years of confused soul-searching wherever humans were making movies. We can best view the talkie era (roughly 1926 to 1936) as a period of linguistic experimentation in terms of writing, narration, and translation, a decade in which all the studios in all the territories of the world sorted themselves out. In the end, many of the larger countries opted for dubbing, while smaller ones often chose subtitling as the standard. This has typically been attributed to economies of scale, because dubbing is significantly more expensive. The cost of dubbing varies greatly from country to country. What costs five thousand dollars in Hungary can require fifty-five thousand dollars in Italy, and American dubs employing popular stars undoubtedly cost millions.[3] Thus, dubbing would seem to be an option only for national cinemas with a significant market and, by extension, substantial box-office returns. Another factor would seem to be the relationship to the foreign, with certain forms of nationalism preferring the cultural and linguistic insularity capable in dubbing. And somewhere in this mix, aesthetics and fickle predilection sneak in.

Thus, in the short period between the invention of practical sound technologies and their widespread accommodation and the forces of capitalism, aesthetics, nationalism, technology, and the relationship to the other determined which way to go as every film industry on Earth strove for standardization. Moreover, the chaos did have structure—an interface between gradations of economic rationalization and nationalism where the spectrum of degrees of foreignness neatly corresponds to cost.[4] In this manner, the world cinemas shook out in favor of dubbing or subtitling between 1929 and 1936.

The choice one way or the other appears fateful. It created an inertia difficult to stop or deflect. Back when Americans took over the film industry during the occupation of Germany, the American consul general reported that Germans *wanted* more films dubbed in German. This implies that they were used to the convention by this point.[5] It has been assumed that the continuation of dubbing into the postwar era had to do with Hollywood conspiring with the American government to ensure that German filmmakers could not resurrect the glories of the Weimar cinema. Enforcing a policy of dubbing would level the playing field for Hollywood, making the distinctions between American and German films a matter of scale and quality of production and not linguistic difference. However, were this the case, it would not explain why the occupation in Japan chose subtitles. Furthermore, the archives reveal that the U.S. government was hardly in the palm of the Motion Picture Association of America (MPAA) (or the Motion Picture Producers and Distributors Association [MPPDA] up to 1946). The American administrators of the occupation were concerned about cultural imperialism and a weakened bourgeoisie with little control over cultural industries, so they actually intervened in some bald attempts by Darryl Zanuck and Paramount to buy up huge numbers of German theaters.[6]

These examples illustrate how, at their most basic level, preference for either subtitling or dubbing is none other than a naturalized convention. Audience research has shown that people tend to prefer whatever form of translation they grew up with.[7] If the preference for dubbing, where it exists, is nothing but conventionalized predilection, lovers of subtitling would probably reach the conclusion that efforts must simply be made to overcome the inertia of historical disposition. Where spectators cannot be convinced to switch, all we need to do is attack and destroy all dubbing operations.

However, it must always be recognized that both subbing and dubbing are far more complex than they appear at first glance. As I have demonstrated, subtitling has actually been conducted in a domesticating mode for most of its history. Here I want to emphasize the less obvious merits of dubbing in the same way. That dubbing has a deep relationship to nationalism and fascism at its formative moment is significant, as it seems to confirm our worst, even paranoiac, suspicions that it is essentially deracinating, deodorizing, imperial. Since MLVs fell by the wayside, dubbing remains our extreme case and that is why we despise it. But I am committed to Yomota's challenge to love dubbing, so I will plow on and search for its hidden treasures.

A Proliferation of Form

In the strictest sense, dubbing refers to a surprisingly wide variety of forms. Probably because of its considerable expense and the fundamental malleability of the sound track, dubbing practices have proliferated since their invention. In addition to a greater heterogeneity of styles, there is a heterogeneity of quality as well. How much time will they put into each stage of the production process? Can the best translators, directors, actors, technicians, studios, and laboratories be secured? How many weeks (or days!) will the translator have to work? Is the translation double-checked by bilinguals? Will the actors have a chance to view the original film? How many takes may the director demand before making do with the performances at hand? All the decisions on all these criteria produce different qualities and styles of dubbing. In comparison, subtitling has remained relatively homogeneous throughout its history, probably because of its relative simplicity and minimal cost.

The method most spectators immediately think of is generally referred to in the translating business as "voice replacement." As the most common and demanding form of dubbing, I want to concentrate on this; however, it is worth considering the other approaches as well. For many people, this is the only dubbing they know and for the most part it is also the lowest of the low. (Although I will draw from a variety of geographic contexts and genres, many of the following citations come from Japanese animation. Aside from offering continuity across a wide disparity of examples, I find myself continually attracted to anime fan culture for its remarkable sensitivity to translation issues.)

One of the oddest forms of dubbing is *intralingual,* although we may question whether it is fruitful to think of this as translation. Perhaps the best examples of this are the first two films of the Mad Max series, *Mad Max* (1979) and *The Road Warrior* (1981). Both films were redubbed into less-Australian Australian English for their American releases. It was thought that no one in the malls could understand a straight-ahead Australian accent, and thus they received a domesticating dubbing. There are many other curious examples. *Gregory's Girl* (1981) had such strong

Glaswegian accents that Sam Goldwyn Jr. would buy it only on the condition that it was dubbed into more intelligible English, much to the consternation of director Bill Forsyth. One finds intralingual subtitles as well. Ken Loach showed *My Name Is Joe* (1998) without subtitles at Cannes, but his distributor added them. Loach was indignant. Needless to say, intralingual dubbing is unusual, and unusually domesticating.

Far more typical are the standard practices of Hong Kong and parts of Europe. In the strictest sense, all films from Hong Kong are dubbed domestic films. On location, sync sound is relatively uncommon and simultaneous dubbing in Cantonese and Mandarin is built into the postproduction process from a film's very inception, problematizing the notion of a simple bifurcation of "original" and "dub." A side benefit of this is that actors from anywhere in China can be drafted for work. European directors have also taken advantage of their culture of dubbing to draw on an international pool of acting talent. One can shoot a film with actors from a number of countries without worrying about accents or translation, or even without writing a shooting script, for that matter. Thanks to monolingual dubbing, they don't have to be marked as foreigners because a domestic voice is attached to the face. Within the rhetoric of the European Union and the trend toward international coproduction, some directors predicted that intralingual dubbing could prove dangerous. At the beginning of the 1990s, Hans-Jürgen Syderberg said:

> I hope the future of art in Europe is not an international film in English with actors from every country speaking lines they can't understand. That is not a good film and not a good Europe ... My other fear for Europe is that it will become like American films, which use American actors who are then dubbed with German voices. If this becomes the case, we cannot speak of a flourishing economy here, because everyone will simply be employed as a *well-paid puppet* or well-behaved slave in the service of foreign inventions, alien spirits [my emphasis] ... Certainly there should be dialogue between cultures; but not as part of some multicultural ensemble where everyone speaks a different language and where no one understands each other—except the foreign director, who gains personal advantage from this story that is no longer our own.[8]

Another form of dubbing involves *adaptation*. This is an extreme form of domestication, so excessive that the translators have significantly departed from the source text. Sometimes this involves transformation of other, nonlinguistic aspects of the film as well. Adaptive dubbings are more common than one might think, although for ideological reasons they rarely present themselves as such. In the era of radical cinema concentrated around the events of 1968, newsreel collectives in various parts of the world performed dubbings that wore their adaptation with pride. Until recently, one of the few dubbing jobs I could manage to love was that of the Japanese film collective Ogawa Productions, which used a radical theater troupe to turn the French May '68 newsreel *Les Chiminots* (1968) into *Ore wa robotto ka* (Am I a robot?). One can vaguely hear the original sound track beneath the strident screaming of the Japanese actors. Even where the original sound track involves calm interviews, the Japanese is delivered as shrill agitprop. Likewise, Chris Marker's 1960s adaptations of the Cuban documentaries of Santiago Álvarez are famous for analogous departures from the original text in order to serve pressing local needs. The pressures of the domestic political situation overrode any conventional impulse to tailor the dubbing to the original sound track.

Historically, however, adaptive dubbing has more to do with market forces and the opposite end of the ideological spectrum. For example, in the face of French rejection of Americanness of films back in the 1930s, directors names were Frenchified—Robert Wyler became Robert Villers—and the scripts underwent thorough revision to hide their foreign origins. Well-known film people like Yves Mirande, Marcel Pagnol, Sacha Guitry, and Saint-Granier "localized" Paramount's films at Joinville.[9] However, more recent Japanese animation provides the perfect example of an adaptive dubbing performed strictly for the sake of profits, and what makes it a fascinating example is how its target audience rejected the translation on the grounds of domestication.

Although Japanese anime starts back in the teens of the twentieth century, American audiences did not take serious notice until the 1980s broadcast of *Robotech* (1985). For most American fans there is no "anime" before this, only "animation" they could care less about. The rights were originally bought by a company called Harmony Gold, which hired a man named Carl Macek to translate the texts and manage their distribution. His problem was that the U.S. networks had hard-and-fast structures for all programming to fit into. One structure was the flow of the episode slot, which had specific times for commercials and credits and the like. The other was the television season, which demanded a minimum of sixty-five outings for any series. His Japanese show, however, consisted of only thirty-six episodes. The solution for Macek was to take three animated shows—*Super Dimension Fortress Macross* (*Chojiku yosai Macross,* 1982), *Super Dimension Cavalry: Southern Cross* (*Chojiku kidan Southern Cross,* 1984), and *Genesis Climber Mospeada* (*Kiko soseiki Mospeada,* 1984)—and suture them into one series with eighty-five half-hour episodes. This required changing names and imagining new relationships for characters from different diegetic worlds; he also had to write in new plot threads and creative transitions to cover the disparate sources, sometimes using shots that had already appeared in previous episodes. Most important for our consideration was Macek's mode of translation. He would watch the series with the volume off and imagine the narrative transpiring. This imaginative narrative would become the object of translation. The relatively small fandom of the time found this unforgivable, although it was basically a demand and precondition of the televisual distribution in the first place, so Macek became the object of venomous criticism and abuse in anime fandom.[10]

A form of dubbing with affinities to this is *parodic,* the most famous example being Woody Allen's *What's Up, Tiger Lily?* Originally a low-budget Japanese spy thriller, Allen rewrote the script for laughs and dubbed a new sound track. In this case, the parody relied deeply on the cultural enmity of elite American audiences toward dubbing—as well as their association of cheap Japanese films with sloppy translation. The idea is better than the end result.

Anime parodies are far more interesting, mostly because they involve subcultural poaching. Unfortunately, most of the sub-dub parodies are poor pornography, but there are exceptions. The best dubbing parodies come from a group called Sherbert Productions (led by Corellian Jones and Phillip Sral). Anime fan dubbings are at an enormous disadvantage because they have no access to separate sound tracks, forcing them to add their own music and sound effects (mostly campy performances using the human voice). However, Sherbert goes to great length to use real sound effects, either creating them or taking them off CD packages like the one from *Star Trek* (1966–69). It also inserts graphics from other beloved series, for example, *Star Trek* and *Babylon 5* (1994–98). Needless to say, they are very complex texts.

Sherbert's first attempt was the 1989 *Dirty Pair: The Arrest of Mr. Macek.* They take the original story—the prison episode from the OAV (straight to video) where the two heroines struggle against evil forces as usual—and revise it into a fabulous revenge fantasy aimed at none other than

Carl Macek (a popular object of catharsis in these parodies). In the tape, Macek has gone around the country to various conventions and kidnapped fans and brought them to his preview house/prison on the planet Jupiter, forcing them to watch *Robotech* until he gets a favorable review. Carl's old pal, *Robotech*'s Exador (who was locked up after demanding a raise), has had enough, and organizes a preview house riot to break into Macek's Japanese animation vault to acquire some "real" anime, which people have been deprived of for so long. Kei and Yuri are sent out to arrest Macek for "the ruthless butchery of Japanese animation," and they arrive on Jupiter just as the riot is under way. The tape ends in complicated chaos, much like the original, with the Dirty Pair declaring, "We're going to Disneyland!"

Unlike Allen's parody, these dubs are done by people who have an intense relationship to the original. They are not translations in the strictest sense, but the English-language scripts are extremely attuned to the original text while embedding it in a complex network of current events and popular culture. As we have just seen, the fans use the foreign objects of their obsession to critique areas of the domestic intertext—Macek as enemy—all the while inserting their new text into current events in popular culture such as popular Hollywood science fiction, American animation, and the Gulf War.

This may be a minor mode of quasi translation within a diminutive niche of (what was at the time) a negligible subculture within American popular culture, but this is part of its fascination. A deep enjoyment of the parodic dubbing depends on a familiarity with the original text in the first place, a familiarity itself dependent on other forms of translation. Today, this relationship to the original text may be readily accessed through voice replacement dubbings and subtitled tapes on both commercial and fan tapes. However, back in the early days of anime fandom, translation was performed on the fly. Untranslated tapes brought straight from Japan were shown publicly at science-fiction conventions. Only a few audience members could understand the sound track. Even if their Japanese was rudimentary, they would shout out snatches of the dialogue they managed to understand or bark out rough explanations of the action. It was a kind of revival of the talkie era *benshi*'s function, only scattered throughout the auditorium and highly participatory.

We can call this an odd form of *commentary dubbing*. Although the anime version sounds rather enjoyable, the typical example from mainstream media is anything but. Because a precise dubbing or subtitling requires considerable time and expense, many media cultures around the world, particularly televisual ones, deploy commentary dubbing. For example, in Polish television all of its foreign product—American dramas and sitcoms, Mexican *telenovelas,* foreign films, and the like—is dubbed by a single person. As in most parts of the world, this narrator is male, and he simply reads a translation of the script over the original sound track. Except for notable exceptions such as some British and Japanese television, this narrator makes few *benshi*-like attempts to imitate voices or modulate the grain of the voice. Imagine the German *Simpsons* (1989–present) with a single, monotone, male narrator/translation. It allows access to snatches of the original language, either before or after or even behind lines of dialogue, but rather than delectable tastes of the remainder, it can only be seen as a cut-rate translation that reduces the film to barren information.

This brings us to the mode of translation usually associated with "dubbing," what is technically referred to as *voice replacement.* This is when a team of actors, shepherded by a director, translator, and team of technicians, voice a translation linked as closely as possible to the gestures and lip movements of the image track. One voice actor likened the process as *crawling into the body* of the screen actor.[11] Ideally, one actor will be assigned to one character, and careful rehearsal can produce a new text masquerading as an original. The actors attempt to deliver what they feel is a natural performance, although this "naturalness" is highly codified and bound to limits set by both the original actor's performance and the demands of the final marketplace. Interestingly enough, they simultaneously assert the specificity of voice acting and disparage productions that employ stars for their fame as opposed to their dubbing skills (as is common in the United States for high-profile translations).[12] Ohira Toru was the first dubbing star in Japan, and is known for his work as Superman, Darth Vadar, the voice from the tape recorder in *Mission Impossible,* and Telly Savalas. Ohira explains the craft of the voice actor with what he calls his "Ninja Theory":

> Whether I am dubbing Telly Savalas or Gary Cooper, if the audience feels my face, it's over. It's that character that Telly Savalas is playing that is talking. One needs only to be able to feel that. On the other hand, if my face flickers in and out from behind, it's a failure. *I am always hidden, and only when absolutely necessary and as little as possible do I enter in.*

Figure 28. Czech actors Andrea Elsnerová and Filip Jančék performing the boating scene from *Howards End* (1992), where Helen and Leonard passionately kiss. Describing a similar situation for the dubbing of *Last Tango in Paris* (*Último tango a Parigi*, 1972), Klaus Biedeerstaedt writes: "You cannot relate to your partner during a session. We must keep our eyes on the screen at all times; otherwise we would miss a cue and the synchronization will be off. When Brando kisses Maria, I kiss the back of my hand. It's not very exciting, but dubbing is an exact science."

In other words, in the Way of the Samurai *[inyo bushido]* there is the saying, "It is by throwing away the body that one floats the rapids"— sorry this is getting serious, but it's the idea that you float to the degree you drown your body. In other words, when you render yourself nothing *[mu]* and immerse yourself in the performance, the audience goes, "Eh, who's that? Eh? Ohira Toru?" That's the award they give you. That's my policy, although I suppose it's over the top.[13]

Ohira was one of the first voice actors for dubbing in Japan. Because Japanese audiences initially rejected dubbing after hearing *The Man Who Came Back* in Hiroshima dialect, voice acting finds its roots in radio drama with the founding of the NHK Broadcasting Troupe (NHK Hoso Gekidan) in 1943. During the U.S. occupation, both NHK and TBS maintained their own radio drama troupes to perform what they called *koe no shibai*, or "voice drama." This *koe no shibai* quickly migrated to television when NHK and others began broadcasting immediately after the occupation in 1953.

In Japan, dubbing was restricted to television, where it was the translation mode of choice. Some reason that this was because the resolution of the Braun tube simply could not make subtitles legible. Other explanations point to the fact that in the 1950s television sets had yet to penetrate the intimate space of the home, so most people were watching broadcasts in public spaces like restaurants where they sat a considerable distance from the screen.

The first dubbed television show in Japan was *Superman,* which began broadcasting in 1956 with Ohira Toru voicing George Reeves's superhero.[14] Most voice actors, or *seiyu,* came from the theater, and in the early days they hid their lives as ventriloquists for television. However, although they found no prestige in their work, their growing importance to the industry was undeniable as newly forming audiences desired foreign television and made-for-TV anime like *Astroboy* (*Tetsuwan Atomu,* which started broadcasting in 1963). A number of other factors led to the voice actors' emergence from obscurity. First of all, the invention of storage technologies like kinescopes and videotape made live dubbing unnecessary and the quality of performance and synchronization steadily increased. At the same time, because these technologies committed the original performance to permanent media, it allowed networks to rebroadcast shows without having to rehire the actor. Soon the voice actors clamored for residuals. They organized the Nihon Haiyu Rengo (Actors' Union of Japan) in 1971 around this very issue, demanding payment every time a network used their past performances. Their demonstrations paid off in a labor agreement in 1973.

Another factor that affected the prestige of voice actors was the release of *Space Cruiser Yamato* (*Uchu senkan Yamato*) in 1974, a wildly popular anime series on television. Suddenly, fans of TV shows and movies wanted to know more about the voices behind their favorite characters, and began to appreciate the art of dubbing. The most popular of them began organizing events at which they would appear, concerts where they would sing, and appearances to sign their autographs. In 1979, Tomiyama Kei (a voice actor on *Yamato* and *Galaxy Express 999* [*Ginga tetsudo 999*], and the voice of Eddie Murphy) released the first album by a voice actor. Soon many were mounting traveling shows. An event at Tokyo's Budokan featuring the voice actors of *Future Boy Konan* (*Miraishonen Konan*) drew more than twelve thousand fans.

By the late 1980s, the concept of *seiyu* was popular knowledge, the importance of the voice actor's role was widely recognized by general audiences, and viewers also started associating specific voices with specific actors/characters. Shortly after *Sailor Moon* appeared in 1988, two magazines with wide circulation were dedicated to voice acting (their largest group of readers were male fans). Very unusual books—without analogues in the U.S. publishing world—were written, including histories of voice acting and training manuals or how-to books.[15] Companies specializing in managing voice actors appeared, and aside from the theme song CDs, special events, autograph parties, and the like, popular voice actors also started their own Web sites, photo albums, and made their own videotapes. Women in particular became "voice idols."

The voice actors with the most rabid fandoms are inevitably connected to anime; however, many working on live-action films achieve national recognition, a phenomenon wherever dubbing is a standard.[16] Some voice actors are irrevocably attached to certain actors, becoming the voice belonging to a given screen persona. Japanaese examples include Aka Kinya as Jack Lemmon, and Otsuka Chikau as Richard Widmark. Every dubbing country has its voice stars. Of course, the gap between the real and virtual voices of those personae can be great. For example, before Peter Falk became Columbo, any number of voice actors played the actor's voice in Japan. Then NHK bought the rights to the TV show and signed a well-respected stage actor, Koike Masao, who has a very different sound and style. In other words, it went for the prestige of the name and not the voice; this is not a translation attending to the material quality of that show's language, especially considering Falk's idiosyncratic delivery. Koike, however, proved extremely popular with Japanese audiences. People thought he was so perfect that they didn't like Falk's (subtitled) movies because they had to listen to the actor's actual voice.

As this example suggests, the performance of voice actors can achieve the authenticity of an original, a paradoxical state in the world of translation. Shi Banyu is popularly known as the (Mandarin) voice of Stephen Chow in twenty-eight of the Hong Kong star's films, including *Shaolin Soccer* (*Siu lam juk kau*, 2001) and *Kung-fu Hustle* (2004). Shi capitalized on his complete identification with Chow by putting his voice on auction at eBay. The winners of his ten auctions could have Shi/"Chow" phone the person of their choice for a two-minute conversation. He even went so far as to present a "certificate of authenticity" on the auction page. The auctions closed at 14,542 yuan (U.S.$1,795), half of which the voice actor donated to a school for the deaf (but half of which he presumably pocketed).[17]

Most voice actors never achieve such fame, and basically use the work to support acting careers in other forums, stage or screen. Then there is an entire stratum of voice acting that is nonprofessional, summoned into instrumental existence by producers cutting corners. Stanley Kauffmann, the powerful critic for the *New Republic*, spent six months in Rome back in the late 1950s and became serendipitously involved in the Italian dubbing world. He rode the phenomenon known as "dubbing bums," young men who drifted across Europe, going wherever they could find work dubbing.[18] They performed mostly for European films on their way to late-late-night television in the United States. (The dubbing bums eventually organized and called themselves the English-Language Dubbers Association, which was established in 1954 and continued into the 1970s.)[19] Kauffmann saw the people next to his studio, the professional voice actors voicing famous American stars, and he wondered, "It seemed to me an odd fate: to be half a star all your life, without even the billing of a radio performer: to know that when two girls next to you on a bus sighed about Gable, they were talking half about you and would never know it."[20] It must indeed be frustrating, although German voice actor Klaus Biederstaedt tries to think about it from a different perspective; he thought of his career as "borrowing the faces" of Marlon Brando, Marcello Mastroianni, and Yves Montand.[21] But the reality of their position is best evidenced by the fact that voice actors are often denied residuals for their performances.

Voice actors are only the most visible elements of dubbing. Their ability to crawl into another actor's body is only possible through teamwork. As in subtitling, the dubbing process demands close cooperation between actors, translators, and technicians with specialized skill sets and a significant measure of control over their domain. To this add the crucial contributions of directors and sound editors. The process has changed quite a bit over the years, particularly in the epic struggle to achieve sync between voice and lip. One possible reason for the rejection of dubbing by Borges's generation could be that image and sound track were unusually out of sync during the talkies era. In 1930, even the sound technicians were pessimistic. A writer in General Electric's sound-system newsletter observed: "The temporary experiments of fitting foreign words to English lip movements and other make shifts have been tried and hastily abandoned. The foreign language features of the future will be recorded in each tongue."[22]

This prediction was, of course, quite incorrect, and in the next decades various devices were invented to achieve closer sync. In the 1930s, some of these centered on a conductor who was "perched on a pulpit or at a high desk, conducting what is in effect an orchestra of voices."[23] In one system, the dialogue and song lyrics were written on a disk, which could be up to three feet in diameter. Mounted vertically, the conductor cued the actors to speak or sing. A variation projected the spinning disk onto a screen with a fixed-mark cuing delivery—a precursor to the rhythmoband, which I will describe shortly. In yet another early system, the conductor listened to the original sound track and manipulated two "Morse Keys," one for stressed syllables and the other for unstressed. When accenting was decided upon, a "projection record" was made to indicate the values. Sometimes, when four or five characters have to speak, they wore colored glasses of different colors, so that they could only see their own lines.

As strategies for sync developed, so did sound technologies. Initially, the talkies used single tracks, forcing dubbers to junk everything and build a new sound track from scratch. Soon the postproduction process started mixing multiple tracks during editing, eventually resolving them all into three final ones: dialogue, music, and sound effects. This conveniently allowed dubbers to retain the special effects and music, and concentrate on replacing just the voices. Even this track required manipulation to match the quality of the dialogue track to the visual setting. Before the age of easy digital manipulation of sound, the ambient sound backing the voices could be controlled through opening and closing wall panels that reflected sound, the difference between talking in a phone booth or a cathedral.[24]

Television dubbing was always a step or two behind the process for film because of the newness of the technology, the most significant difference being the fact that all broadcasts were live in the first few years. In the Japanese case, all programs arrived on 16mm film, sans sound track. As in the early days of film, the sound track was not split into discrete tracks. Erasing the voices meant dispensing with all the music and sound effects. Because the broadcasts were live, the voice actors had to deliver their performance on the fly. Sometimes they were handed their scripts only minutes before going on air, and because the prints were sent without sound tracks they had no way of listening to the original actors beforehand. The sound effects and music, supplied from whatever records happened to be on hand, were also performed live, as were the commercials. Our dubbing ninja Ohira was the perhaps the first voice actor to garner a fandom, as he would appear in those commercials, Superman outfit and all. American producers finally started using separate tracks in 1958, but they used special 17mm tape decks that were in short supply in Asia, so audiences did not have regular access to the original sound and music until the broadcast of *Sunset 77* in 1960. Even then, the dubbers could not pause these tape recorders, so the actors had to perform the episode start to finish without interruption. If someone made a mistake, he or she had to start from the beginning again. Despite these difficulties, there are apocryphal stories about speechless Japanese spectators thinking, "My, those foreigners speak amazing Japanese!"

Conceptualizations of the translator's task transformed along with the technological change. For one thing, dubbers tend to be attuned to aspects of language and its performance that subtitlers tend to overlook in their quest for rooting out sense. Paulette Rubinstein, Ingmar Bergman's dubber, has said, "You have to have a grasp of language, a grasp of acting and directing, and a sensitivity to what it is the actors and the director were doing. It's not just a matter of calculating word to word."[25] In some countries, this attitude led to a disregard for sync altogether. One American translator working in Europe described what she found in Italy in the early 1970s:

> Italian producers and distributors feel that it is more important to capture the spirit of the word rather than the letter, and they are willing to sacrifice sync for concept. Consequently, most of their product is either out of sync or imperfectly "sunk," but the dubbing performances are generally just as good as, if not better than, the original. Because sync is not paramount, the Italian dubbing director can call upon a wider range of actors who need not be specialists at lip-synchronization but whose voices more closely fit the faces they are portraying. Having worked in the dubbing industry in Rome, I initially found Italian-dubbed films irritating—often voices began well before the on-camera actor had a chance to part his lips—but once I overcame my petty annoyances with the technicalities I truly appreciate the fine quality of the dubbing performances.[26]

This writer feels a sense of liberation from denying the grip that desire for sync had over her praxis. Interestingly enough, an analogous commitment to the "spirit, not the letter" becomes theorized in the 1980s to the paradoxical end of achieving sync. This debate draws on linguistic theory coming out of pragmatics, which puts an emphasis on the context of utterances. In "A Pragmatic Translation Approach to Dubbing," Thomas Herbst writes:

> I would argue that a pragmatic, plot-oriented translation approach would contribute greatly to achieving higher text quality. The idea is quite simply to translate scene by scene rather than sentence by sentence, to identify the plot-carrying elements and to create a dubbed version containing these elements and the general tone of the scene. The freedom gained through such an approach can not only be used to increase the amount of lip- and nucleus-synch, but also—and this is very important—to achieve a dialogue that is consistent in style and much more natural than dialogues based on the sentence-for-sentence approach.[27]

This conception of dubbing has been influential among translators. By placing equivalence in such a broad context, the translator feels a sense of liberation. Suddenly, the seemingly impossible demands of sync seem so much easier to meet. Even cultural explanations can easily be inserted on the sly. Today, dubbing translators tend to align themselves with either the scene-by-scene or the sentence-by-sentence approach.

In either case, the challenge posed by sync pivots around the shape the mouth takes for all the phonemes of language. It was not until the mid-1930s that translators strove to conform translation at this minute a level; when they started, the technique was called "revolutionary."[28] In some contexts, a powerful intermediary figure stands between the translator and the performer, someone who ensures that whatever the translator produces conforms to the lip movements of the original actor, particularly with regard to labials (m's, b's, and p's) and fricatives (f's, v's, w's, and wah's), the sounds that invariably produce dramatic lip movements. This interloper in the translation process may have no knowledge of the source language, and need not be "so much a writer as a cross between a thesaurus and a crossword puzzle expert."[29] Tom Rowe describes the problem succinctly:

> Take, for example, the old standby "I love you," which is bound to creep into the flick at some point. On the silent screen *Je t'aime* looks like *Who's Abe?* Strictly synching, "I lub you" will work on this, only if the actor on the screen opens his mouth after the labial and has a head

cold. *Io ti amo* is graphically "Also I lub you," which makes the passion somewhat parenthetical, and *Ich liebe dich* really synchs only if the beloved is a mensch named Dick.[30]

Ideally, of course, the dubbing translator includes this role in his own toolbox, and when combined with certain technologies the results are a marvelous discovery for those of us that grew up with subtitles and associate dubbing with the non-sync of Shaw Brothers kung-fu flicks. The finest example I have come across is that in French-speaking Canada, which uses a brilliant contraption called the Rhythmoband.[31] Essentially an elaboration of the 1930s disk systems, here is how it works.

In the first step, a specialist sits at a flatbed film editor with the film and original sound track. One of the reels on the flatbed unspools a roll of 35mm white leader, which is interlocked with the original film. This leader runs across a thin black bar called the sync line, which indicates the exact position of the strip in relation to a given frame of the film. At the very frame where a character begins to utter a phrase, this person begins transcribing on the white leader, writing on the sync line. He ends the transcription precisely on the frame where the actor finally closes her mouth and ends her utterance. Thus, the transcription of a fast talker results in cramped, narrow script, while a drawl stretches out along the strip (Figure 29). At the same time, every closed-mouth labial or fricative is marked with a symbol, as are sighs, hmmmm's, breaths, and any other human noise. Even if someone moves his or her lips inaudibly in the background, this mouth movement is added to the transcription (as we will see, the image demands a sound). This is called "detection."

When the detection is complete, the white leader is handed to a translator. While referring to the original film and its postproduction scenario, the white leader becomes the translator's main tool. Because it references mouth shape, he can craft target-language sentences that produce a structure of sync at the level of phoneme. When the source language uses a word containing a labial, the translator endeavors to place a target-language word that similarly features a closed mouth at the very same point. The process allows for such precision. The translator writes this translation directly on the white band, just above or below the transcription of the detector. This is called the "mother band."

A calligrapher then transcribes the mother band onto clear 35mm film (see cover photograph), including only the translation and aspirations so

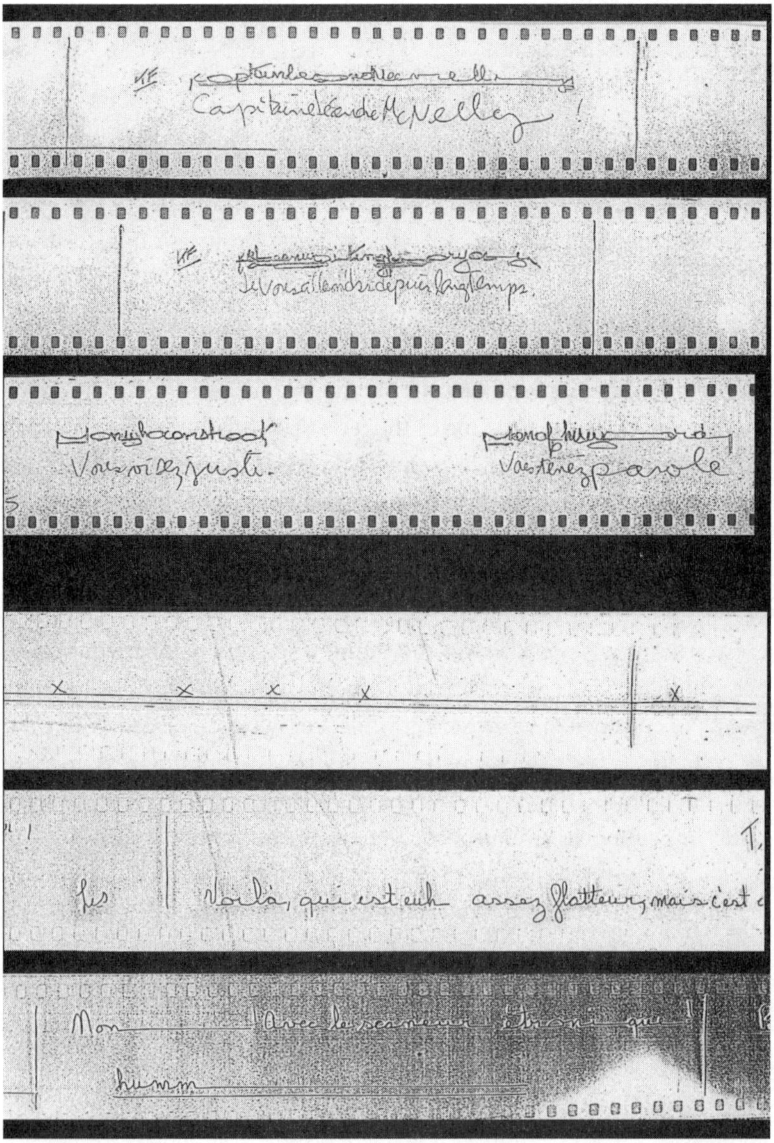

Figure 29. The top three strips are from a mother band, with the "detected" English transcription on top and the French translation written underneath. The vertical lines signify cuts between shots. Offscreen utterances and sounds are underlined. Note how circles of various widths in the English indicate "o" sounds, and the length and speed of utterances is graphically evident from the density and length of the script. The bottom three strips are from the calligrapher's final rhythmoband. The Xs signal the voice actor to grunt.

that actors know when to sigh, hmmm, breathe, or grunt. The graphic expansion and contraction of the handwriting indicates the temporal flow of speech, cuing the actor when to speed up or slow down. In the recording studio, a director—generally an actor and/or translator herself—works with the actors and a sound engineer. The calligraphic band is run on a projector linked to an interlocked video projector, computer, and soundboard. As the scene to be dubbed runs, a second screen displays the calligraphic rhythmoband, and another sync line marks the point at which actors start and finish their lines. The detector has also indicated offscreen speech with an underline, and indistinct on-screen mouth movements (such as in long shots) with a dotted line; these inscriptions help the translator and voice actor know when they are relieved from the obligation to sync. The results are remarkably impressive, virtually rendering sync a nonissue (providing each link in the human chain performs his or her role to perfection).

Actually, sync may soon be a thing of the past as the dizzying speed of technological development overtakes long-entrenched dubbing practices. Computer programmers are busy writing programs that switch the burden of sync from the translator and voice actor to the original actor's image. I cannot resist quoting the following one-sentence description of this process from one of the patents:

A cinematic work having an altered facial display made in accordance with a process that includes substituting a second animated facial display for a first animated display and in which the displays have lip movements corresponding to the languages used and wherein the languages of the two displays are sufficiently different to result in different lip movements for each display, and which process further comprises: generating data in digital form representing the configuration of the second facial display over a plurality of cinematic frames, generating data in digital form representing the configuration of the first facial display over a plurality of cinematic frames of said work, and altering under the control of both sets of said data and a programmed digital computer which provides numerical interpolation of lip distance data, the configuration of said first facial display to produce substantially the configuration of the second facial display.[32]

Translated, the aim is to morph the lips on the image to conform with whatever flapping is invoked by the performance of the dubber's translation. It's vaporware at the time of this writing, but its potential to free translators to concentrate more on traditional translation problems than sync are intriguing, to say the least. However, even in the utopian world of perfect digital sync imagined by these programmers, there will always be dubbers who opt for easier, cheaper routes and produce translations that fill the theaters with chimeras and other perverse monsters. It is to this persistent problem that we will turn next.

The Ventral Art

The pervasive rhetoric of death in Ohira's Way of the Samurai theory of dubbing indicates the centrality of the uncanny in dubbing. I think a key reason we find dubbing despicable is because it turns actors (and, we suspect, spectators as well) into dummies, which is to say that dubbing is like *ventriloquism*.[33] The first person to compare dubbing to ventriloquism was Jesse Zenser, a critic in the 1960s who dubbed dubbing "the Schizophrenic Stunt of Disembodied Performances . . . grafted voices hemstitched onto other actors' faces."[34] However, the dynamic was noticed from the start. In 1932, Jorge Luis Borges famously wrote:

> The possibilities for the art of combination are not infinite, but they are apt to be frightening. The Greeks engendered the chimera, a monster with the head of a lion, the head of a dragon, and the head of a goat; the theologians of the second century, the Trinity in which the Father, the Son and the Holy Ghost are inextricably linked; the Chinese zoologists, the *ti-yiang*, a bright red, supernatural bird equipped with six feet and six wings but with neither face nor eyes . . . Hollywood has just enriched this frivolous, teratological museum: by means of a perverse artifice they call dubbing, they offer monsters that combine the well-known features of Greta Garbo with the voice of Aldonza Lorenzo. How can we fail to proclaim our admiration for this distressing prodigy, for these ingenious audio-visual anomalies?[35]

In the very same year, Claire Rommer commented from the perspective of the actor: "My colleague's voice had wandered away from him— had disappeared into a stranger—from whose mouth it now runs on incessantly—DESPITE his tongue not uttering those words—despite his lips never framing them! A strange Homunculus-like being has been summoned into existence by a conjuring trick."[36]

Interestingly enough, the ventriloquist-like quality of dubbing is even built into the Japanese word for the term, *fukikae*. Originally from kabuki, it refers to when one actor plays two roles, or when a stand-in substitutes for the star. It *also* means the prop used for a corpse, and a secondary meaning has to do with cheating while gambling—the old switcheroo.

Thus, unlike the English term, *fukikae* condenses many of the ideas I am playing with here in an interesting package. However, rather than fake corpse or homunculus, today we are more likely to feel that the experience of dubbing is like watching a bad ventriloquist—granted, one who disturbs the depths of our souls.

So, what do ventriloquist translators do besides striving for sync—matching body movement to voice? For one thing, the humans behind the dummy must suppress their selves, their very being. Douglas Houlden's *Ventriloquism for Beginners* reads like a manual for film translators: "You must remember, however, that your partner will play the lead in your act and usually have the best lines. His *voice and personality should be richer and stronger than yours.* That internationally famous ventriloquist, Edgar Bergen, is not so well known as his partner, Charlie McCarthy. Bergen is, or seems, quite a shy person while Charlie has all the cheek in the world."[37] However, as Jean Renoir suggests in the epigraph at the beginning of this chapter, this attempt all too often results in scandal.

I'm taking a cue here from an article by Rick Altman, who uses the trope of ventriloquism to reverse film studies' privileging of the image over sound. For Altman, mainstream cinematic narrative involves the repression of two "sources"—the apparatus and the screenwriter—each repressed to preserve the complementary, pseudo-unity of the human subject (which was a topic of contentious debate when he was writing in 1980).[38] Rather than elaborating his Lacanian theories of subject positioning, I instead point to one more repressed threatening to return: the translator.

The thing about dubbing is that it calls attention to the mediation of translation in the most troubling of ways. One of the most interesting of Altman's observations is about the tension always produced by sound, where it serves as a discursive source for visual information: "The image says *where?* And sound says *here!*"[39] Altman continues: "We are so disconcerted by a sourceless sound that we would rather attribute the sound to a dummy or a shadow than face the mystery of its sourcelessness or the scandal of its production by a non-vocal (technological or 'ventral') apparatus."[40] In the ventriloquist's dubbing, the image says *where?* The sound says *here!* And we say *No, thank you!* Here, in the gap between the ventriloquist's thrown voice and the flapping of the dummy's lips, the hegemony of the target language is laid bare as *we* speak through *them*.

In this section, I want to analyze the ventral art of a particularly famous ventriloquist in Japan, Wakayama Genzo, to make some tentative observations about the voice-replacement approach to dubbing. Wakayama was born in Russia in 1932, but came back to Japan after the end of World War II. Between 1952 and 1957 he was in NHK Sapporo's Broadcast Theater Troupe, after which he moved to Tokyo. He started his career as an actor in television dramas like *Marimo no kage ni* (*In the Shadow of Marimo*, 1958) and *Daiyaru 110 ban* (*Dial 110*, 1959) before turning to dubbing foreign television shows. He was immediately popular for his low voice, and came to be known as Raymond Burr's voice on *Ironsides* (1969), as well as *The Lone Ranger* (1958) and the lead of *Name of the Game* (1972). Fans of Japanese monster films might remember him as the voice of the boss in *Destroy All Planets* (aka *Gamera against the Space Monster Bairus, Bamera tai uchu kaiju Bairusu*, 1968). He achieved such fame as a voice actor that he hosted his own radio show on TBS Radio, *Wakayama Genzo's Dial Tokyo 954* (*Wakayama Genzo' no Tokyo Daiyaru 954);* running from 1973 to 1995, it holds the all-time record for the number of broadcasts in Japanese radio at 5,734 programs. However, Wakayama's greatest role was as Bond, the Sean Connery Bond.

Let's look at Wakayama's versions of *Dr. No* (1962) and *From Russia with Love* (1963). *Dr. No* was the first Fleming book to be adapted to the screen (and, in fact, Ursula Andress's own voice was dubbed in the original English version). The novel initially hit the streets of Kanda as a pirated version titled *Isha ga Iranai* (literally, *I Need No Doctor*), and this bizarre transliteration pretty much set the tone for the text's translation as it made its way to Japanese television. Unfortunately, I have not been able to access videotapes of Wakayama's performance because they were shortened versions produced for television broadcast. The analyses that follow are based on Wakayama's personal scripts, nine thousand of which are housed in Waseda University's library. Based on these, along with a few other texts, I want to analyze specific instances of translation in order to isolate some basic observations about dubbing.

The first observation is that *ventriloquists mistake their script for an original*. The most striking aspect about these scripts is Wakayama's own, often liberal, revisions of the translation. For example, when Dr. No invites Bond to join the Spectre and its plot to dominate the world, the British spy replies:

BOND: Very flattering. I'd prefer the revenge department. Of course, I'd want to start with the man responsible for killing Strangways and Quarrel.

The script's translation is tailored quite close to the original line, but Wakayama has penciled it out and revised it freely; to return the line to English, it comes out, "I'm honored. What I could do is seduce women spies and while I'm kissing them I could get information. That kind of thing I could do." This kind of revision is not unusual in dubbing, and is often the result of collaboration by the entire staff. However, a voice actor of Wakayama's prestige has the authority to do it on his own (and probably knows better than the rest of the staff anyway). These changes often amount to departures from the lines on the sound track, suggesting that Wakayama's debt lies elsewhere. In an interview in year 2000, he expressed his desire to preserve on film a *seikaku* (correct) Japanese for future generations, suggesting a conservative debt to his own language and culture.[41]

The issue of debt brings us to a second observation, that the ultimate debt of the ventriloquist is probably to the *body* of Bond. In the first instance, this may be attributed to the desire for synchronization between mouth and voice. Québécois translator Robert Paquin explains, using his translation of *Titus* (1999) as an example:

> There must be a close correspondence between the actor's interpretation and the translation. Indeed, while recording in the studio, dubbing actors always carefully listen to and watch the screen actors, trying to imitate them, and following them as closely as possible, just as the translator attempts to walk in the author's tracks. Likewise, the screen translator must watch attentively and take his or her cues from the actors on the screen. There were a few cases in the writing of the French script for *Titus* where the actor's interpretation of the lines helped me understand the true meaning of the text, which had eluded the two previous French translators.[42]

Paquin takes the dubbing of *Titus* as seriously as François-Victor Hugo and J. B. Fort took their print translations of Shakespeare's play. This is precisely why his own quest for sync afforded him a new perspective on the play unavailable to the literary translators of old. The problem is that the matching mandate can become a tyranny of synchronization, where harmonizing mouth to voice threatens to take precedence over translation itself. Wakayama's revision points to a translation scene evacuated by the translator, a scene in which the text is subjugated to the whims of voice actors, whose sense of debt finds its locus in the body first and foremost—form before content! "What I could do is seduce women spies and while I'm kissing them I could get information. That kind of thing I could do," says Bond/(Wakayama). The source of this text is nothing other than the hypersexualized body of the Connery Bond.

A third observation is that *ventriloquists can't take a joke.* They translate past humor, the surest sign of a domesticating translation that zeroes in on the most literal of meaning without accounting for linguistic play and the materiality of language. In *Dr. No,* Bond is chased up a treacherous mountain road by some heavies in a hearse. Suddenly, a large crane appears in the middle of the road, and Bond drives right under its arm; the much larger hearse is forced to veer off the road and it plunges down a long cliff, bursting into explosive flames. On the original sound track, here is what happened when Bond and the truck driver look over the edge at the burning wreck:

TRUCK DRIVER: How did it happen?
BOND: I think they were on their way to a funeral.

The dubbing script calls for the truck driver to say, "Korya hidoi ya" (This is terrible), to which Bond replies, "Jigoku o gyakuotoshi da" (literally, They're going back down to hell). What is significant here is not only that the ventriloquist has ignored the typical Bond irony, but that the translation *refers instead to the image:* the reference to hell comes from the explosion, and *gyakuotoshi* to the downward movement of the spectacular crash.

This seeming inability to take a joke naturally affects what kind of comedy gets exported *and even produced*—it's to be physical and simple. But I'd like to share an interesting comment by Harada Masato, an actor in *Last Samurai* (2003) and director of major Japanese films like *Gunhead* (1988), *Kamikaze Taxi* (1994), *Bounce-ko Gals, aka Leaving (Bounce ko gyaru,* 1997), and *Spellbound (Jubaku,* 1999). A fluent English speaker, Harada also translated and directed the Japanese dubbings of *Star Wars* (1977), *The Empire Strikes Back* (1980), and *Full Metal Jacket* (1987). As Harada notes, "Film translators ignore all the jokes, probably because they don't get them in the first place. Basically, their translations contain no irony. No sarcasm. And since 80 percent of all American films' lines are sarcastic, virtually nothing is translated!"[43] Although this has not exactly imperiled Hollywood, it has probably affected foreign impressions of American screenwriting. As for Bond, he comes off as an even more outrageous womanizer because his comments on women and sex are rendered so straight, when in reality they're riddled with irony and sarcasm. For example, after a series of assassination attempts in *Dr. No,* Bond boards the boat of CIA agent Felix Leiter (Jack Lord) to sneak onto the mad scientist's island. Pushing off, he exclaims:

> BOND: For me Crab Key is going to be a gentle relaxation.
> LEITER: From what, dames?
> BOND: No, from being a clay pigeon.

In the Japanese script, this is rendered in the following manner:

> BOND: "Kani ga Shima" ha pikkunikku rando da. Honeyasume dekiru
>   zo. ("'Crab Island' is a picnic ground. I'll be able to relax.")
> LEITER: Onna ga inai kara ka? ("Because there are no dames?")
> BOND: So! Onna wa kirai sa. ("That's right! I hate dames.")

Still a joke, but the new lines contain only a simplistic irony that inflates his image as a womanizer, while basically concentrating blame for his assassination attempts on a Chinese woman from the preceding scene.

This leads me to my next observation: *ventriloquists hate double entendre*—which is why the Bond films provide such rich texts. Consider this far more complex example (because the sound–image relationship is so important, I shall add a few annotations):

> BOND *(looking through a periscope into a room):* Just a moment. A girl's
>   just come in.
> BEY *(Bond's point of view through the periscope):* Probably Romaldava.
>   She's the only one that's allowed to. How does she look to you?
> BOND *(a table obscures all but her legs):* Well, from this angle, things are
>   shaping up nicely. I'd like to see her in the flesh. Yes. Could you get me
>   a plan of that place?
> BEY: I wish I could.
> BOND: But there must be the original architect's drawings registered
>   somewhere.
> BEY: I'll get on to that.

The ventriloquist's script calls for:

> BOND: Chotto matta. Onna ga haite kita zo. ("Wait a second. A girl's
>   come in.")

BEY: Kitto Romaaba da yo. Hoka no onna ha hairenai n da. Do da bijin daro? ("I'm sure it's Romaldava. Other girls can't go in. What do you think? Isn't she a beauty?")

BOND: A. Bijin mo bijin. Mabushikute kao mo ogamenai ya. Ashi kara zentai o sozo suru no mo otsu na monda ne. Ryojikan no mitorizu ga hoshii na. ("Ah, the most beautiful of the beautiful. Her face is so dazzling I can't worship it. It's thrilling to imagine her entire body from her legs. I sure would like the consulate's floor plan.")

BEY: Muri da yo. Soriya. ("That's impossible.")

BOND: Ano onna o riyo sureba te ni hairu ka mo shirenzo. ("Maybe we can get our hands on it if we use that girl.")

BEY: Yoshi. Atatte miyo. ("OK. Let's try.")

The translation accounts for the business of the table blocking Bond's view and strives to include well-worn expressions: the original screenwriter has tampered with "shaping up nicely" and "seeing in the flesh" and this finds analogous treatment in *ogameru,* to worship—often a face of a god or a woman. However, where the original lines involve pleasurable leaps of meaning from the original expressions to the sexual innuendo, the Japanese is right out there. The implicit is rendered explicit throughout this film. Furthermore, the outright revision of the last lines about "using the woman" give the entire passage, if not the entire film, the stench of misogyny.

As a corollary to this example, *ventriloquists can't stand silence.* To illustrate this, let us look at a rather remarkable illustration from the Japanese version of *The Godfather* and one of the most famous scenes in film history. At the beginning of the film, the Godfather has left his son's wedding to entertain a request from a distant relative. The relative explains that a man who hurt his family escaped punishment by the American legal system:

DON CORLEONE: Why did you go to the police? Why didn't you come to me first?

RELATIVE: What do you want of me? Tell me anything. But do what I beg of you to do.

DON CORLEONE: What is that?

The man looks at the other people in the room, stands out of his chair, walks around the Godfather's enormous desk, and bends over to whisper the request in the Godfather's ear. We hear nothing, but understand the nature of the request when Brando waves in the air and says, "That I cannot do." In the Japanese dubbed version, when the relative comes close to Don Corleone's ear, we hear (we are told): "Koroshite itadakitai n desu" (I want you to kill him for me). Just after this, the cat on Brando's lap jumps off with a "meow!" that is not on the original sound track.

Bresson once famously said, "A sound always evokes an image; an image never evokes a sound."[44] However, this example shows that ventriloquists operate under a different logic, one that feels compelled to compensate for the inertness of their dummies by filling in silence and rendering the implicit explicit, even giving away the secrets! It is not only lips that demand sound. Sometimes it is a head-toss shot from behind. A passionate kiss seems to require extra hmmmmms and heavy breathing (Figure 28). Such sounds find their source text in the image, not the sound track. These examples reveal an ethic of domination that discounts the original text, the specificity and materiality of its language, as well as the culture from which it emerged. The following examples pursue some of the ideological implications of this dynamic.

For instance, *ventriloquists are prudes.* They are often complicit in scandalous censorship. Examples are virtually ubiquitous in the history of dubbing, but my favorites are the ones that result in unintended perversity. Back in the Franco era, adultery was offensive to Franco. Spanish ventriloquists erased the adultery in John Ford's *Mogambo* (1953) by turning Grace Kelly and her lover into siblings. It made her flirtations with Clark Gable OK, but inserted an incestuous subtext![45] Similarly, American ventriloquists and network executives nervous about the homoerotic relationship between sailors Neptune and Uranus have turned the two into cousins. Interestingly enough, the image can betray the ventriloquist. Thus, in the 1948 *Arch of Triumph*, Ingrid Bergman checks into a hotel with a man and when asked if they're married she shakes her head; in the Spanish version, she says, "Sí" at the same time.[46] Likewise, the German distributor of a James Bond film fretted about a scene in which Bond is discovered in the bathtub by an unsuspecting chambermaid. "May I wash your back?" she asks with a knowing look. "Please," responds Bond, handing her his bar of soap. The distributor had the German dubbers change the response to a friendly and innocuous, "No, thank you," and the ventriloquists did their best to match the lip flapping. But there was nothing they could do about the dirty little smile on the hero's face when he handed her the soap.[47]

Because they are prudish, *ventriloquists ignore obscenity.* Wakayama did not have to worry about this problem, because back then the studios squelched coarse speech at the point of production. After films like *The Last Detail* (1973) brought the whole flowery range of human speech to Hollywood movies, the translators stepped in to take the censorship role previously held by the studio system. Typically, film translators confront a "dirty word" by either cleaning it up or replacing it with terms so highly conventionalized that they have lost the force of their obscene power. In Japanese, for example, these substitute words are typically *kuso-yaro* (literally, "shit-bastard") or *okama-yaro* (literally, "faggot-bastard"). More often than not, they are simply, silently skipped over.

Japanese translators would deny their prudishness, pointing to various theories to justify their actions. These theories are explicated, defended, and naturalized through pedagogy and publishing. These discourses basically call for a kind of rarefied, literary language for film translation, which is why obscenity is cleaned up; it is not beautiful speech (and thus would not be worth learning). When the subject of obscenity is taken up, it is usually dismissed as "untranslatable" in Japanese language. Toda Natsuko once told the *Hollywood Reporter,* "We just don't have any real swear words in Japan. If you directly translated the sexual obscenities used in foreign films, no one would understand."[48] This is precisely why she got into trouble with Stanley Kubrick when she was hired to translate his Vietnam film.

Full Metal Jacket (1987) must have been a daunting task for translators everywhere. Kubrick's film is notorious for its first half hour of boot camp where a drill sergeant subjects his recruits, and by extension the audience, to nonstop verbal abuse. Aside from his onslaught of words your mother told you never to use, the drill sergeant has a knack for producing scandalous imagery with the skill of a surrealist poet. (A former drill sergeant from the U.S. Marines who was hired as an adviser so impressed Kubrick with his ad-lib rants that the director gave him the role.) Few films have achieved such dizzying dirtiness through language.

The first attempt at a Japanese translation was undertaken by Toda Natsuko, the superstar translator of the Japanese film world. Once Toda completed her manuscript, the film's director was not pleased. Kubrick was one of the few directors to take an active role in the translation of his films, thanks to an unusual four-column, *en-face* script performed by a second, independent translator. The first column contained the proposed Japanese translation, the second a transliteration into *romaji*

(Roman letters), the third a word-for-word translation (English words in the Japanese grammatical order), and the fourth a full translation back into natural English. The problem with Toda's translation was the way it tampered with the original language script. Toda, not surprisingly, excised all the obscenity. Kubrick immediately fired her and asked for someone who knew cinema intimately as a producer and also spoke English fluently. Twentieth Century–Fox asked Harada Masato, one of the few people in Japan who fit that bill.

As already mentioned, Harada is a director in his own right. Before taking the director's chair, he spent many years studying in the United States, writing film criticism, and working in the Hollywood system. Having directed the dubbings of *Star Wars* (1977) and *The Empire Strikes Back* (1980) early in his career, he had translation experience as well. Thanks to this unusual personal profile, his English was unusually good and his command of film language was unquestionable. His translation of *Full Metal Jacket* is superb.

As an outsider to the highly professionalized world of ventriloquists, Harada did not feel constricted by the conventions of film translation I have been outlining. Aside from his treatment of the linguistic obscenity, which I will discuss in more detail, Harada wrote a translation that eschewed simplification for an unusually dense prose (for both subtitles and dubbing). He did not limit himself to the restrictive time and space rules of conventional subtitling. For both versions, he proved willing to make his audience work, using imagery and phrases that may not have made crystal clear sense, but which had the tremendous force of the original.

Upon completion of his own translation, Harada submitted it to a second translator for the production of the *en-face* script and waited for Kubrick's response. When it came, it was in the form of a flurry of extended international phone calls from Kubrick himself. Harada sat at the table with Warner's Japan representative and Ikui Eiko, a critic and well-known scholar of the Vietnam War. The four pored over the script together, discussing every individual line in the context of characterization, theme, adjacent scenes, *and writing*. They hashed out alternatives until a satisfactory translation emerged from their collaboration. The result was a translation that caused a media sensation. No one had ever heard a foreign film like this, despite the aggressive use of obscenity by American filmmakers since the 1970s.[49]

Like Kubrick and his actor, Harada pulled no punches in his prose. Harada's favorite line from the drill sergeant was ad-libbed on the fly while shooting. When Kubrick yelled "cut," everyone present burst out laughing, although the actor couldn't even remember what he had said. When Matthew Modine visited to Japan on a press junket and met Harada, he immediately asked how this line was translated. Here it is:

> SOUND TRACK: I'll bet you're the kind of guy that would fuck a person in the ass and not even have the goddamn common courtesy to give him a reach around!
>
> TRANSLATION: Kisama wa hitosama no kama o horu dake hotte, mawashite de ikasete yaru shinsetsushin mo nai yatsu da!
>
> TRANSLATED BACK INTO ENGLISH: You're the kind of bastard that would fuck a man (literally dig a pot) as hard as possible without being so kind as to give him a reach around.

For "reach around" Harada coins a similar word in *mawashi te*. This condenses many meanings into a compact package. Based on the verb *mawasu/*"to turn" (a handle or key, among many other things), its stem *(mawashi)* is often used as a prefix and combined with other words— *te/*"hand" in this case. However, *mawashi* also stands alone as a noun signifying the loincloth wrapping the groin of sumo wrestlers. Unfortunately, we do not have Toda's translation to see how she dealt with these kinds of lines, but we can assume it cleaned them up and excised their tacit acknowledgment of the military's ambivalent (love–hate?) relationship to homosexuality. What is left of that sequence without it?

Aside from Harada's unflinching translation of the fearsome obscenity pouring from the drill instructor's mouth, he admirably ignored the common sense of dubbers when it came to casting actors. He prefers to use actors from the stage or live-action film wherever possible, although in Japan this is unusual outside of the blockbuster animation from Disney. Voice actors, complains Harada, have developed a highly conventionalized style used exclusively for their trade: "No one actually speaks that way. It's as if they've created a 'foreigner's language.' They are speaking in fluent Japanese, but they seem to think it has to be a little different because its coming out of the mouths of foreigners." For this reason, Harada draws on actors without experience as voice actors. *Full Metal Jacket* featured actors who were relatively unknown at the time, such as Riju Go as Joker, Saito Haruhiko as Hartman, and Shioya Shun as Cowboy.

Furthermore, Harada does not cast strictly by voice. When we spoke, he was preparing to direct the dubbing of Kubrick's last film, *Eyes Wide Shut* (1999). Mulling over the casting of the Tom Cruise character, all of Harada's choices had a small mouth and short build, "because short people have a special kind of energy that gets expressed in their speech." Thus, even physique plays into the audition process. Harada is not alone in this strategy. Film producer Kato Satoshi says, "Overweight people have overweight voices because the vocal chords are different, while skinny people have skinny voices, which tend not to be so deep. It's hard to find a person to fit Schwarzenegger. The dubber must have a voice that is strong, manly and wild."[50] Dubbers in other parts of the world, such as Czech Republic, also base casting partly on body typage.

This suggests that a certain kind of acting is necessary as well. As Paris dubbing bum Lee Payant put it in 1966, "A Method actor might never catch on. There's no time to build a role."[51] What sets Harada Masato apart from the typical film translator is his lack of devotion to the apparatus of rules that buttresses the professionalization of dubbing and subtitling. He demonstrates that it only takes a creative mind and a flexible approach to translation problems to change the rules.

A final observation: *ventriloquists fear the other*. This is probably the main reason we condemn dubbing as the lowest form of translation. It is too often a domesticating form of translation as it is generally practiced. Whereas subtitles grant one access to both meaning and the foreign grain of the voice, dubbing retains only sound effects and music. The foreign language is completely extracted, replaced with sameness. Of course, the image often betrays the ventriloquist with signs of difference: race, gesture, fashion, even road signs. One can bet that this is going on at many levels whenever characters' names are domesticated, as in the anime classic *Gigantor* (1963), where "Kaneda Shotaro" becomes "Jimmy Sparks." In highly capitalized projects, dubbers can go to extraordinary lengths to excise any trace of the remainder. For example, the producers of *Pokemon* regularly redraw images that contain signs in Japanese. For a while they even eliminated (translated!?) the squinty eyes of one character because (white) American test audiences felt he looked too Asian.

Back in the 1960s, the distributors of Japanese animation were cash poor, so redrawing cels was out of the question and they had to rely on cheaper means for this visual erasure of otherness. One episode of *8th*

Man (1963–64) is set at an art museum. The ventriloquists work over-time to account for all the signs in Japanese. When a guard strolls past the entrance sign, the narrator intones, "They pass the authentic Orien-tal sign." Hearing a suspicious noise, another guard grabs his flashlight to check it out; when its beam illuminates an arrow sign reading "*Chin-retsu Kaijo*" (Exhibit Hall), he mumbles to himself, "Making those signs Oriental sure doesn't help you find your way!" At the end of the episode, 8th Man (in civilian garb) inexplicably reads a Japanese newspaper over breakfast; his wife asks if the robberies were reported, adding, "I'll bet the people of those Oriental countries are upset!"

This kind of textual gymnastics may seem like an extreme case, but I assert that the *impulse* to domesticate is built into the standard conven-tions of dubbing. In other words, most dubbing is every bit as corrupt as its subtitling counterpart; they are hardly the kind of polar opposites they have always been assumed to be. This is not to say that corruption is necessarily essential to dubbing (the attitude with which I began this project), but we may have to find translators striving for alternatives before we can come to love it. Anime fandom is acutely aware of this problem; thus, its long-running debate over sub versus dub pivots on this very issue. However, Harada Masato said something to me that sug-gests that this issue of otherness might be more complex:

> Japan was complicit in Vietnam, but we don't have a film like *Full Metal Jacket*. I prefer subtitles as a rule, but when I watched my own dubbing I was so moved. If it is subbed, the people on the screen are really foreign because they look different and speak a language you can't understand. There's a built-in distance. But with dubbing it's close. They are white, but when Cowboy dies at the end, it was like a friend died because he was speaking Japanese. I want Japanese to feel that kind of pain, but they won't if it's subtitled. It's simply not the same.

This comment raises a knot of vexing issues, all of which we cannot hope to resolve here. If it is indeed the case that spectators can more readily identify with characters in a dubbed film—overcoming various forms of difference—then what are the factors that enable this? Are they extrafilmic? Do they involve a powerful identification with the appara-tus itself, what 1970s screen theory referred to as primary identification? Perhaps they are related to physiological differences in the reading pro-cess. We know that subtitles force viewers to scan the frame very differently, thanks to studies that have connected spectators to headsets that track their eye movements with gaze monitors.[52] It should be no surprise that much of the time viewers' eyes track back and forth at the edge of the frame, flicking up to the middle only between subtitles. If the composition of the image has anything to do with spectators' involvement in the filmic experience, as has often been theorized, then this may be an important, underlying factor in Harada's observation.

Finally, how we figure in the issue of convention and its naturalization in light of all this is yet another thorny problem. Note, for example, that it is primarily lovers of the subtitle who complain about sync. This is because a little lip flapping does not faze people who grew up with dubbing. Furthermore, their eyes are not glued to the actors' lips; they tend to look at characters in the eyes, as in face-to-face conversation. I have found that training myself to maintain eye contact was the first step on the road to loving dubbing.

I raise these questions to emphasize that I am not claiming that dubbing is simply "bad translation" or only a matter of competence. Rather, these issues serve to point out the complexity of our relationship with moving-image media from other parts of the world. For the most part, the problems outlined here are symptomatic of a corrupt conception of translation. One that domesticates the other. One in which the "translator"—that team of technicians, translators, and actors—feels a stronger debt to the bodies of the actors (or the image in general) than to the original text, which is a sound/image complex.

Fucking It Up with Love and Respect

I have complicated our notion of dubbing—what it is and how it came to be this way—but Yomota's question remains: "Can we come to love dubbing?" Can we dub without ourselves becoming dummies? As I prepared this essay I kept flashing on the dummies gone berserk in films like *The Great Gabbo* (1929), *Dead of Night* (1945), *Devil Doll* (1964), *Magic* (1978), and *Dead Silence* (2007). The motivations behind the decision to dub are all too often crazy ones: raking in the dough, destroying entire foreign national cinemas, easy censorship, yokel ignorance, fascism! However, a graphic novelist provides a hint at a slightly different stance, drawn from his experience dubbing Miyazaki Hayao's *Princess Mononoke* (*Mononoke hime*, 1979):

So my first experience with *Mononoke* was sitting in an empty screening room in L.A. watching a subtitled version. I'd never seen anything like it. I came out of it saying this is absolutely wonderful. I don't know if [my translation] can do it justice, but on the other hand, if I don't do it, they'll get someone else. To put it bluntly, if I fuck it up, I'll fuck it up with respect and love. I would rather it were me fucking it up with respect and love than somebody who was doing it as a job.[53]

At the most *basic* level, I am calling for respect and love—for quality, attentiveness, rigor, and cognizance of the ideological dimensions of the practice. In other words, the field of dubbing is also ripe for abuse. Perhaps all ventriloquists know this in their guts. There are plenty of remarkable dubbers such as Robert Paquin who don't flinch at the challenges coming their way—who get the joke. Unfortunately, I suspect more are like Herbert Fielden-Briggs, a translator, dubbing director, and voice actor otherwise known as "Robert Duvall" in French-speaking parts of the world, who puts it bluntly: "Dubbing is a lie. You lie from beginning to end. It's a complete invention, so it can be more or less faithful to a given market."[54] This dishonesty is precisely what got Toda Natsuko into trouble with Stanley Kubrick. The deliciously abusive translation resulting from Kubrick's collaboration with Harada demonstrates just one of the possibilities available to the ventriloquists when they stop living the lie.

For dubbers, this is a smaller step than one might imagine, and it has something to do with the production process itself. In the translation of literature, the translator takes on a mimetic relationship to the author. Regardless of the conception of translation, both author and translator sit at a desk with pen and paper, computer and keyboard. Dubbing is similarly mimetic. As in the original production process, there are a producer and a director who manage schedules, budgets, and casting. The director has a hand in the technical process of sound capture, all the while coaching actors to deliver the best performance possible. The recording process is just as fragmented and achronological as the original production. Finally, the postproduction process gives acoustic nuance to the raw sound captured at the studio. Where famous actors are employed, the stars often help with the film's advertising campaign as well. It is no wonder that dubbers are more in tune with the performative and aesthetic aspects of cinema, as dubbing represents a mimetic rearticulation of the process of filmmaking itself. By way of contrast, subtitling may resemble the work of the screenwriter; however, it stops short there, diverting the work of textual production to an entirely novel place. This helps explain why subtitlers obsess on simple sense to the exclusion of all else. The process itself is thoroughly out of sync with the nature of film production.

Ventriloquists can stray from the path of duplicity and corruption by recognizing that dubbing produces a new (hopefully artful) text. But it is also more than this. We need to flip-flop the hierarchy of debt, putting the screenplay first rather than adapting and abandoning the original linguistic text for the sake of filling silence or the maintenance of domestic common sense. Where the translator confronts seemingly untranslatable cultural difference, the remainder is allowed to leak into the text. Where the screenplay plays with language or creates knots of signification that seem to defy translation, the dubber brings similar moments of stress to bear in the language of the voice actors.

I suspect that ventriloquists are likely to be more open to abusive translation than subtitlers simply by virtue of the fact that many already

Figure 30. Dubbers will probably be more receptive to abusive translation. This dubbing of *Monty Python's Flying Circus* (1969–74) in the late 1980s deploys abusive subtitles for graphic text: "Osoji obasa~n!"/("Clea~ning Woman!"). The woman swings, Tarzan-like, behind the Japanese title, which uses a similarly shadowed font, an identical color palate, matching mise-en-scène, and punctuation like "~" and "!" to match the movement and the sound track.

deploy abusive strategies. They often exploit moments when characters turn their backs to add explication or deal with tricky translation problems. The entire project of sound editing is sympathetic to abusive translation; the sound editor's job is nothing other than attending to the material qualities of speech. As for actors, they *act;* there is no correlative to the inert, nondescript subtitle. Casting often attends to the original's soundscape. The Japanese voice actor chosen to replace *The Godfather*'s Don Vito Corleone delivers the spitting (aural) image of Marlon Brando's raspy delivery. At the same time, the corrupt ventriloquist from Italy reveals the depths of his deceit when he gloats, "In Italian, we got rid of [Brando's] scratchy American voice. He has a good voice now, and now he is a great actor."[55] This is to say that there is an curious ambivalence at the heart of dubbing, a circulation between corruption and other possibilities.

As we proceed deeper into the third epoch of film translation, there are hopeful signs that ventriloquists will indulge more freely in abusiveness. One occasionally finds intimations that this is precisely the case. One of these hints is Stephen Chow's *Shaolin Soccer* (*Sui lam juk kau,* 2001). At first glance, it would seem to be a typically poor dubbing job from Hong Kong. The sloppiness, however, is parodic by design. Chow did his own dubbing in his distinctive Hong Kong accent, and Chinese-born actress Bai Ling dubbed the film's mainland character. This gave the English version a strange linguistic purity for Chinese-language speakers who could recognize the difference. The rest of the characters were voiced in inscrutable Chinese accents by American actors who mimic the other two. The film itself is a send-up of 1970s kung-fu films, which received similarly strange dubbings with slapdash lip-synch. The effect is half parody, half tribute. A brilliant example of abusive dubbing, *Shaolin Soccer* provides a foreignizing translation deeply engaged with the sensibility of the creators of the film and its audiences.

Lest abusive dubbing become simplistically identified with bad lip-synch, we should remember how abusive subtitles have sometimes been unfairly reduced to graphic play and little else. Abusive translation here is both stance and strategy, so its possibilities for creative ventriloquists are only as limited as their own imaginations. Let us look at some other films and television shows that seem more abusive than deceitful. Some are actual examples of abusive dubbing; others strike me as films just crying for abuse.

A clever dubber should welcome sound experiments such as the beginning of *Weekend*, which I described in the introduction, *The Conversation* (1974), or pretty much any Robert Altman film. There are films where the image–language relationship is off-kilter in other ways. Perhaps only a dubbing could duplicate the power of Anthony Burgess's inventive English in *A Clockwork Orange* (1971). Similarly, wouldn't the best translation of *Othello* be a careful adaption of the standard foreign-language translation dubbed onto the sound track? Surely the integrity of Shakespeare's words is more important than the voice of Orson Welles? (The casting director will attend to that small but crucial issue.) These films are nothing other than opportunities to experiment and ply the craft.

Recently, we have also seen the welcome emergence of the hybrid translation. In the past, dubbers have used everything from voice of God narrators to subtitles to translate visual signs (letters, billboards, headlines, etc.). This hybridity is available to capitalize upon. There is, for example, the English version of the Japanese television show *Iron Chef* (*Ryori no tetsujin*, 1993–99), which mixes subbing and dubbing. The inane chatter of the jury is dubbed in quite natural English, freeing one's eyes to caress the images of cooking food. However, what is most impressive is that the master of ceremonies is *subtitled*, because he's *performing*. Unlike the jury of dummies, the grain of his voice—the materiality of his language—is every bit as important as what he says. Furthermore, the subbed introduction and conclusion bookend the show with the remainder.

Then there are the films containing unreasonable speech, a virtual license for abuse. For example, in the setting of a silly film like *Gladiator* (2000), no one spoke English in the first place, so why not dub? Many of the dubbings for *Babe, the Gallant Pig* (1995) adopted an abusive strategy by assigning each animal species a different dialect or accent. The Austrian dub has the piglet star speaking Viennese, while the cow reportedly sounded more like Arnold Schwarzenegger's Alpine idiom. We can also find this on what Hamid Naficy would call "accented television"; for example, Welsh dubbing for Channel 4 has been known to use various Welsh accents to connote cultural differences in the source text.

Although it is a rather exceptional example, Werner Herzog demonstrated that the practice of MLVs could be resurrected. He shot *Nosferatu the Vampire* (*Nosferatu: Phantom der Nacht*, 1979) with the same actors in both English and German.[56] We are beginning to see this in the world of anime, where *Ghost in the Shell* (*Kokaku kidotai*, 1995) and other films have been simultaneously released in English and Japanese. Here the issues of the original and debt evaporate (at least for everyone except the nationalists, the Orientalists, and their ilk).

Finally, one of the purest examples of ventral abuse I have come across is the Spanish dubbing of *Power* (1986). The first half of the film places Richard Gere in Mexico, speaking English to people who cannot understand a word he is saying. The Spanish dubbing leaves Gere untranslated throughout this extended sequence, only bringing out the Spanish ventriloquists when Gere moves north across the border.[57]

I draw this last example from Michael Watt's condemnation of dubbing titled "'Do You Speak Christian?'" Regarding this innovative strategy in *Power*, he writes, "It's best not to even try to figure out what the intention was here."[58] Quite the contrary, Watt is fairly condescending to an audience that surely knows exactly what mischief the translator was up to. In general, Watt's essay provides an excellent example of the way the lovers of subtitling project the values of corruption onto dubbing, demanding, for example, that it resolutely conform to the norms of Hollywood motivation while letting subtitlers off the hook. He argues that, subtitles, unlike dubbing, "more or less confess their true nature as a tool to aid understanding. They're not pretending to be the dialogue. They're not pretending to exist inside the film. They're not trying to convince the spectator that the characters are speaking in a different language than they originally spoke in."[59] Actually, as I argued in the preceding chapter, this is precisely the pretense of the subtitler. Those condemning the dub simply must look as closely at the subtitling as they do the flailing of mouths—and then look once again at dubbing without looking at the lips.

In my own close examination of dubbing, I find myself returning to Harada's example of Cowboy's death throes in *Full Metal Jacket*. What he is ultimately talking about in this example—the reason he chose this scene in particular—is that both director Kubrick and translator Harada are struggling to represent the unrepresentable. This indicates our key coordinate: the Limit. And this itself is most often rendered through the trope of death, which always circulates around the issue of translation like a hungry vulture.

The limits of *film* translation are imposed, first and foremost, by the apparatus itself, the unforgiving turn of the gears and reels. For sub-

Figure 31. *Full Metal Jacket* (1987). Translator Harada singled out Cowboy's death to advocate dubbing because both he and director Kubrick struggle here to represent the unrepresentable. This indicates our key coordinate: the Limit. And this is most often rendered through the trope of death, which always circulates around the issue of translation like a hungry vulture.

titling, this forces the translator to deal with severe time limitations as the act of reading and hearing synchronize in an often-uncomfortable fit. There's also the way the eye's embrace of the screen is forcibly locked on its edge by the hand of the translator. Thus, for many spectators what is left is, precisely, the remainder, a dead text, a *fukikae,* and thus they prefer the tricks of the ventriloquist.

On the other hand, there are also people who find dubbing disconcerting, because they locate the Limit at the word, not the body—and this can be traced all the way back to the invention of dubbing. Back in 1930, a critic writing on Hitchcock's *Blackmail* (1929) couldn't stand Anny Ondra's dubbing of Joan Barry's voice: "What if the voice, tired and resentful of anonymity, clamors for publicity, to be featured as itself? Like the Siamese twins, Face and Voice are inseparable, the death of one implying the death of both."[60] Those of us mourning this death, along with the loss of the foreign voice in a world where contact with otherness is a value, opted for subtitles; all the while, others grew accustomed to the ventriloquist's act.

We may start to understand the proponents of the dub, and the ventriloquists who cater to them, by centering our attention on the Limit, where it is located, and how conventions of translation come to protect us from it. What dub lovers value is less an accurate translation of the foreign original than the obscure integrity of the cinematic narrative space. These spectators feel a fatal attraction to that sublime immersion in the film's diegesis. It is between the words of a filmic text and that inscrutable understanding of their significance that the lovers of dubbing locate their limit; the subtitle violently reduces that experience to dry verbiage. However, as limits are often described with death, we may locate ours somewhere else and look at the very same scene dubbed and see nothing but dummies.

If the two historically winning strategies for film translation are, at the most basic level, naturalized, prophylactic conventions protecting us from the death of the text, then the question we must pose is whether dubbing can be rescued from its duplicitous self. From its debt, which is skewed to the image and the actor. From its domesticating tendencies. And from its complicity with nationalism in an age of self-reflexive globalization. Only when I get answers to these questions can I decide if I can love the dub.

CONCLUSION

Genesis

If the U.S. spoke Spanish, Britain might still have a film industry.
— Samuel Goldwyn

Since there were no fixed wage agreements for our dialog writers, we created our own: Action is cheap. Humor is expensive. Culture is impossibly expensive.
— Matthias Müntefering

Prophylaxis

Readers more familiar with literary translation may have been taken aback by all the discussion of money in the preceding chapters. Particularly striking are the often mind-boggling production budgets, the balances of which teeter on the delicate apex of translation. Film, along with architecture, is one of the most expensive art forms. To make films and television programs fine and competitive, and to traffic them expeditiously and profitably, requires muscular investment. The budgets of American blockbusters have broken the $100 million mark. A modest narrative film can require a cool million—or two—to produce, and this is to say nothing of the cost of promotion and distribution. Before the era of high-quality digital video, even the artisanal arenas of the avant-garde and documentary demanded precious treasure. Now that video is edited on personal computers, one of the most expensive lines in an independent producer's budget can be for translation. Thus, it is the nature of the medium, being so capital intensive, that corners will be cut. The bare minimum will be spent. This goes for films with staggering budgets as well; Hollywood filmmakers spend more on catering than on translation.

This economic equation inflects every question of quality in the realm of moving-image translation. This is to say that one must ask how—in this delicate balance of economic, technological, literary, and ideological pressures—one can regulate traffic for quality. In these pages, I struck a stance wary of received traditions. My historical investigation was committed to the search for translation modes that exploited the toys in the filmmaker's toolbox and self-consciously explored the specificities of moving-image media. I have drawn on these historical examples to advocate a translation ready and willing to experiment, to tamper with tradition, language, and expectations in order to inventively put spectators into contact with the foreign—a translation that is, in a word, abusive.

These final pages return to the translation factor in the globalization of cinema and television. They consider the regulation of traffic with an eye on the technological and material working conditions of translators. The question is how the finest translators can be nurtured while protecting them from the twin forces of rationalization and domestication.

As we have seen, cinema was a global phenomenon within a few years of its invention. It spread unevenly, so it would never extend into many rural areas of the world before broadcast television and the videotape substantially completed this process after World War II. However, in its infancy the motion-picture medium was largely conceptualized and organized on a planetary scale. That the circulation of moving pictures was characterized by unevenness indicates political, economic, and cultural difference. So it should come as no surprise that as producers extended their geographic reach, accumulating and redeploying capital, the energies backing this penetration met growing counterforces of protectionism. Budding industries sought help from their home states to fend off competition (or interfere in such efforts in other national cinemas on their behalf). At the same time, these products of other cultures inspired anxieties over contamination, often identified with the "vacuous" and "salacious" product of Hollywood.

After only a few decades, the hegemony of American film was felt globally. This single industry enjoyed such power thanks in part to the happy coincidence of its linguistic market. According to Kristin Thompson, French producers could directly target 75 million French speakers around the world through approximately five thousand far-flung theaters. On the other hand, the English-language audience was 225 million strong, with some thirty thousand cinemas.[1] Translation strategies expanded these markets considerably. For example, dubbing allowed American studios to flood Europe with handsome, large-scale productions for far less money than domestic industries could manage to gather. Dubbing's leveling of linguistic difference between domestic and foreign films contributed to Hollywood's domination of Europe.

At the same time, translation can also be deployed as a prophylactic. As an example, we could wade into the mind-boggling array of rules and regulations a 1930s producer faced wherever he tried to distribute a film. In many regions, he was free to use his translation method of choice, a selection generally based on market preference. For instance, a dubbed film in Japan simply did not sell, so all films were subtitled on the basis of a marketing decision. The story was different in Europe. Germany, Spain, and Italy legislated dubbing as the standard method.[2] France did as well, and the producer had to make that dub within French territory.[3] Around the same time, Belgium tried to enact a similar set of laws requiring domestic dubbing *into its own brand of French;* however, the producer was eventually relieved of such restrictions thanks to the French government, which let it be known that Belgian dubs would be banned in retaliation. The American Motion Picture Producers and Distributors Association (MPPDA) also exerted pressure by using the U.S. State Department to threaten an embargo and informing Belgium-based Gavaerts that Hollywood would simply use competitor Kodak's film stock. Late in the decade, when the Nazis took control of Belgium, films had to be in German.[4] In Spain, films not only had to be dubbed, but at least 90 percent of the voice actors had to be Spanish nationals, disallowing the possibility of cheap dubs made south of the border in Mexico City. In Austria, the producer could avoid import restrictions by dubbing in-country, and quota laws allowed him a free import for every foreign-language version of an Austrian film he produced. Among all these markets, Italy may have been the most onerous to deal with. The producer's Italian distributor paid twenty-five thousand lira in taxes to dub a film; however, for every Italian film distributed the distributor received a "dubbing coupon," relieving him of the import tax for three (and later four) foreign films. Every country in the world presented a particular set of problems, both logistical and legalistic.

The case of Mexico provides a particularly useful example of the global/national dynamic linked to Hollywood's hegemony, thanks to its geographic proximity to California. Even before decolonization and advances in transportation technologies enabled the emergence of a globally mobile workforce, Mexico City and Los Angeles were close enough to commute between. In 1944 there was a row between the United States and Mexico over Hollywood's use of Mexican actors for dubbing in Los Angeles. The American industry was seducing the country's finest talent across the border, much to the detriment of the health of the local film community. The problem escalated to the point where projectionists in Mexico threatened to stop showing films from the north.[5] Negotiations ensued between the Mexican Actors Guild and the American Screen Actors Guild. The Mexican side sent a uniformed officer of the Mexican army, who evidently left the arbitration with a contract to return to dub the name role of *Don Q, Son of Zorro*.[6] The two industries finally reached an entente cordiale when the American producers agreed to confirm that actors had no outstanding contractual obligations in Mexico before importing them to Hollywood. This was at the height of the collaboration between the U.S. government and the Hollywood studios to treat their southern allies with respect (while propagandizing them into the American vision of the hemisphere); significantly, the mover and shaker behind the negotiations was Francis Alstock of the Office of the Coordinator of Inter-American Affairs. The Americans no doubt felt in a uniquely weak position in 1944.

After the war, Mexico hosted much of the dubbing for Central and South American markets, particularly after the spread of broadcast television in the mid-1950s.[7] However, the Mexican industry continued to wither under the intense competition from the neighbor to the north. This helps explain why, when the country finally instituted a comprehensive film law, its eighth article prohibited dubbing as a defense of its domestic national cinema. By forcing American distributors to plant subtitles on their films, it strategically forced the films to maintain an otherness that (supposedly) offset the higher production values of Hollywood. Supporters of article 8 pay lip service to protecting the integrity of foreign art, but everyone knows it is about circling the wagons around their own artists. Hollywood's Motion Picture Association of America

(MPAA) is lobbying to change Mexican law on the presumptive logic that its regulations limit market access under the North American Free Trade Agreement (NAFTA). The MPAA's lawyers are also arguing that the protective measures of the Mexican film industry are unconstitutional because they violate free speech protections![8] This is simply the latest chapter in Hollywood's greatest story ever told, its maintenance of hegemony over world cinema. Few national industries stood a chance without such drastic (top-down) measures, the most successful of which have often been linked to rabid nationalism and the exploitation of language difference.

Genesis

The preceding section examined the many ways in which language difference provides filmmakers with a tool to protect industries or national cultures from competition and contamination. This is translation as global battleground, where border crossings involve altercation and contamination, prophylaxis and destruction. Were we to accept this pessimistic view of globalization, we would edge toward the simplified worldview of national chauvinists. However, the nature of globalization is far more complex and contradictory, as is the transnational circulation of the moving image. The continuing intensification of globalization deeply affects film translation practices. The big picture presents us with a vast number of prints trafficking the planet, moving through a system that networks, rationalizes, and homogenizes, but inevitably works with products marked by foreignness—marking that can either help or hinder circulation.

Thanks to the forces of globalization, the nodes and routings of this network are proliferating, their traffic accelerating. This means ever more opportunities for translators, and on increasingly exploitative terms. We must not lose sight of the fact that all this interaction requires work. So, any critique of cinema's global environment should also pay attention to organizational underpinnings and working conditions. I can sum up these developments with the example of the "genesis file."

Dreams of combining more than one translation in a single product package have been around since the silent era's bilingual intertitle. Sync sound spoiled these efforts, although in the 1960s technicians in Hollywood invented a special color sound track that could contain three languages on 35mm and two on 16mm. This was a by-product of experiments in stereo sound, but it was never adopted. In the end, the dream resurfaced with the DVD, which can contain several sound tracks and many subtitle tracks on a single disk. This invention had little to do with the analytic impulses underlying the tradition of interlinear versions of printed texts. Rather, draped in the glow of a new technology capable of collapsing the world into a package that can be held in one's hand, the DVD seemed to symbolize the brighter side of globalization. No doubt the DVD's linguistic abilities are convenient, but this has less to do with the lofty rhetoric than with rationalization of the distribution network. Unfortunately, the genesis file injects these rationalizing energies into the translation scene.

The genesis file is the invention of translation clearinghouses modeled on the one-stop, take-no-prisoners approach of Wal-Mart. No longer must a studio take the route of our hypothetical 1930s producer, relying on countless foreign distributors and translation companies to navigate the global traffic lanes. Instead, a film, television show, or promotional video can be sent to one of these new translation companies. After a short wait, they return a single DVD with made-to-order language tracks.

This "one-stop shopping" is largely possible thanks to the invention of the genesis file and swift communication technologies like e-mail. The genesis file is essentially an English-language scenario/spotting list—a compilation of all the dialogue is annotated with precise timings of all the subtitles. The translation house maintains relationships with translators scattered across the planet, enabling clients to choose their target languages from a menu. Upon completion of the genesis file, the company sends the computer file to its translators as an e-mail attachment. These translators simultaneously open the genesis file and substitute each line of dialogue with a translated subtitle in their own language. After the substitutions are complete, the new files are sent back to the translation house by e-mail, where they are converted into discrete subtitle tracks on a single DVD, or any format from theatrical release, to television broadcast, to the World Wide Web. It is as simple as that.

This new practice thrills the companies adopting it while frustrating translators no end. At a 2002 conference on moving-image translation, the "advance" of the genesis file was roundly celebrated on a panel devoted to globalization, a panel constituted mainly by businessmen at the bleeding edge of new translation technology. As the panelists boasted about the convenience and speed of the service they offered, the darker side of globalization began to leak out. For example, the genesis file is invariably an English-language dialogue list, no matter the source language of the film itself. To take a hypothetical example, a Brazilian studio would send its film to an Australian translation house, which would have a Portuguese translator create an English-language genesis file; the Australian company would then forward this file to translators in Germany, Spain, Japan, India, and Egypt. In effect, subtitles for texts from countries other than the United States—the United Kingdom—Australia—Canada are actually translations of translations.

Vanessa Bathfield, a champion of this method from Hollywod Gelula translation house, exclaims, "*Everything* starts with a good English list."[9] In fact, one might argue the opposite. When that 2002 globalization panel turned to questions and answers, I suggested that the "genesis file," with its overtly Judeo-Christian image of prelapsarian fertility, was perfectly named for a neo-imperial translation project positioning English as the source of all meaning. The panelists were predictably defensive; however, I spent the rest of the conference being pulled aside by translators who wanted to thank me for standing up to these increasingly powerful companies.

These translators also related strikingly similar horror stories. As this globalized business strategy goes mainstream, media translators find the genesis file increasingly difficult to evade. Working with them becomes unavoidable for those trying to make a living exclusively by subtitling. Aside from the English problem, the companies find other ways to rationalize the translation process at the expense of quality. Sometimes they give translators only a genesis file of English subtitles and no script of the original dialogue. Those asking to see non-English source texts are refused. Occasionally, translation companies forward the genesis file without a video of the text under translation, forcing the translator to work blind. Deadlines get shorter and shorter as wages freeze or fall. Conscientious translators who ask to change the timing of subtitles to accommodate target-language specificities are not allowed to, a mighty snub to their expertise and professional pride. Apparently, one does not mess around with Genesis.

The genesis file is an exemplary instance of collapsing space and time in the current episode of the globalization of the moving image. Like manufacturers of tennis shoes, the translation house has come to transcend national borders, crisscrossing the planet through cheap shipping and computerized communication networks to exploit cheap labor and develop new markets for its services. It is a vicious irony that the same technologies that provide so much new work for translation workers simultaneously subject them to a global system of exploitation. It is highly unlikely that translators can turn back the clock, so somehow it is a matter of how they manage the forces and to what ends.

Managing the Forces: The Czech School of Dubbing

With its laboratory-like shift from Communism to capitalist social and political systems, the Czech Republic provides an inspiring illustration of translators taking matters into their own hands when flung into the global marketplace. First a little history.[10] For much of the 1930s, MLVs were the region's method of choice. Subtitling eventually became the standard mode of translation, until the early 1950s. Dubbing was reintroduced for children's films in 1949, starting with an obscure Soviet film, and gradually the entire industry followed suit. Television was a decisive factor in the switch to a dubbing culture. Broadcasts began in 1953 with voice-overs. The Czechs started using live dubbing in 1960, again with a Soviet film, Mikhail Sholokhov's Destiny of a Man (Sudba cheloveka, 1959). The era of live dubbing was short-lived as dubbing studios with tape technologies were established in Bernal (Moravia) and Prague. Soon broadcasters and distributors avoided subtitling because audiences rejected the method for voice replacement. The reason was clear: the Czechs had established and nurtured one of the highest-quality dubbing cultures in the world.

A number of factors enabled the establishment of high standards. Broadcasters, translators, and actors strove for fine performances. As dubbing director Zdeněk Coufal put it, "Although we are a small country, we always had high cultural ambitions. Poor technology, but high ambitions." Accordingly, the best Czech actors openly dubbed films. It was never considered something to hide through pseudonyms, so, beginning in the era of live dubbing, even popular stars from the stage participated. Most of the first films in the 1950s were bad Russian productions, but this gave actors a chance to puzzle through the specific challenges of voice acting. By the time higher-quality films arrived in the 1960s, particularly from places like Russia, Hungary, and Poland, the Czechs were prepared to deliver incomparably excellent performances. With the country's finest actors working, a unique synergy developed between dubbing studio, stage, and screen. One veteran actor explained, "We learned a lot about acting from dubbing. In the 1950s, I did a lot of John Osborn's *Entertainment*. I vividly remember doing the dubbing for a show featuring Lawrence Olivier. It was such a great experience. Inspirational—like looking into the kitchen of a great actor."

In the 1960s, dubbers came to realize the unusual level of quality they had achieved. Pan-European translation conferences allowed them to compare their work to other countries (they were, and still are, fond of contrasting Czech dubbing to that of Germany, which is always characterized as technically precise but cold as ice). Foreign producers praised their work, and soon the Czechs developed a reputation for exceptionally fine translation. By the end of the 1960s, an identity developed around this practice and it even took a name: "The Czech School of Dubbing."

It is highly unlikely that this "school" would have developed had Czechoslovakia not been Communist. Both television and cinema were state-run industries. This necessitated certain ideological adjustments; for example, Russian spies in thrillers would be changed into Italians. On the other hand, as long as political land mines were sidestepped in the translation act, dubbers found themselves in an enviably supportive working environment. As translator Jiřina Hradecká remembers it, "Back then it wasn't about profit. After all, it was a Communist system. The pressure to toe the ideological line was often ridiculous—we couldn't even translate the expression 'Oh God!'—but the studio was not thinking about profit, a marketplace, or even speed. We had very reasonable deadlines and the emphasis was on quality." When Hradecká joined the throngs in Wenceslas Square in 1989 to shake her keys, she could not have predicted what was in store for her as a translator.

After the Velvet Revolution, the floodgates opened for decades of film and television from the capitalist world. In the early 1990s, this amounted to more than five thousand films and TV shows a year. Naturally, most of these had sound tracks in English, a language the previous regime's education system had offered but hardly encouraged. The few translators capable of English were quickly overwhelmed by the workload and the overall quality of the Czech School devolved into bland voice-over. There were simply too many films and too little talent. It took four to five years to achieve reasonable quality after the revolution. What is fascinating about the Czech School is the creativity with which they met these challenges. The most significant efforts arose from the Czech Film and Television Association (FICAS). Translators, directors, and actors brainstormed through their problems and came up with two novel ideas.

First, they began consciousness-raising in the reception context. FICAS convinced Prague's major newspaper to publish a new kind of movie review. The organization found five critics to write critiques of foreign film dubbing. The target of their critiques and the standards they used were roughly identical to the conventional film review: direction, acting, writing (translation), editing (sound), and the like. However, these reviews concentrated exclusively on the translations. They educated audiences while simultaneously raising their expectations. This in turn exerted pressure on distributors, producers, and artists to deliver the best dubbing possible.

FICAS designed its second strategy to reward the best dubbers for their hard work. It created the annual Přelouč Awards. Modeled after the Oscars and held in a castle town outside of Prague, the awards sport all the familiar categories: best picture, director, actor, translator, and many more. FICAS brings together a selection committee of eleven professionals—two from FICAS, six from the largest dubbing producers, two from the actors' guild, one from the town—and three co-organizers. The committee meets regularly throughout the year to exchange entry tapes and opinions. In 2004, thirty films underwent this layered review process. The outsider conditioned by the glamour of the Academy Awards or other national competitions may be tempted to dismiss the Přelouč Awards as quaint or kitschy—in effect redisciplining the invisibility of the translator. However, the Czech School takes the awards seriously. Winning a Přelouč is a point of pride and garners the respect of colleagues and employers. In my casual inquiries around Prague, I also found that regular spectators were quite cognizant of the annual awards, and that they admired the work of the Czech ventriloquists.

It could very well be that these strategies to manage for quality will become increasingly important as the 1989 Velvet Revolution recedes into history. At the beginning of the new century, dubbers increasingly dismiss or even ridicule the notion of a Czech "school." This is un-doubtedly connected to the way the conditions of translation finally became integrated into the new market economy and the scene admit-tedly looks more like an "industry" than a "school." Just as dubbers man-aged to bring the post-1989 situation under control, new challenges abound. Reforms of the education system have produced a new genera-tion of English speakers. These are young people enamored of Ameri-can pop culture. They are just starting their careers and perfectly willing to work faster for less money to enter a fascinating career like moving-image translation. Awash in English speakers, the old pros are finding their salaries falling and deadlines shortening. The translation skills of the new generation may be questionable, but when it comes to time and money, they represent formidable competition.

This is mainly because a new kind of company has emerged that pri-oritizes cost cutting and turnover time. The Czech School was nurtured by the cozy environment of the dubbing studios and Czech TV. The lat-ter continues to dub in the old approach. It has a producer managing schedules, budgets, and contracts; a director sits in the studio itself, coaching actors who perform together in the same space (Figure 28). It uses a loop method that painstakingly records short, predetermined seg-ments one at a time. In contrast, the new independent companies clearly emphasize speed. Actors perform alone, even for dialogue. They use nonlinear, computerized systems, not segmented loops. So the actor per-forms a scene continuously until he or she stumbles. With these small independent companies providing the competitive comparison, people increasingly complain about the budgets of Czech TV dubbings. One old hand at the network, Zdeněk Coufal, told me, "Looking at dubbing only through the prism of the market is spoiling it. No artistic discipline is directed by money as dubbing is—although dubbing is the cheapest form of production in television."

Nostalgia for the good old days of the Czech School is widespread. In 2005, I met a group of the best translators and adaptors from the Czech School of dubbing. I explained my fascination for their response to the unusual challenges posed by the transition from planned to market economy, how the entire situation represented a grand laboratory for understanding the economic and industrial dimensions of translation practice. I also expressed my surprise at the palpable desire of many to return to the 1980s. Screenwriter and adaptor Josef Eismann responded,

"Are you surprised that people could be nostalgic for the Communist era? Communism was like kindergarten; you couldn't cross the street, but you were safe."

"The Way a Man Moves, Mirrors the Meaning of His Life"

These are the words of Alfred Adler, a Weimar era psychologist, and they remind us of the ethical dimensions of traffic.[11] As I intimated at the beginning of this book, translation is built into the very substance of the moving image, enmeshed as it is between the structuring forms of the nation and the more disseminating forces of both the local and the global. It follows that we all share a stake in the history, theory, and practice of translation. And because the situation is, as I have argued, historically compromised on every level, I wrote this book with a broad audience in mind. We all need to rethink our relationships to translation—especially if we have yet to contemplate it at all.

This helps explain why the example of the Czech School is so inspiring—translators took matters into their own hands, and audiences recognize it. However, as the business of translation adopts more and more globalized structures and strategies, translators who want to agitate for change find their inevitable geographic separation a seemingly insurmountable obstacle. Furthermore, on the more theoretical points raised in this book, many translators take ambivalent or resistant positions. As my historical inquiry suggests, the common assumptions about good translation are contingent and thoroughly informed by the inertia of practices inherited from the past. Things are indeed changing, but that change often comes hard. And, as I have indicated in this conclusion, many translators have other things to worry about, such as deadlines and paychecks.

Naturally, this book is for audiences and film lovers. I am fascinated by a fan insurrection over Toda Natsuko's 2001 translation of *Lord of the Rings: The Fellowship of the Ring* (as well as a second controversy surrounding her *Phantom of the Opera* [2004] subtitles).[12] Translators often dread the reader who checks their translation. This is something subtitlers rarely need worry about, as audiences are usually content to keep the translator invisible and are pessimistically resigned to the limits imposed by the apparatus. Furthermore, for most of film history, the translation was only available for the split second it hit the projector's light. Fans, however, are a unique segment of the audience with a special passion for the objects of their affection. Japanese fans of the Tolkien trilogy were shocked by Toda's translation. Judging from the way she treated foreshadowing, it became evident that she had not read the original novels. And although director Peter Jackson had gone to great lengths to preserve Tolkien's use of English—and in the same spirit the Japanese translator of the novel used various archaicisms—Toda felt that a more modern, lighter writing style would be more appropriate for young audiences.[13] Web sites analyzing every line of the film proliferated, in both Japanese and English. Finding the distributor unresponsive, they petitioned Peter Jackson directly.[14] Shortly after this, the director dropped a bombshell during a French TV interview. He casually remarked, "We've got someone else to do the Japanese translations this time around." Subsequently, the distributor convinced Jackson that Toda was too powerful and her prestige too profitable to sack. Instead, they teamed her up with the novels' translator to redo the subtitles and collaborate on the two sequels. But this is clearly a highly unusual situation. As I said in the introduction, most spectators do not give dubbing or subtitling a second thought unless overt intransigence inspires the desire for revenge.

I also write for distributors, inspired by this comment by Matthias Müntefering of Deutsche Synchron in Berlin:

> Sometimes we receive requests from small, independent distributors. Their films have not been produced for commercial purposes and are only screened nationally in minor cinemas with 25 copies. Although we know that we will have to wait a long time for payment, we try to help, and regard this as a form of cultural sponsoring. In the case of low-budget films without commercial prospects we try to preserve the cultural content, which deserves to be retained and reflects the interests of only a minority of viewers. This sympathetic attitude is not shared by most other dubbing companies, but, in this line of work, this is a necessary sacrifice if cultural variety is to be maintained.[15]

How enlightened! And how atypical. Distributors and the international divisions of major studios do monitor translators to find the finest and most reliable in their particular market. However, it is the marketplace that typically concerns them. They devote themselves to forms of translation aimed at the most massive of mass audiences, no matter the film. Toda is the pet subtitler for Japanese distributors because she effectively targets a lucrative demographic that even recognizes her name. Historically, there has been a productive tension between producers and their creative staffs. Producers relieve artists from the responsibility of finding and managing the vast treasure demanded by film and television production. It is this tension between producers (who keep things under control) and filmmakers (who make the most of every penny) that often produces great filmmaking. Strikingly, this tension evaporates upon the domestic release of a film. Regrettably, the vast majority of filmmakers leave foreign versions to the vagaries of unrestrained bottom-line thinking.

Of course, it does not have to be that way. In the last instance, I deliver *Cinema Babel* to the artists. It is they who are in a particularly muscular position to agitate for the translations their hard work and talent deserve. Their power is both collective and individual—collective because it takes the form of unions for screenwriters, actors, and directors, and individual because contracts are flexible and fine-tunable by design.

Film lore is filled with stories of filmmakers putting up the good fight to save their films from bottom-line thinking that puts commerce before art. Thus, DVDs are filled with director's cuts that restore the original vision that proved impractical for one reason or another. DVD technology has also given birth to a new practice of directors letting go of their desires, knowing that a director's cut disk with restored scenes or multiple endings is always a possibility, even a lucrative one. Few of these same filmmakers give a thought to the "cuts" performed by all the translators that stand between them and their vast foreign audiences.

Subtitlers, for example, take it as a point of pride that they are masters of condensation. In any form of translation, change is inevitable. Although "loss" is only one way of characterizing the transformative properties of translation, it may be more appropriate for subtitling than any other form of translation. Simultaneously, no matter the degree of loss, there are also all manner of productive transformations. So film artists should learn about translation and find out who these people are. What do they actually know about cinema in the first place? What do they understand about narrative? Performance? Sound? History? The majority of film translators see their task as nothing other than the transference of meaning from one language to another. The unforgiving speed of the projector and the constant moving of mouths are privileged over other aspects of the text before them. This is to say, the craft of the screenplay routinely goes unacknowledged. The tools of the screenwriter—things like foreshadowing, alliteration, metaphor, vulgarity, and so on—go largely untouched by translators striving for the anonymously straightforward prose of the subtitle or dubbing. In subtitling, the craft of the actor, with its timing, force, and volume, goes similarly ignored. If the studios demanded this kind of reduction and restraint of their artists, the creative unions would strike in an instant!

Some filmmakers have cared enough to supervise the translations of their films. Fellini went so far as to sue his French distributor to stop the release of *Intervista* (1987), which he thought distorted and diminished his work. He demanded $18,500 for every day the film was shown in France.[16] After being "burned" when an impoverished translation damaged the overseas reception of one of his films, Martin Scorsese and his long-time editor Thelma Schoonmaker now examine the subtitle lists before they are irrevocably committed to celluloid.[17]

Filmmakers must involve themselves in translation because the contribution of the translator is every bit as profound as that of the screenwriter, actor, or director. The translators are creating a new text from their original films, and there are myriad cultural, industrial, and ideological pressures exerting themselves on that act of creation. Thus, it behooves artists to understand the process and get involved if they care at all about their work.[18] They should make themselves available to translators, demand the best, and participate in the process like Kubrick, Fellini, and Scorsese. They should adopt the respectful attitude demonstrated by Hitchcock and Truffaut and develop relationships with their translators, as do novelists and poets. After all, in an age when no film is complete until it crosses the frontier of language, it is the translator who has the last word.

Global cinema is the translator's cinema.

Notes

Notes to Introduction

1. "Saban, SAG Struggle over *Digimon* Dispute," *AWN* (April 14, 200): www .news.awn.com/index.php?newsitem_no=2485.

2. The first film studies book dedicated to film translation would probably be Atom Egoyan's and Ian Balfour's fascinating *Subtitles: On the Foreignness of Film* (Cambridge: MIT Press, 2004). However, it would seem to be difficult to get authors to actually write about translation as such. Roughly half of the contributors write primarily about the idea of foreignness. The most compelling work on film translation thus far comes from Nataša Ďurovičová: "*Los Toquis,* or Urban Babel," in *Global Cities,* ed. Patrice Petro and Linda Krause (New Brunswick, N.J.: Rutgers University Press, 2003), 71–86; online at *Rouge* 7 (2005): www.rouge.com.au/7/ urban_babel.html; "Local Ghosts: Dubbing in Early Sound Cinema," *Moveast* 9: www.epa.oszk.hn/00300/00375/00001/durovicova.html; "Introduction," *CINEMA&Cie* 4 (spring 2004): 7–16; and "Translating America: The Hollywood Multilinguals 1919–1933," in *Sound Theory Sound Practice,* ed. Rick Altman (New York: Routledge, 1992), 138–53, 261–66.

3. For excellent bibliographies collecting this work, see Yves Gambier's appendix to Henrik Gottlieb's entry "Subtitling" in *The Encyclopedia of Translation Studies,* ed. Mona Baker (New York: Routledge, 1998), 244–48; and Zoe de Linde and Neil Kay, *The Semiotics of Subtitling* (Manchester: St. Jerome Publishing, 1999). Yves Gambier also lays out the recent history of this heterogeneous research in his introduction to a special issue of the *Translator* on screen translation: "Screen Transadaptation: Perception and Reception," *Translator* 9.2 (2003): 171–89.

4. Benjamin J. Barber, *Jihad vs. McWorld: How Globalism and Tribalism Are Reshaping the World* (New York: Ballantine Books, 1996).

5. Eric Cazdyn, "A New Line in the Geometry," in Egoyan and Balfour, *Subtitles,* 416.

6. Ritva Leppihalme, *Culture Bumps: An Empirical Approach to the Translation of Allusions* (Clevedon, U.K.: Multilingual Matters, 1997); Lawrence Venuti, *The Scandals of Translation: Towards an Ethics of Difference* (New York: Routledge, 1998).

7. Koichi Iwabuchi, *Recentering Globalization: Popular Culture and Japanese Transnationalism* (Durham, N.C.: Duke University Press, 2002), 24–28.

8. Cazdyn, "A New Line in the Geometry," 417.

9. Filmmaker Jon Jost actually demonstrates the potential of the running subtitle for interlingual translation at the beginning of *Six Easy Pieces* (2000): "I found that putting the translation in a continuous crawl produced a kind of violence. The text competed for primacy with the image to the point that one couldn't watch one without losing the other. It was very discomforting" (conversation with director). Elsewhere in Jost's film, we find other kinds of subtitling strategies. For example, in a scene where two people swim in and out of the frame, Jost fades his subtitles to near invisibility as the swimmers reach the end of their laps and their dialogue becomes virtually inaudible. He also plays with font and positioning in this film that explores the new aesthetics made possible (and affordable) by digital video. This is precisely the kind of emergent subtitling practice I call abusive in chapter 5.

10. Helmut Lethen, *Cool Conduct: The Culture of Distance in Weimar Germany*, trans. Don Reneau (Berkeley: University of California Press, 2002), 26. I am thankful to Alexander Zhalten for directing me to Lethen's work.

11. Ibid., 27.

12. Tom Rowe, "Help, I've Been Dubbed," *Weekly Variety* (May 3, 1972): 99.

13. Nataša Ďurovičová gives a sense for the debates that took place in Europe with the coming of sound in "Translating America."

14. *Shukan Asahi* (November 24, 1957).

15. Jeff Matthews, "Hey, You Sound Just like Marlon Brando, Robert Redford and Paul Newman!" (www.faculty.ed.umuc.edu/~jmatthew/Dubbing.htm).

16. Gerald Blank, "Dubbing Protest," *New York Times*, July 7, 1966, D5.

17. India is a country that has resisted the domination of American cinema. One reason is probably that until the enormous success of a dubbed *Jurassic Park* (1993), the miniscule, middle-class audience for English-language films preferred subtitling. A generalized shift to dubbing is currently allowing Hollywood to make inroads in the Indian market. See Don Groves and Uma da Cunha, "India's Dino-Size Legacy," *Weekly Variety* (August 15–21, 1994): 41–42.

18. Paul Rotha, "Paul Rotha," *Films and Filming* (January 1967): 66.

19. Bosley Crowther, "Subtitles Must Go! Let's Have Dubbed English Dialogue on Foreign-Language Films," *New York Times*, August 7, 1960, sec. 2, X1, 3.

20. Philip K. Scheuer, "On Foreign Films: To Dub Is to Flub—Critic Crowther's Argument Raises Storm of Disapproval," *Los Angeles Times*, September 26, 1960, C9.

21. For an excellent example, listen to the second explanatory audio track on the American DVD of *Godzilla 2000* (*Gojira ni-sen mireniamu*, 1999) released by Columbia Tri-Star.

22. Vincent Canby, "A Rebel Lion Breaks Out," *New York Times*, March 27, 1983, H22.

23. Egil Törnqvist, "Fixed Pictures, Changing Words: Subtitling and Dubbing the Film *Babettes Gæstebud*," *TijdSchrift voor Skandinavistiek* 16.1 (1995): 63.

24. Bosley Crowther, "Should Foreign Films Be Dubbed?" *New York Times*, August 28, 1966, D14. This is the critic's response to a letter to the editor, itself provoked by his article "Tower of Babel Again," *New York Times*, August 14, 1966, D1.

25. Mike Nowak, "Thinking about Disterbing Subtitles," The-inbetween.com (February 1, 2004): www.the-inbetween.com/archives/2004_02.php. One of the com-

ments to this blog post points to a key pleasure here: "I tend to think that crap dialogue is better under a haze of nostalgia. That's why 'All Your Base' got so popular. When that stuff ceases to be the norm, it opens up the possibility of someone recalling it and concentrating the badness in a way that's more pleasurable than being subjected to it over and over." "All Your Base" refers to the most famous English localization of a Japanese video game. One of the most charming lines was from an alien descending from space to conquer the Earth: "All your base are belong to us." This line became a cult phenomenon on the Internet, and then spilled out onto material world signs and secret messages embedded in the code of popular software packages. The phenomenon attained renewed vigor during the post 9/11 Bush administration.

26. We could also say that fans find analogous pleasure in the dubbings of pre-1980s kung fu films and Japanese monster movies. Won't most viewers agree that they are vastly superior in their sloppily dubbed versions?

27. Sharptongue's Theatre (http://members.ozemail.com.au/~sharptongue/hksubs.html). A similar kind of list can be found on paper in Stefan Hammond and Mike Wilkins's *Sex and Zen: Hong Kong Cinema* (London: Titan Books, 1997). The new frontier for misprision collection is the localization business for the video-gaming industry. See note 15.

28. Michael X. Ferraro, "Eeee-Yow! That Translation Hurt!" *Los Angeles Times*, August 2, 1998, 24.

29. Tejaswini Niranjana, *Siting Translation: History, Post-Structuralism, and the Colonial Context* (Berkeley: University of California Press, 1992); Eric Cheyfitz, *The Poetics of Imperialism: Translation and Colonization from* The Tempest *to* Tarzan (New York: Oxford University Press, 1991); Douglas Robinson, *Translation and Taboo* (DeKalb: Northern Illinois University Press, 1996) and *Translation and Empire: Postcolonial Theories Explained* (Manchester: St. Jerome Press, 1997); Lydia Liu, *Translingual Practice: Literature, National Culture, and Translated Modernity* (Stanford, Calif.: Stanford University Press, 1995); and Vicente Rafael, *Contracting Colonialism: Translation and Christian Conversion in Tagalog Society under Early Spanish Rule* (Durham, N.C.: Duke University Press, 1993). Robinson has summarized these writers in and how they fit into the greater landscape of translation studies in his elegant little 1997 book, so I do not feel compelled to recap their work here.

30. George Steinar, *After Babel: Aspects of Language and Translation* (New York: Oxford University Press, 1975); Lawrence Venuti, *The Scandals of Translation* (New York: Routledge, 1998) and *The Translator's Invisibility* (New York: Routledge, 1995); Antoine Berman, *The Experience of the Foreign: Culture and Translation in Romantic Germany,* trans. S. Heyvaert (Albany: State University of New York Press, 1992).

31. Vachel Lindsay, *The Art of the Motion Picture* (New York: Modern Library Edition, 2000).

32. Miriam Hansen, "Fallen Women, Rising Stars, New Horizons: Shanghai Silent Film as Vernacular Modernism," *Film Quarterly* 54.1 (fall 2000): 12.

33. Ibid., 13.

34. Hamid Naficy, *An Accented Cinema: Exilic and Diasporic Filmmaking* (Princeton, N.J.: Princeton University Press, 2001). Naficy attends more specifically to the question of translation practices in "Epistolarity and Textuality in Accented Films," in Egoyan and Balfour, *Subtitles,* 131–51.

35. Walter Wanger, "120,000 American Ambassadors," *Foreign Affairs* 18.1 (October 1939): 45–59.

36. Ella Shohat and Robert Stam, *Unthinking Eurocentrism: Multiculturalism and the Media* (New York: Routledge, 1994), 191.

37. *Hitchhiker's Guide to the Galaxy: The Guide*, www.bbc.co.uk/cult/hitchhikers/ guide/babelfish.shtml.

38. David Trottier, *The Screenwriter's Bible: A Complete Guide to Writing, Formatting, and Selling Your Script*, 3d revised and expanded ed. (Los Angeles: Silman-James Press, 1998).

39. Linda Williams, "Introduction," in *Viewing Positions: Ways of Seeing Film*, ed. Linda Williams (New Brunswick, N.J.: Rutgers University Press, 1994), 11–12. See also Tom Gunning, "The Cinema of Attractions: Early Film, Its Spectator, and the Avant-Garde," in *Early Cinema: Space Frame Narrative*, ed. Thomas Elsaesser (London: British Film Institute, 1990), 56–62; Tom Gunning, "An Aesthetics of Astonishment: Early Film and the (In)Credulous Spectator," *Art and Text* 34 (spring 1989): 31–45. Gunning himself presages Williams's argument when he writes, "In fact, the cinema of attractions does not disappear with the dominance of narrative, but rather goes underground, both into certain avant-garde practices and as a component of narrative films, more evident in some genres (e.g. the musical) than in others" (Gunning, "Cinema of Attractions," 57).

40. Laura Marks, *The Skin of Film: Intercultural Cinema, Embodiment, and the Senses* (Durham, N.C.: Duke University Press, 2000), 105.

41. I owe this observation to Bob Rehak of Indiana University, who responded to my query for examples on Screen-L (June 30, 2004). Thanks also to Donald Larsson and Dava Simpson from the same thread.

42. Margaret Morse, *Virtualities: Television, Media Art, and Cyberculture* (Indianapolis: Indiana University Press, 1998).

43. This "sober" representation of reality is most forcefully theorized by Bill Nichols in *Representing Reality* (Bloomington: Indiana University Press, 1991).

44. Steven Lee Myers, "A Silent Act of Rebellion Raises a Din in Ukraine," *New York Times*, November 29, 2004, A12.

1. Interpreters with Attitude

1. Lawrence Venuti, *The Translator's Invisibility* (New York: Routledge, 1995), 2.

2. Michael Watt, "'Do You Speak Christian?'—Dubbing and the Manipulation of the Cinematic Experience," *Bright Lights Film Journal* 29 (July 2000): www .brightlightsfilm.com/29/dubbing1.html.

3. Anthony Pym, "Interpreters at the O. J. Simpson Trial," *Translator* 5.2 (1999): 265–83.

4. Erving Goffman, *Forms of Talk* (Oxford: Basil Blackwell, and Philadelphia: University of Pennsylvania Press, 1981). Also influential was P. Brown and S. Levinson, *Politeness: Some Universals in Language Use* (Cambridge: Cambridge University Press, 1987).

5. The breakthrough book in translation study was probably Basil Hatim and Ian Mason, *Discourse and the Translator* (London: Longman, 1990). Another work I have found particularly useful is Cecilia Wadensjö, *Interpreting as Interaction* (London and New York: Addison-Wesley Longman, 1998).

6. Francesco Straniero Sergio, "The Interpreter on the (Talk) Show," *Translator* 5.2 (1999): 308.

7. Goffman, *Forms of Talk,* 67.

8. Straniero Sergio, "The Interpreter on the (Talk) Show," 307–8.

9. Letter, Kurosawa Akira to Elmo Williams, n.d. (Elmo Williams Collection, Folder 67; Margaret Herrick Library, Academy of Motion Pictures Arts and Sciences).

10. Letter, Elmo Williams to Darryl Zanuck, June 23, 1967 (Elmo Williams Collection, Folder 159; Margaret Herrick Library, Academy of Motion Pictures Arts and Sciences).

11. Notes from story conference, May 8, 1967 (Elmo Williams Collection, Folder 159; Margaret Herrick Library, Academy of Motion Pictures Arts and Sciences).

12. *Runaway Train* was another Kurosawa coproduction that went sour. It was eventually completed in the 1980s by Russian director Andrei Konchalovsky.

13. Letter, Aoyagi Tetsuro to Elmo Williams, April 11, 1968 (Elmo Williams Collection, Folder 67; Margaret Herrick Library, Academy of Motion Pictures Arts and Sciences), 4–5.

14. Letter, Aoyagi Tetsuro to Elmo Williams, April 11, 1968 (Elmo Williams Collection, Folder 67; Margaret Herrick Library, Academy of Motion Pictures Arts and Sciences), 4.

15. Report, Elmo Williams, Week October 28–November 1 (Elmo Williams Collection, Folder 156; Margaret Herrick Library, Academy of Motion Pictures Arts and Sciences).

16. Report, Elmo Williams, Week December 2–December 15 (Elmo Williams Collection, Folder 156; Margaret Herrick Library, Academy of Motion Pictures Arts and Sciences).

17. Stuart Galbraith III, *The Emperor and the Wolf: The Lives and Films of Akira Kurosawa and Toshiro Mifune* (New York: Faber and Faber, 2002), 459. An exception is Tajima Ryoichi, but he read Ito Kosuke's book. See Tajima Ryoichi, "Kurosawa Akira Eiga no Henbo— *Tora Tora Tora!* no Kantoku Kainin Jiken o Megute," *Nihon Daigaku Geijutsu Gakubu Kiyo* 23 (1993): 248–35.

18. Shirai Yoshio, "*Tora Tora Tora!* to Kurosawa Akira Mondai 5," *Kinema Junpo* 493 (April 15, 1969): 27.

19. Shirai Yoshio, "*Tora Tora Tora!* to Kurosawa Akira Mondai 12," *Kinema Junpo* 505 (September 15, 1969): 33.

20. Perhaps the sole exception was publicist Ito Kosuke. See his *Kurosawa "Ran" no Sekai* (Tokyo: Kodansha, 1985). In a series of interviews by Kurosawa's longtime staff member Nogami Teruyo (who was excluded from this production because Kurosawa felt a war film was no place for a woman), seven of the core staff continued to defend Kurosawa's behavior while placing blame on American intolerance of cultural difference. See *Akira Kurosawa: Kuno to Sozo,* ed. Nogami Teruyo (Tokyo: Kinema Junpo, 2001).

21. A vague report of this incident was used by Sato to contrast Kurosawa's demand for precision and authenticity with Hollywood's business as usual, where the bottom line determines everything.

22. Insurance report, Elmo Williams, January 7, 1969 (Elmo Williams Collection, Folder 157; Margaret Herrick Library, Academy of Motion Pictures Arts and Sciences), 13–14.

23. Report, Elmo Williams, Week November 4–November 8 (Elmo Williams Collection, Folder 156; Margaret Herrick Library, Academy of Motion Pictures Arts and Sciences).

24. Insurance report, Elmo Williams, 6.

25. Shirai Yoshio, "*Tora Tora Tora!* to Kurosawa Akira Mondai 14," *Kinema Junpo* 502 (August 15, 1969): 30.

26. Ibid., 31.

27. "Summary of the First Production Meeting between the Kurosawa Staff and the Fox Staff Set Up by Elmo Williams, December 4, 1968," supplement to insurance report, Elmo Williams, January 7, 1969 (Elmo Williams Collection, Folder 157; Margaret Herrick Library, Academy of Motion Pictures Arts and Sciences), 1.

28. Shirai Yoshio, "*Tora Tora Tora!* to Kurosawa Akira Mondai 6," *Kinema Junpo* 505 (May 1, 1969): 33.

29. Shirai Yoshio, "*Tora Tora Tora!* to Kurosawa Akira," *Kinema Junpo* 489 (February 15, 1969): 22.

30. Ibid., 23.

31. Ibid.

32. "Summary of the First Production Meeting between the Kurosawa Staff and the Fox Staff Set Up by Elmo Williams, December 4, 1968," 3.

33. Shirai Yoshio, "*Tora Tora Tora!* to Kurosawa Akira Mondai 3," *Kinema Junpo* 491 (March 15, 1969): 23.

34. Ibid.

35. This would be the infamous white uniform incident. Standard practice for costumes is to always have at least one identical spare on hand. Matsue claimed that Aoyagi told the wardrobe man to make only one formal white uniform, against his wishes, just to cut corners and save some money (ibid., 24–25). However, according to the American line producers and Kurosawa's own crew, it was actually Kurosawa's doing. As Williams relates the story, "The wardrobe man told me that Kurosawa had originally ordered two white uniforms for Yamamoto. Then, just a week before shooting started, Kurosawa had insisted on canceling the order for one of the uniforms. The wardrobe man thought this highly irregular but fearing Kurosawa, he cancelled the second uniform. Later on, on his own initiative, he decided that this was foolish and placed a second order without telling Kurosawa about it. Kurosawa did not check Yamamoto's uniform until the day that Yamamoto appeared on the set in it. Kurosawa took one look at the uniform and immediately complained about four small, black threads showing where one of Yamamoto's naval decorations had been attached to the tunic. The wardrobe man immediately offered to remove the four threads, but Kurosawa insisted that the holes where the threads had been would then show and that the uniform was not usable under these conditions. He now asked for the two additional uniforms and was told that there was only one other uniform ready and this was only available because the wardrobe man had ordered it on his own initiative. Kurosawa immediately shut the wardrobe man up and told him that he wanted no backtalk from him, that from now on all the wardrobe man had to do was to see that there were three complete uniforms for everyone ready at all times and that these uniforms must stand up to Kurosawa's most careful inspection" (insurance report, Elmo Williams, 8).

36. Letter, Elmo Williams to Matsue Yoichi, July 18, 1969 (Elmo Williams Collec-

tion, Folder 67; Margaret Herrick Library, Academy of Motion Pictures Arts and Sciences).

37. Shirai Yoshio, "*Tora Tora Tora!* to Kurosawa Akira Mondai 12," 33.

38. Letter, Aoyagi Tetsuro to Elmo Williams, March 3, 1969 (Elmo Williams Collection, Folder 67; Margaret Herrick Library, Academy of Motion Pictures Arts and Sciences), 3.

39. Telex, Darryl Zanuck to Elmo Williams, March 9, 1970 (Elmo Williams Collection, Folder 142; Margaret Herrick Library, Academy of Motion Pictures Arts and Sciences).

40. Letter, Aoyagi Tetsuro to Elmo Williams, April 28, 1969 (Elmo Williams Collection, Folder 67; Margaret Herrick Library, Academy of Motion Pictures Arts and Sciences), 1.

41. François Truffaut, "Introduction," in *Hitchcock* (New York: Simon and Schuster, 1967), 15.

42. Winston Dixon Wheeler, *The Early Film Criticism of François Truffaut* (Bloomington and Indianapolis: University of Indiana Press, 1993), 91.

43. Letter, François Truffaut to Alfred Hitchock, June 2, 1962 (Alfred Hitchcock Collection, Folder 1482; Margaret Herrick Library, Academy of Motion Picture Arts and Sciences).

44. Hedda Hopper, "Entertainment," *Los Angeles Times*, August 20, 1962, C16.

45. "The Talk of the Town," *New Yorker* (October 31, 1963): 45–46.

46. Letter, Helen Scott to Alfred Hitchcock, October 9, 1962 (Alfred Hitchcock Collection, Folder 1482; Margaret Herrick Library, Academy of Motion Picture Arts and Sciences).

47. Truffaut, "Introduction," 8.

48. Dilys Powell, "The Importance of International Film Festivals," *Film Review* 3 (1947): 60.

49. Blake Murdoch, "'Living Subtitlers' Cross Fest's Great Divide," *Hollywood Reporter* (May 21–23, 1999): 9, 52.

50. Bill Nichols, *Representing Reality* (Bloomington: Indiana University Press, 1991).

2. The Circulation of Ideas

1. Giorgio Bertellini, "Introduction: Early Italian Cinema," *Film History* 12 (2000): 235.

2. See Iris Barry, review of *Documentary Film*, *Saturday Review* (August 12, 1939), which discusses how people are nervous about Rotha's politics and his immodest pontification. See also Frank Evans, "How the Film Can Help Democracy," *Evening Chronicle* (Newcastle on Tyne) (May 12, 1939), a book review that discusses only documentary's social function (nothing on style), and Elizabeth Laine, "About Documentary Films," *Transcript* (Boston) (June 10, 1939), "*Documentary Film*," *Times*, August 11, 1939, "*Documentary Film*," *Lady* (August 3, 1939).

3. Imamura's postwar *Introduction to Film Theory* contains the best Japanese overview of Rotha. In contrast to the wartime debates, its reasoned, overall critique reveals how narrowly the discussion was focused in 1940. This suggests how other

issues were at stake besides the one explicitly on the table in 1938. See Imamura Taihei, *Eiga Riron Nyumon* (Tokyo: Itagaki Shoten, 1952), 184.

4. Paul Rotha, *Dokyumentarii Eiga*, revised and expanded ed., trans. Atsugi Taka (Tokyo: Misuzu Shobo, 1960); Paul Rotha, *Dokyumentarii Eiga*, revised and expanded ed., trans. Atsugi Taka (Tokyo: Misuzu Shobo, 1976); Paul Rotha, *Dokyumentarii Eiga*, refurbished ed., trans. Atsugi Taka (Tokyo: Miraisha, 1995). The 1960 edition involved a fairly extensive revision of the translation itself, although this translation has its own problems. The 1995 outing is billed as a "refurbished edition" *(shinsoban)*, but the only apparent difference is a new color on the jacket.

5. Nothing in his personal files suggests that Rotha knew what the Japanese thought of his work. Quite the opposite, he clearly shared fears about the menace Japan posed to the West. In a letter to Eric Knight written at the height of his prestige in Japan, Rotha wrote, "I agree that the sooner America sees her immediate danger the better and that now more than ever is the time to come into this business... She actually (it sounds) trying to appease the Japs which seems odd after all the examples of appeasement she's had before her *[sic]*. I agree with all your beliefs about the cementing of the English speaking peoples—at least that would be a beginning basis for reconstruction" (Letter, Paul Rotha to Eric Knight, August 28, 1941 [2001 Box 26; Paul Rotha Collection, UCLA]). After the war (in the 1960s, from the look of the paper and adjacent documents), in a statement written to someone in Japan, Rotha wrote, "One day, perhaps, if I am still alive, I will come to visit to the land of Hokusai and Kurosawa and Ozu" (no mention of any Japanese documentarists, let alone his translation by Atsugi) (Letter, Paul Rotha to unspecified recipient in Japan, n.d. [2001 Box 82, Folder 3; Paul Rotha Collection, UCLA]).

6. Paul Rotha, *Bunka Eiga-ron*, 1st Japanese ed., trans. Atsugi Taka (Tokyo: Dai'ichi Geibunsha, 1938), 108.

7. Rotha, *Dokyumentarii Eiga* (1960), 68.

8. In her postwar autobiography, Atsugi Taka's embarrassment for rushing the translation prematurely to print is clear. See Atsugi Taka, *Josei Dokyumentarisuto no Kaiso* (Tokyo: Domesu Shuppan, 1991), 103–5.

9. Okamoto Masao, *Bunka Eiga Jidai + Jujiya Eigabu no Hitobito* (Tokyo: Unitsushin, 1996), 62–63.

10. Atsugi also married Yuiken philosopher Mori Koichi.

11. Rotha, *Bunka Eigaron* (1938). The original volume is Paul Rotha, *Documentary Film* (London: Faber and Faber, 1935).

12. Paul Rotha, *Bunka Eigaron*, 3d Japanese ed., trans. Atsugi Taka (Kyoto: Dai'ichi Geibunsha, 1939).

13. Paul Rotha, *"Bunka Eigaron* Josetsu," trans. Ueno Ichiro, *Eiga Kenkyu* 1 (1939): 54–84 (covers chapter 1 in Rotha's *Documentary Film*); Paul Rotha, "Dokyumentarii no Jyakuha to Sono Shiteki Kosatsu," trans. Ueno Ichiro, *Eiga Kenkyu* 2 (1939): 50–85 (covers Rotha's chapter 2). Although there were many reports on the British documentary movement, Ueno probably wrote the best; this study certainly contributed to his translation: Ueno Ichiro, "Eikoku no Bunka Eiga," *Eiga Kenkyu* 1 (1939): 146–61.

14. Paul Rotha, "Bunka Eiga-ron," *Chosa Shiryo* 4 (Kyoto: Toho Kyoto Satsueijo, undated; Makino Mamoru collection). This mimeographed publication completes the Ueno translation, covering the final chapter 4.

15. Makino Mamoru, "Kiroku Eiga no Rironteki Doko o Otte 41," *Unitsushin* (June 19, 1978).

16. Tanikawa Yoshio, *Dokyumentarii Eiga no Genten—Sono Shiso to Hoho*, 3d ed. (Tokyo: Futosha, 1990), 194–95.

17. Rotha, *Documentary Film* (1935), 70.

18. Okada Shinkichi, *Eiga Bunkenshi* (Tokyo: Dai Nippon Eiga Kyokai, 1943), 39.

19. Tsumura Hideo, "Poru Ruta no Eigaron Hihan—Sono Cho 'Documentary Film' ni Tsuite," *Shineiga* 9.12 (November 1939): 17.

20. Takagiba Tsutomu, "Kyoko no Riron—Tsumura Hideo-shi no 'Poru Ruta Hihan' o Yomu," *Bunka Eiga Kenkyu* 3.1 (January 1940): 525–28.

21. Kubota Tatsuo, *Bunka Eiga no Hohoron* (Kyoto: Dai'ichi Geibunsha, 1940).

22. Rotha, *Documentary Film* (1935), 156.

23. Atsugi Taka's personal copy of Rotha, *Bunka Eiga-ron* (1938), 150–52 (Atsugi Taka Collection, National Film Center of the National Museum of Modern Art, Tokyo). Original text is Rotha, *Documentary Film* (1935), 135–36.

24. Ibid., 132. Original text is Rotha, *Documentary Film* (1935), 108.

25. Ibid., 198. Original text is Rotha, *Documentary Film* (1935), 143.

26. I have deposited this book in the Makino Collection (Columbia University).

27. Sekino Yoshio, "Tadashiki 'Documentary' Riron no Ninshiki no Tame Ni," *Bunka Nyusu Weekly* 110 (January 18, 1940): 1 (Makino Collection).

28. Sekino Yoshio, "*Kyo Made no Eiga* to Ashita no Eiga (1)," *Bunka Eiga Kenkyu* 3.2 (February 1940): 8–11; Sekino Yoshio, "*Kyo Made no Eiga* to Ashita no Eiga (2)," *Bunka Eiga Kenkyu* 3.3 (March 1940): 58–60; Sekino Yoshio, "*Kyo Made no Eiga* to Ashita no Eiga (3)," *Bunka Eiga Kenkyu* 3.4 (April 1940): 109–12; Sekino Yoshio, "*Kyo Made no Eiga* to Ashita no Eiga (4)," *Bunka Eiga Kenkyu* 3.5 (May 1940): 176–79; Sekino Yoshio, "Dokyumentariiron Kento no Tame Ni (1)," *Bunka Eiga Kenkyu* 3.6 (June 1940): 236–39; Sekino Yoshio, "Dokyumentariiron Kento no Tame Ni (2)," *Bunka Eiga Kenkyu* 3.7 (July 1940): 304–7; Sekino Yoshio, "Dokyumentariiron Kento no Tame Ni (3)," *Bunka Eiga Kenkyu* 3.10 (October 1940): 563–67. The other major series of articles by Sekino is Sekino Yoshio, "Poru Rosa: Dokyumentarii Eiga no Sonogono Shinten 1," *Nihon Eiga* 5.7 (July 1940): 22–29; Sekino Yoshio, "Poru Rosa: Dokyumentarii Eiga no Sonogo no Shinten 2," *Nihon Eiga* 5.8 (August 1940): 68–73, 120; Sekino Yoshio, "Poru Rosa: Dokyumentarii Eiga no Sonogo no Shinten 3," *Nihon Eiga* 5.10 (October 1940): 72–77, 14.

29. Sekino Yoshio, *Eiga Kyoiku no Riron* (Tokyo: Shogakkan, 1942).

30. Rotha, *Documentary Film* (1935), 66; Sekino, *Eiga Kyoiku no Riron*, 163. By way of contrast, Ueno Ichiro's translation is complete and correct in Rotha, "*Bunka Eigaron Josetsu*," trans. Ueno, 79.

31. STS, or the "Square Table Society," was an influential study group composed of a variety of intellectuals interested in film education. They published their own independent journal: *Eiga Zehi* and *Eiga Dai-issen*. For a history, see Makino Mamoru's column in *Unitsushin* between September 26, 1977 and November 21, 1977.

32. For an extensive discussion of Sekino's Children's Film Days, see Gonda Yasunosuke, *Minshugorakuron* (Tokyo: Ganshodo Shoten, 1931), especially 309–28.

33. Yamada Hideyoshi, *Eiga Kokusaku no Zenshin* (Tokyo: Koseisho, 1940), 216.

34. Rotha, *Documentary Film* (1935), 48.

35. Rotha, *Bunka Eigaron*, trans. Atsugi (1938), 34.

36. Rotha, "*Bunka Eigaron* Josetsu," trans. Ueno, 56.

37. Sekino, *Eiga Kyoiku no Riron*, 136.

38. One of the young scholars was Asanuma Keiji, who is Japan's best-known film semiotician.

39. Further evidence that Atsugi did not recognize the mistranslation can be found in the various copies she deposited at the Film Center. None of them contains any corrections here, although she did underline the *adjacent* sentence in her 1960 edition.

40. This is not the only place where Atsugi's misprision reveals the nature of her (mis)reading of Rotha. Her translation provides many examples. Most critics refer only to how "bad" it is. For example, in the afterward to his *Eiga Riron Nyumon* Imamura Taihei points out how thankful we should be for the work of translators like Iijima Tadashi, Sasaki Norio, and Atsugi Taka. He also warns the readers to be cautious when it comes to trusting translation; ultimately, they must refer to the original, as Imamura has. He cites one example of misprision, and he singles out Atsugi: Rotha refers to some "modern authorities" who call dialectical materialism "out-of-date," but Atsugi translates this *saishin* ("latest" or "newest"). Although Imamura picks a good example of mistranslation he—like everyone else—does not ask what factors led to this misreading. It does seem rather obvious. See Rotha, *Documentary Film* (1935), 182; Rotha, *Documentary Film*, trans. Atsugi (1938), 270; Imamura, *Eiga Riron Nyumon*, 184.

41. Letter, Paul Rotha to Eric Knight, November 8, 1938 (Paul Rotha Collection, 2001 Box 26, UCLA).

42. This is how the great documentarist Kamei Fumio described his own relationship to Rotha's book. Various people had criticized *Fighting Soldiers* by claiming that Kamei was Rotha's disciple. However, Akimoto Takeshi introduced the original book to Toho studios when Kamei was in China shooting the film. Rotha was less a guidebook than simple inspiration, especially the second half of the book on practical matters (this was the section translated and circulated within Toho). See Kamei Fumio, Akimoto Takeshi, Ueno Kozo, Ishimoto Tokichi, Tanaka Yoshiji, "Nihon Bunka Eiga no Shoki Kara Kyo o Kataru Zadankai," *Bunka Eiga Kenkyu* 3.2 (February 1940): 16–27.

43. Kuwano Shigeru, *Dokyumentarii no Sekai—Sozoryoku to Hohoron* (Tokyo: Simul Shuppankai, 1973), 201–2.

44. Ibid., 201.

45. Shirai Shigeru and Kano Ryuichi, "Kameraman Jinsei," in *Kinema Seishun*, ed. Iwamoto Kenji and Saiki Tomonori (Tokyo: Libroport, 1988), 73.

46. See Takagiba Tsutomu, "*Dokyumentarii Firumu* no Oboegaki," *Bunka Eiga Kenkyu* 3.4 (April 1940): 112–13; Atsugi Taka, "Story-film no Yakugo ni Tsuite," *Bunka Eiga Kenkyu* 3.4 (April 1940): 118–19; Takagiba Tsutomu, "Eiga no Honshitsu ni Kan Suru Ronmo," *Bunka Eiga Kenkyu* 3.10 (October 1940): 577–80; Kubota Tatsuo, "Gekiteki Yoso to Kirokuteki Yoso," *Bunka Eiga Kenkyu* 3.10 (October 1940): 575–76.

47. See, for example, Ueno Kozo, "Eiga ni Okeru Geijutsu to Kagaku—Bunka Eigaron no Kisoteki Mondai 1," *Nihon Eiga* 5.2 (February 1940): 24–35; Ueno Kozo, "Eiga ni Okeru Geijutsu to Kagaku—Bunka Eigaron no Kisoteki Mondai 2," *Nihon Eiga* 5.3 (March 1940): 25–35.

48. Ueno, "Eiga ni Okeru Geijutsu to Kagaku—Bunka Eigaron no Kisoteki Mondai 1," 33.

49. Atsugi Taka, "Kiroku Eiga no Kyoko—'Jijitsu' wa Sono Mama 'Shinjitsu' de wa Nai," *Nihon Eiga* 5.2 (November 1940): 82.

50. Atsugi discusses this phenomenon in her translator's afterward to the 1960 edition of *Documentary Film*. See Atsugi Taka, "Yakusha no Atogaki," in Rotha, *Dokyumentarii Eiga*, trans. See Atsugi (1960), 329–34.

51. Tanikawa, *Dokyumentarii Eiga no Genten*, 195.

52. See Kamei Fumio, "Bunka Eiga Geppyo," *Nihon Eiga* 5.12 (December 1940): 24–26. Kamei et al., "Nihon Bunka Eiga no Shoki Kara Kyo o Kataru Zadankai," 16–27.

3. Voices of the Silents

1. "Scattered Meller with More Subtitles Than Scenes," *Wid's* 4.6 (February 7, 1918): 922.

2. Quoted in "The International Cinema," *New York Times*, May 16, 1920, X4.

3. Eileen Bowser, *The Transformation of Cinema, 1907–1915* (Berkeley: University of California Press, 1994), 23. See also Charles Musser, "American Vitagraph," in *Film before Griffith*, ed. John Fell (Berkeley: University of California Press, 1983), x.

4. Charles Musser, *The Emergence of Cinema: The American Screen to 1907* (Berkeley: University of California Press, 1994), 364, 412.

5. Bowser, *The Transformation of Cinema*, 232.

6. Denise J. Youngblood, *Soviet Cinema in the Silent Era, 1918–1935* (Ann Arbor, Mich.: UMI Press, 1980), 23.

7. A historical summary this short necessarily results in the roughest of periodizations. For a nuanced look at the problem, the best place to start would be Ben Brewster's "Periodization in Early Cinema," in *American Cinema's Transitional Era* (Berkeley: University of California Press, 2004), 66–75.

8. My sources in this section are wide-ranging, but I am particularly indebted to Musser, *The Emergence of Cinema*; Barry Salt, *Film Style and Technique: History and Analysis*, 2d ed. (London: Starword, 1992); Kristin Thompson, "Narration: The Functions of Intertitles," in David Bordwell, Janet Staiger, and Kristin Thompson, *The Classical Hollywood Cinema: Film Style and Mode of Production to 1960* (London: Routledge, 1985), 183–89; and Francesco Pitassio and Leonardo Quaresima, eds., *Scittura e immagine: La didascalia nel cinema muto* (Udine: Forum Udine, 1998). One can get a sense for the semiotics of intertitles just before their demise in Brad Chisholm, "Reading Intertitles," *Journal of Popular Film and Television* 15.3 (fall 1987): 137–42.

9. See Musser, *The Emergence of Cinema*, 221–23, 258–61; Charles Berg, "The Human Voice and the Silent Cinema," *Journal of Popular Film* 4.2 (1975): 165–79.

10. Quoted in David Robinson, *From Peep Show to Palace: The Birth of American Film* (New York: Columbia University Press, 1996); also see Kemp Niver, *The First Twenty Years: A Segment of Film History*, ed. Bebe Bersten (Los Angeles: Artisan Press, 1968).

11. G. W. Beynon, *Musical Presentation of Motion Pictures* (New York: published privately, 1921), 8–9; quoted in Berg, "The Human Voice and the Silent Cinema," 174 n. 39.

12. "Musings of the Photoplay Philosopher," *Motion Picture Story Magazine* 4.10 (November 1912): 142.

13. "I Want Smooth Titles," *Wid's Films and Film Folk* 1.5 (October 7, 1915): n.p. Also see "Rewriting the Films," *Wid's* 2.19 (May 11, 1916): 562.

14. Gertrude Allen, "The Function of the Sub-title," *Kinematograph Weekly* (December 1, 1921): 65; quoted in Christine Gledhill, *Reframing British Cinema 1918–1928: Between Restraint and Passion* (London: British Film Institute, 2003), 161.

15. Frederick James Smith, "Truth on the Screen," *Motion Picture Classic* 12.2 (April 1921): 36.

16. "The Emerson-Loos Way," *New York Times*, February 29, 1920, X7.

17. Malcolm Stuart Boylan, "Nine Star Title Writers," *New York Times*, June 17, 1928, X4.

18. Luigi Pirandello, "Pirandello Views the 'Talkies': The Cinema, Says the Noted Italian Playwright, Will Never Take the Place of the Theatre; the Proper Field, He Believes, Lies in the Realm of Music Rather Than That of the Spoken Word," *New York Times Magazine* (July 28, 1929): 1.

19. "Should They Speak English?" *Wid's Films and Film Folk* 1.11 (November 18, 1915): 1–2.

20. See William Selig Collection, Folder 487; Margaret Herrick Library, Academy of Motion Picture Arts and Sciences.

21. Letter to E. H. Montague, London, from F. A. Nöggerath, Amsterdam, December 6, 1915 (William Selig Collection, Folder 504: Correspondence [Netherlands]; Margaret Herrick Library, Academy of Motion Picture Arts and Sciences).

22. See, for example, the folder of correspondence with Selig's Spanish distributor.

23. "Pictures All Over," *Motion Picture Story Magazine* 3.4 (May 1912): 96.

24. "How Pictures Are Sold Explained by Executive," *New York Times*, September 19, 1926, X5.

25. "Retaliation," *Variety* (1929), 6.

26. Abel, "*Seduction (Erotikon),*" *Variety*, October 30, 1929.

27. See, for example, Pearl Bowser, Jane Gaines, and Charles Musser, eds., *Oscar Micheaux and His Circle: African-American Filmmaking and Race Cinema of the Silent Era* (Bloomington: Indiana University Press, 2001); Pearl Bowser and Louise Spence, *Writing Himself into History: Oscar Micheaux, His Silent Films, and His Audiences* (New Brunswick, N.J.: Rutgers University Press, 2000).

28. Antoine Berman, *Les Tours de Babel: essais sur la traduction* (Mauvezin: Trans-Europe-repress, 1985), 48; translated and quoted in Peter Fawcett, "Ideology and Translation," in *Routledge Encyclopedia of Translation Studies* (London: Routledge, 2001), 110.

29. See, for example, "*Daughter of Israel,*" *Variety*, May 30, 1928.

30. Quoted in Anthony Slide, *Aspects of American Film History Prior to 1920* (Metuchen, N.J.: Scarecrow Press, 1978), 132–33.

31. Salt, *Film Style and Technique,* 107.

32. Genevieve Harris, "*The Aryan,*" *Motography* 15.14 (April 1, 1916): 766; quoted in Thompson, "Narration," 187.

33. C. A. LeJeune, "Meet Alfred Hitchcock," *New York Times*, December 15, 1935, X7.

34. *In the Motion Picture Studio* (July 30, 1923): 10; quoted in Gledhill, *Reframing British Cinema,* 161.

35. It must be pointed out that there are more and more distributors who conscientiously duplicated the visual aesthetics of the intertitles while performing re-

translations. Kino's DVD of *The Cabinet of Caligari* (*Das Kabinett des Dr. Caligari,* 1920) is a case in point.

36. The pattern continued into the sound era, when the theaters of Havana and Vedado screened English-language films; when those prints moved on to their second and third runs, they played only two to three days, while Spanish features ran two to three times as long. See C. J. North and N. D. Golden, "The Latin American Audience Viewpoint on American Films," *Journal of the Society of Motion Picture Engineers* 17.1 (July 1931): 19–20.

37. This material on the linguistic complexity of Transylvanian cinema comes from Sergio Grmek Germani, "The Cinema of Jeno Janovics," *Le Giornate del Cinema Muto,* www.cinetecadelfriuli.org/gcm/previous_editions/edizione2002/Transilvanica.html.

38. Ibid.

39. Priya Jaikumar, "More Than Morality—The Indian Cinematograph Committee Interviews (1927)," *Moving Image* 3.1 (spring 2003): 102.

40. Much of my information on this film comes from Lucia Saks, *The Race for Representation: Cinema in a Democratic South Africa* (forthcoming), 72–115; Edwin Hees, "*The Voortrekkers* on Film: From Preller to Pornography," *CinemAction* (Durban, South Africa: University of Natal, 1985), www.und.ac.za/und/ccms/publications/articles/articles.htm.

41. Musser, *The Emergence of Cinema,* 489.

42. Daniel Haber, "When the Lights Go Down Low in Lao" (www.mekongexpress .com/laos/articles/dc_1294_lightsgolow.htm), describes the Odeon Rama Theater in Vientiane: "Say [the owner] brought me upstairs to the little booth next to the projectionist where four readers sit hunched over scripts reading simultaneous Lao translations to the original dialogue which must be switched off whenever a character speaks." Also see Ron Gluckman, "Lights, Camera, Laos" (www.gluckman .com/LaosCinema.html).

43. This activity is centered on Matsuda Film Productions, which has a large collection of silent film prints. With this core collection, it sells videos and holds regular screenings. The screenings often feature the performances of the most famous working *benshi* in Japan, Sawato Midori. Here is the company's home page: www.infoasia.co.jp/subdir/matsudae.html. In recent years, Sawato has cultivated a repertoire of English-language translations for Japanese films, which she is performing at foreign film festivals and retrospectives.

44. The key writings are Noël Burch, *To the Distant Observer: Form and Meaning in the Japanese Cinema,* ed. Annette Michelson (Ann Arbor: University of Michigan Center for Japanese Studies Publication Program, 2004), www.umich.edu/~iinet/cjs/publications/cjsfaculty/filmburch.html; Komatsu Hiroshi and Charles Musser, "Benshi Search," *Wide Angle* 9.2 (1987): 72–90; and J. L. Anderson, "Spoken Silents in the Japanese Cinema; or, Talking to Pictures: Essaying the *Katsuben,* Contextualizing the Texts," in *Reframing Japanese Cinema: Authorship, Genre, History,* ed. David Desser and Arthur Noletti Jr. (Bloomington: Indiana University Press, 1992), 259–311. More recent contributions are Jeffrey A. Dym, *Benshi, Japanese Silent Film Narrators, and Their Forgotten Narrative Art of Setsumei: A History of Japanese Silent Film Narration* (Lewiston, N.Y.: Edwin Mellen Press, 2003), and Aaron A. Gerow, "Writing a Pure Cinema: Articulations of Early Japanese Film," dissertation, University of Iowa, 1996 (forthcoming from the University of California Press under

a new title). I am particularly indebted to the last three for the background of this chapter.

45. Dym, *Benshi*, 186, and Joseph Anderson and Donald Richie, *The Japanese Film: Art and Industry* (Tokyo: C. E. Tuttle Co., 1959), 25.

46. Matsui Suisei, "Taitoruto Setsumeisha," *Sakkaku* 1.1 (June 1925): 32; quoted in Dym, *Benshi*, 107.

47. Tamura Yukihiko, "Chikagoro Zakkan," *Kinema Junpo* 173 (October 1, 1924): 31; quoted in Dym, *Benshi*, 107.

48. "Arashi no Koji Gappyo," *Katsudo Gaho* 7.8 (August 1923): 107; quoted in Dym, *Benshi*, 108.

49. Dym, *Benshi*, 113–15.

50. John C. Catford, *A Linguistic Theory of Translation: An Essay on Applied Linguistics* (London: Oxford University Press, 1965).

51. John Dryden, "On Translation," in *Theories of Translation: An Anthology of Essays from Dryden to Derrida*, ed. Rainer Schulte and John Biguenet (Chicago: University of Chicago Press, 1992), 17.

52. Ibid., 20.

53. Bowser, *The Transformation of Cinema*, 19.

54. "Survivors of a Vanishing Race in the Movie World: 'Lecturers' on the Lower East Side—Five of 'Em—Still Explain Eloquently What Is Happening on the Screen, and Regard Their Work as Art," *New York Times Magazine* (January 18, 1920): 3.

55. See Miriam Hansen, *Babel and Babylon: Spectatorship and American Silent Film* (Cambridge: Harvard University Press, 1991), especially 97.

56. Tom Gunning, *D. W. Griffith and the Origins of American Narrative Film* (Urbana: University of Illinois Press, 1991), 92–93; quoted in Gerow, "Writing a Pure Cinema," 85.

57. Hansen, *Babel and Babylon*, 97.

58. Gunning, *D. W. Griffith and the Origins of American Narrative Film*, 93.

59. Gerow, "Writing a Pure Cinema," 231. See also Gonda Yasunosuke, "Eigasetsumei no Shinka to Setsumei Geijustu no Tanjo," *Gonda Yasunosuke Chosakushu* 4 (Tokyo: Bunwa Shobo, 1974): 128.

60. Takeda Kokatsu, "Setsumeisha no Shimei," *Kinema Kurabu* 4.12 (December 1921): 96; quoted in Gerow, "Writing a Pure Cinema," 85.

61. Musobei, *Eiga Setsumei no Kenkyu* (Tokyo: Choyosha, 1923), 63–64; translation modified from Gerow, "Writing a Pure Cinema," 239.

62. Dym, *Benshi*, 105.

63. Germain Lacasse convincingly argues that the translation role for lecturers is the decisive factor in their durability in a given country or minority community. See Germain Lacasse, "The Lecturer and the Attraction," in *The Cinema of Attractions Reloaded*, ed. Wanda Strauven (Amsterdam: Amsterdam University Press, 2006), 182–203.

64. Musobei, *Eiga Setsumei no Kenkyu*, 94; quoted by Gerow, "Writing a Pure Cinema," 223.

65. During the silent era, expository intertitles were generally called "sub-titles" because they were "beneath" the main title of the film. "Spoken titles" were intertitles for dialogue.

66. Bertram Reinitz, "The Subtitle Interpreter," *New York Times*, March 7, 1926, XX2.

67. "Survivors of a Vanishing Race in the Movie World," 3.
68. Ibid.
69. Richard Abel, *The Red Rooster Scare: Making Cinema American, 1900–1910* (Berkeley: University of California Press, 1999).
70. Sheila Skaff, "The History of Cinema in Poland and the Transition from Silent to Sound Film" (Ph.D. dissertation, University of Michigan, 2004), 100.

4. Babel—the Sequel

1. Takeyama Masanobu, "Tokii o Karera wa Do Suru?" *Tokyo Asashi Shinbun* (July 20, 1930): 5.
2. Mitsubayashi Takayoshi, "Tokii Tanhyo," *Kinema Junpo* 342 (September 11, 1929): 70.
3. Ishimaki Yoshio, "Hassei Eiga no Hiai 3," *Kinema Junpo* 415 (October 11, 1931): 48. Other examples include Takada Masaru, "Hassei Eiga no Bokko," *Kinema Junpo* 303 (August 1, 1928): 59, and Takahashi Hotaru, "Tokii Zeze Hihi," *Tokyo Asahi Shinbun* (June 2, 1929): 5.
4. Kristin Thompson, *Exporting Entertainment: America in the World Film Market 1907–1934* (London: BFI Publishing, 1985), 123.
5. "Latins Demand Talkies—South America Clamoring for Sound Pictures—Delay Will Lose Market to Americans," *Hollywood Filmograph* (March 16, 1929): 1.
6. Kristin Thompson, "The Rise and Fall of Film Europe," in *"Film Europe" and "Film America": Cinema, Commerce, and Cultural Exchange 1920–1939,* ed. Andrew Higson and Richard Maltby (Exeter: University of Exeter Press, 1999), 65–66.
7. Quoted in Oketani Shigeichiro, "Furansu ni Okeru Hassei Eiga no Rongi," *Kinema Junpo* 314 (November 21, 1928): 43.
8. For example, Ginette Vincendeau, "Hollywood Babel: The Coming of Sound and the Multiple Language Version," in Higson and Maltby, *"Film Europe" and "Film America,"* 214–15 (originally published in *Screen* in 1988); Dudley Andrew, "Sound in France: The Origins of a Native School," *Yale French Studies* 60 (1980): 94–114; Douglas Gomery, "Economic Struggle and Hollywood Imperialism: Europe Converts to Sound," *Yale French Studies* 60 (1980): 90–93; Martine Danan, "Hollywood's Hegemonic Strategies: Overcoming French Nationalism with the Advent of Sound," in Higson and Maltby, *"Film Europe" and "Film America,"* 225–48.
9. A notable exception to the historiography of the past is Donald Crafton, *The Talkies: American Cinema's Transition to Sound, 1926–1931* (New York: Scribners, 1997), especially 418–41 for the issue of foreign films and markets. I should add that Crafton's historiographic analysis of *The Jazz Singer's* reception resonates strongly against the historical reality of the film's release in Japan. It simply was not as earth-shaking as historians have described it, and in any case the first sound films shown in regular theaters in Japan were the shorts *Song and Dance of Hawaii* (1929) and *Marching On* (1929). They were fourth and fifth bill, respectively, at the Musashinokan on May 9, 1929. Interestingly enough, Japanese historians do not use *The Jazz Singer* as a trope for the change in epochs; instead, they typically make the subtitled version of *Morocco* the historic turning point. Perhaps because of the historical legacy of the *benshi*, the shift to a new era was marked not by sound technology but by a

translation method. This is to say that Japanese audiences always enjoyed talking films, so the real change was that they would be translated by subtitles and not the *benshi*. I will deal more extensively with the case of *Morocco* later.

10. Rudolf Arnheim, "Sound Film Confusion," in *Film Essays and Criticism* (Madison: University of Wisconsin Press, 1997), 33–34. Vsevolod Pudovkin made the same point with an equally compelling metaphor: "Our contemporary film with its superimposed subtitles gives me the impression of an entertaining bus excursion that has been arranged by removing tires, muffler, and springs from our vehicle. Such excursions give me nothing but nervous indigestion" (Vsevolod Pudovkin, "The Global Film," trans. Jay Leyda, *Hollywood Quarterly* 2.4 [July 1947]: 329).

11. Tachibana Takahiro, "The Talkies in Japan," *Contemporary Japan* 1.1 (June 1932): 122.

12. Crafton, *The Talkies*, 431.

13. Erich Pommer, "The International Talking Film," in *Universal Filmlexikon*, ed. Frank Arnau (Berlin, 1932), reprinted in Higson and Maltby, *"Film Europe" and "Film America,"* 394.

14. William Victor Strauss, "Foreign Distribution of American Motion Pictures," *Harvard Business Review* 8.3 (April 1930): 307; quoted in John Trumpbour, *Selling Hollywood to the World: U.S. and European Struggles for Mastery of the Global Film Industry, 1920–1950* (Cambridge: Cambridge University Press, 2002).

15. Nathan D. Golden, "American Motion Pictures Abroad," *Transactions of the Society of Motion Picture Engineers* 12.33 (1928): 41–57. A further example: of the 285 films imported into Japan in 1937, 231 were American; the next closest was France with only twenty-one productions (*Cinema Yearbook of Japan 1938* [Tokyo: Kokusai Bunka Shinkokai, 1938], 54).

16. Takeyama Masanobu, "Oru Tokii no Gaikokuban no Mondai," *Kinema Junpo* 360 (March 21, 1930): 32.

17. *Kinematograph Year Book 1931* (London: Kinematograph Publications, 1931), 18.

18. According to the *Annalist*, "A Journal of Finance, Commerce, and Economics" published weekly by the *New York Times Company* (54.1391 [September 14, 1939]), American film exports went from 274,351,341 feet (and $8,119,000 in receipts) in 1929 to 194,386,495 feet (and $4,212,000) in 1934; cited in John Eugene Harley, *World-Wide Influences of the Cinema: A Study of Official Censorship and the International Cultural Aspects of Motion Pictures*, no. 2 of the University of Southern California's Cinematography Series (Los Angeles: University of Southern California, 1940), 254.

19. William C. DeMille, *Variety* (May 16, 1928), quoted in Crafton, *The Talkies*, 422. Crafton also quotes Winfield Sheehan as saying, "Talking pictures may in time make the English language known throughout the civilized world" (*Film Daily* [October 3, 1929]: 11); quoted in Crafton, *The Talkies*, 422. Curiously enough, learning English through Hollywood movies is practiced in ESL circles the world over since the coming of sound, and it also constitutes a minor genre in textbook publishing.

20. Harold B. Franklin, "Talking Pictures—The Great Internationalist," *Journal of the Society of Motion Picture Engineers* 15.1 (July 1930): 19.

21. Horseu T. Kuraku, "Toyo Kakuchi Eigakai Shisatsuki," *Kinema Junpo* 403 (June 11, 1931): 22.

22. "Talkie Puzzle Seen by Marie Dressler: Actress, Back from Europe, Says Producers Here Face Test on Language in Films," *New York Times*, June 25, 1930, 31.

23. Advertisement for *Sous les Toits de Paris* in *Kinema Junpo*.

24. "A *Benshi* of the Films: Preparing a Version of 'Paramount on Parade' Is but One of His Problems. Saw Five Shows a Day. That New York Climate," *New York Times*, August 3, 1930, X3.

25. "*Paramount on Parade*," *Kinema Junpo* 379 (October 1, 1930): 32.

26. Advertisement for *Paramount on Parade*, *Kinema Junpo* 376 (September 1, 1930): back cover.

27. C. Dodge Dunning, "Composite Photography," *Transactions of the Society of Motion Picture Engineers* 12.36 (1928): 975–79; Carroll H. Dunning, "Dunning Process and Process Backgrounds," *Journal of the Society of Motion Picture Engineers* 17.5 (November 1931): 743–48. Also see Vincendeau, "Hollywood Babel," 213.

28. Crafton, *The Talkies*, 31; Barry Salt, *Film Style and Technique: History and Analysis*, 2d ed. (London: Starword, 1992), 187.

29. Sigfried F. Lindstrom, "The Cinema in Cinema-Minded Japan," *Asia* 31.12 (December 1931): 807.

30. J. L. Pickard, "Old and New Meet in Orient as *Benshi* and Talkies Combine to Entertain Patrons," *Erpigram* (September 1, 1929): 2; quoted in Crafton, *The Talkies*, 423.

31. Tachibana Takahiro, "The Talkies in Japan," 122–23.

32. Jeffrey A. Dym, *Benshi, Japanese Silent Film Narrators, and Their Forgotten Narrative Art of Setsumei: A History of Japanese Silent Film Narration* (Lewiston, N.Y.: Edwin Mellen Press, 2003), 198–99.

33. Kitagawa Fuyuhiko, "Setsumei, Saido Taitoru, Supa Inpozu, Sono Hoka," *Kinema Junpo* 451 (October 21, 1932): 45.

34. Ibid., 3. Also see Tokugawa Musei's somewhat desperate article in *Kinema Junpo*: "Kuo Badisu-ben," *Kinema Junpo* 422 (January 1, 1932): 78–79.

35. "Tokii Muki no Shinjin *Benshi* Yosei," *Tokyo Asahi Shinbun* (February 17, 1931): 7.

36. "Jinyo Dodo to Hoga ni Semaru," *Tokyo Asahi Shinbun* (February 17, 1931): 8.

37. "Yoga Shisha Kozotte: Hobun Jimaku Sonyuan," *Kinema Shuho* 60 (May 8, 1931): 22; "Hikitsuzuki Seisaku ni Chakute," *Kinema Junpo* 405 (July 1, 1931): 14.

38. "Tokii no Gisei—*Benshi* Shutsugyo Zokushutsusu," *Tokyo Asahi Shinbun* (November 2, 1929): 3.

39. Vincendeau, "Hollywood Babel," 212.

40. Takeyama Masanobu, "Oru Tokii no Gaikokuban no Monday," *Kinema Junpo* 360 (March 21, 1930): 32. Takeyama was the publicity manager for Paramount in Japan.

41. "Hobun Jimaku Eishaki o Chumon," *Yomiuri Shinbun* (November 29, 1930): 7; "Gyaku Yushutsu no Saido Taitoru Gentoki," *Kinema Shuho* 94 (February 20, 1931): 10.

42. "Saido Taitoru Gyaku Yushutsu," *Kinema Junpo* 392 (February 21, 1931): 15.

43. *Shochikuza Panfuretto* (program for Shinjuku Shochikuza and Asakusa Shochikuza, September 1929; in the Tsuboichi Theater Museum of Waseda University): n.p.

44. "Metoro no Nihonban ni Tokugawa Museishi," *Kinema Junpo* 403 (June 11, 1931): 8.

45. Dazai Yukimichi, "Doro Gassen: Nihonban Sono Hoka," *Kinema Junpo* 407 (July 21, 1931): 18.

46. Takeyama Masanobu, "Tokii o Karera wa Do Suru?" *Tokyo Asahi Shinbun* (July 20, 1930): 5.

47. The most important single resource is the special issue edited by Nataša Durovičová on the topic "Multiple and Multiple-Language Versions" for *CINEMA& Cie* 4 (spring 2004). For an example of an article written in the short period when dubbing and subbing were no competition for MLVs, see C. J. North and N. D. Golden, "Meeting Sound Film Competition Abroad," *Journal of the Society of Motion Picture Engineers* 15.6 (December 1930): 749–58. Lists of Hollywood's Spanish and French MLVs are published the following articles: Alfonso Pinto, "Hollywood's Spanish-Language Films," *Films in Review* 24.8 (October 1973): 474–83; Alfonso Pinto, "Hollywood's French Language Films," *Films in Review* 29.1 (January 1978): 29–35.

48. Pommer, "The International Talking Film," 396.

49. In one of the most promising strands of research on the MLV, Charles O'Brien is investigating the implications of these kinds of differences for shifts in film style at the level of national cinemas. See his "Multiple Versions in France: Paramount: Paris and National Film Style," *CINEMA&Cie* 4 (spring 2004): 80–88.

50. Mordaunt Hall, "The Screen: Miss Garbo Speaks German," *New York Times*, January 6, 1931, 25; quoted in Crafton, *The Talkies*, 428.

51. *Kinematograph Year Book 1931*, 17.

52. Danan, "Hollywood's Hegemonic Strategies," 236; Vincendeau, "Hollywood Babel," 213.

53. "Foreign Language Films," *New York Times*, November 17, 1929, X5.

54. "Paramount to Film Talkies in Europe: Will Solve Language Problem with Casts Composed of Foreign Actors. Others May Follow Move. Representatives of American Firms Are Already Investigating Possibilities on the Ground," *New York Times*, April 27, 1930, 10.

55. Quoted in Harley, *World-Wide Influences of the Cinema*, 253.

56. Vincendeau, "Hollywood Babel," 212.

57. See Lawrence Venuti, *The Scandals of Translation: Towards and Ethics of Difference* (New York: Routledge, 1998).

58. Paramount also saw its move to Joinville as a cost-saving measure. Foreign versions could be produced for 33 percent below the production budget of the original American film. See Geoffrey Shurlock, " 'Versions': The Problem of Making Foreign-Language Pictures," *American Cinematographer* 11.9 (January 1931): 22. However, it is also claimed that the reason for Joinville's demise was the excessive waste and cost (see, for example, Charles Ford, "Paramount at Joinville: Its Attempt to Make Foreign Language Films in France Was a Failure," *Films in Review* 12.9 [November 1961]: 541–44). Which is correct is hard to say; the economies of the MLV have yet to be explored by careful archival research.

59. Friedrich Schleiermacher, "On the Different Methods of Translating," trans. Waltraud Bartscht, ed. Rainer Schulte and John Biguenet, *Theories of Translation: An Anthology of Essays from Dryden to Derrida* (Chicago: University of Chicago Press, 1992), 42.

60. Richard Maltby and Ruth Vasey, "Temporary American Citizens: Cultural Anxieties and Industrial Strategies in the Americanization of European Cinema," in Higson and Maltby, *"Film Europe" and "Film America*," 49.

61. Robert Paquin interview, Montreal, October 7, 2004.

62. Danan, "Hollywood's Hegemonic Strategies," 230.

63. Ibid.

64. Quoted in Nataša Ďurovičová, "Translating America: The Hollywood Multi-linguals 1919–1933," in *Sound Theory Sound Practice*, ed. Rick Altman (New York: Routledge, 1992), 264. Also see Nataša Ďurovičová, "*Los Toquis*, or Urban Babel," in *Global Cities*, ed. Patrice Petro and Linda Krause (New Brunswick, N.J.: Rutgers University Press, 2003), 82. There is speculation that American companies might have quietly set off the riots to destroy the German competition; see Jaroslav Brož and Myrtil Frída, *Historie Československého filmu v obrazech (1930–1945)* (Prague: Orbis, 1966): 14–16, cited in Ďurovičová, "Translating America," 264.

65. The heavy censorship through dubbing and cutting of *All Quiet on the Western Front* (1930) could not save it from Nazi rioting; on the night of its premiere a mob led by Goebbels himself stormed the theater with stink bombs, mice, and sneeze powder (and the Nazis in the audience even asked for refunds!); described in Andrew Kelly, "*All Quiet on the Western Front*: Brutal Cutting, Stupid Censors, and Bigoted Politicos (1930–1984)," *Historical Journal of Film, Radio, and Television* 9.2 (1989): 139.

66. Ibid.

67. Maxi, "L'Énigmatique M. Parkes (The Enigmatic Mr. Parkes)," *Variety* (November 12, 1930): 45.

68. Maltby and Vasey, "Temporary American Citizens," 46. Subtitles sidestepped these problems by rendering the target language in writing, which reveals an affinity with the silent intertitles.

69. "*Sombres de Gloria*," *Variety* (February 19, 1930): 33.

70. "*Cascarrabias (Grumpy)*," *Variety* (October 22, 1930): 35.

71. For the Hollywood perspective on this issue and early translation practices in Latin America, see C. J. North and N. D. Golden, "The Latin American Audience Viewpoint on American Films," *Journal of the Society of Motion Picture Engineers* 17.1 (1931): 18–25.

72. "*Olimpia (If the Emperor Only Knew)*," *Variety* (October 22, 1930): 35.

73. Maxi, "*Si l'empereur savait ça (If the Emperor Only Knew)*," *Variety* (November 19, 1930): 28. Fox also tried dubbing *Manuela* into French with a distinct Spanish accent (Danan, "Hollywood's Hegemonic Strategies," 231).

74. Jeff Matthews, "Hey, You Sound Just like Marlon Brando, Robert Redford and Paul Newman!" (faculty.ed.umuc.edu/~jmatthew/Dubbing.htm). Matthews also notes that Clarence Nash, the voice of Donald Duck, dubbed himself into everything from Italian to Japanese. Also see Danan, "Hollywood's Hegemonic Strategies," 231.

75. Mario Quargnolo, "Le Cinéma Bâillonné," in *Le Passage du Muet au Parlant*, ed. Christian Belaygue and Jean-Paul Gorce (Toulouse: Cinémathèque de Toulouse/ Éditions Milan, 1988), 43; quoted in Crafton, *The Talkies*, 439. Ironically, at the dawn of the talkie, Mussolini held a double standard vis-à-vis the MLV. After seeing George Bernard Shaw's famous appearance in an Edison newsreel, Mussolini wanted so badly to reach the British public with his political views that he memorized an English-language speech for a newsreel interview, just as Laurel and Hardy would a few years later. See Stuart Chesmore, *Behind the Cinema Screen* (London: Thomas Nelson and Sons, 1935), 58–59.

76. Quoted in James Hay, *Popular Film Culture in Fascist Italy—the Passing of the Rex* (Bloomington: Indiana University Press, 1987), 86–87.

77. Edwin Hopkins, "Re-Vocalizing Films," *Transactions of the Society of Motion Picture Engineers* 12.35 (1928): 851.

78. A Czech producer attempted to revive this approach in the 1980s: "New Twist on Lip Synching," *Weekly Variety* (July 1, 1987): 28.

79. J. Douglas Gomery, "The Coming of Sound to the American Cinema" (Ph.D. dissertation, University of Wisconsin, Madison, 1975), 376.

80. Thompson, *Exporting Entertainment*, 160.

81. "Nowa rewelacja 'dubbing,'" editorial, *Illustrated Kurier Codzienny* 170 (1932); quoted in Sheila Skaff, "The History of Cinema in Poland and the Transition from Silent to Sound Film" (Ph.D. dissertation, University of Michigan, 2004), 90.

82. Oswell Blakeston, "Paris Margin Note," *Close-up* 10.4 (1933): 365–66.

83. Danan, "Hollywood's Hegemonic Strategies," 239.

84. Gomery, *The Coming of Sound to the American Cinema*, 378.

85. Joseph Garncarz, "Made in Germany: Multi-Language Versions and the Early German Sound Cinema," in Higson and Maltby, *"Film Europe" and "Film America,"* 259.

86. Advertisement, *Kinema Junpo* (August 1931).

87. C. V. Heiku, "1932 Nen no Haru o Mukaete," *Kinema Junpo* 422 (January 1, 1932): 69.

88. *"The Man Who Came Back,"* *Kinema Junpo* 422 (January 1, 1932): 55.

89. Adachi Chu, "Kokusan Tokii Jidai," *Kinema Junpo* 425 (February 1, 1932): 56.

90. Examples of the older dictionaries are *Eigagaku Nyumon* (Tokyo: Dai Nihon Eiga Kyokai, 1943), 303; Kitagawa Tetsuo, *Eiga Kansho Dokuhon* (Tokyo: Horitsu Bunkasha, 1955), 213.

91. Shimizu Shunji, "Seiko Shita *Saisei no Minato*," *Yomiuri Shinbun* (December 11, 1931): 3.

92. Paul Rotha, "Paul Rotha," *Films and Filming* (January 1967): 66.

93. Okaeda Shinji, *Jimaku Honyaku Kogi no Jikkyo Chukei* (Tokyo: Gogakushunjusha, 1989), 229.

94. The Moviola also made dubbing easier, as it enabled editors to extract dialogue tracks from music and sound-effects tracks while maintaining sync.

95. Herman Weinberg, *Coffee, Brandy, and Cigars: A Kaleidoscope of the Arts and That Strange Thing Called Life* (New York: Anthology Film Archives, 1985), 107–8.

96. Tamura Yukihiko, "Amerika Nikki 2," *Kinema Junpo* 390 (February 1, 1931): 57–58.

97. Tanaka Jun'ichiro, *Nihon Eiga Hattatsu-shi II* (Tokyo: Chuokoronsha, 1980), 217.

98. Koizumi Yasushi, "Tokii to Setsumeisha: *Morokko* Hobun Jimaku ni Tsuite," *Yomiuri Shinbun*, evening edition, February 9, 1931, 3.

99. Furukawa Roppa, "Tokii Hogoban no Mondai," *Eiga Jidai* 10.4 (April 1931): 32.

100. Kitagawa, *Eiga Kansho Dokuhon*, 45.

101. Yanagida Hide, "Purezenteshon no Mondai," *Kinema Junpo* 424 (January 21, 1932): 22–23. This article includes an interesting survey of theaters and the various combinations of translation methods they were using at the time. Yanagida discov-

ers that theaters were typically unwilling to bank on a single approach and used many combinations of the available methods.

102. Tokugawa Musei, Mori Iwao, et al., "Shakai Mondai ni Natta Hobun Taitoru Mondai Zadankai Sokki," *Kinema Shunho* 48 (February 13, 1931): 31. This fascinating issue also has a report from Tamura, an interview with the local Paramount representative, and comments by theatergoers.

103. Tokugawa Musei, "Hobun Jimaku no Shutsugen to Setsumeisha no Tachiba," *Tokyo Nichi Nichi Shinbun,* February 27, 1931, 6.

104. Quoted in ibid.

105. Tamura Yukihiko, "Henshu Goki," *Kinema Junpo* 414 (October 1, 1931): 92.

106. "Paramaunto Nihonban wa Wagakuni ni te Seisaku," *Kinema Junpo* 469 (May 1, 1933): 6.

107. By way of contrast, Germany was producing 4.4 percent of its films in sound in 1929, but that reached 98.6 percent by 1931 (Garncarz, "Made in Germany," 251).

5. For an Abusive Subtitling

1. I am speaking primarily of the worldview of feature-film subtitlers. We find other motives come to the fore in, for example, the ethnographic film. In this genre of documentary, pleasure is downplayed for the sake of pedagogy. Starting in the silent era and continuing into the 1960s, intertitles and voice-over narration held profilmic people in an interpretive frame. However, starting with the work of Tim Asch in the 1960s, subtitles "let people speak for themselves," or so thought filmmakers and their audiences. Subtitles supposedly rendered the speaking subject's interiority transparently knowable (along with the help of the anthropologist). This mode of translation came under brilliant critique in the filmmaking critical writings of Trinh T. Min-ha, as well as the work of David MacDougall and Brenda Longfellow. See David MacDougall, *Transcultural Cinema* (Princeton, N.J.: Princeton University Press, 1998); Brenda Longfellow, "The Great Dance—Translating the Foreign in Ethnographic Film," in *Subtitles: On the Foreignness of Film,* ed. Atom Egoyan and Ian Balfour (Cambridge: MIT Press, 2004), 337–53.

2. Trinh T. Min-ha, *Framer Framed* (New York: Routledge, 1992), 102.

3. The apparatus for dubbing regularly features analogous reversals of power. Consider *The X-Files* dubbing for Japanese television. Mulder is dubbed by a man with a husky, deep, tough-man voice, while Scully's relatively low, businesslike tone is replaced with the high-pitched voice one usually associates with soap operas and weather report announcers. This manipulation of the material qualities of language—in this case, the grain of the voice—reverses the sexual play and politics of the show. Sheryl WuDunn calls this the "sky-high voice lift," although she is writing about Mukai Mariko's dubbing of Marilyn Monroe (Sheryl WuDunn, "Marilyn Monroe Cooing in Falsetto: Dubbers Bring Foreign Film Stars to Japan's Living Rooms," *New York Times,* February 19, 1996, D4). Although less dramatic, the *RoboCop* example displays the same dynamic. As I will argue, standard subtitles ignore the material aspects of language.

4. Antje Ascheid, "Speaking Tongues: Voice Dubbing in the Cinema as Cultural Ventriloquism," *Velvet Light Trap* 40 (fall 1997): 40.

5. Fujinami Fujiaki, *Nyusu Kameraman—Gekido no Showashi o Toru* (Tokyo: Chuokoronsha, 1977), 81–84.

6. Andrew Martin, "Words to the Wise," *Time Out* (London) (August 7, 1991): 23.

7. Henri Béhar, "Cultural Ventriloquism," in Egoyan and Balfour, *Subtitles*, 81.

8. In this method, a photographic negative containing the subtitles is sandwiched between the raw stock and the original negative while striking the prints. This is costly, and can harm the quality of the prints if not done with care.

9. Rachael Low, *The History of the British Film 1929–1939* (London: George Allen and Unwin, 1985), 100.

10. Ever since the talkies era, filmmakers naturally ran into the perennial problem of white optical subtitles appearing over white backgrounds, rendering them practically invisible (Figure 1). However, *Tora! Tora! Tora!* was no ordinary subtitling job. Whereas most subtitles were virtually the afterthought of an anonymous distributor, these were the end point of three years of constant, arduous translation. Invisible words negated all that effort, so Elmo Williams had his lab technicians experiment by moving the subtitles to different parts of the screen. Late in the process, he had them try the addition of a yellow filter during the final printing process and that solved the problem. Unfortunately, he didn't think of this until after most of the master dupe negative was complete, so these yellow subtitles appeared only on the first reel. However, Williams received many complaints that the rest of the reels were plagued by the white-on-white problem, and he later had them do this for all the reels. Thus, the legible yellow subtitles we now associate with video were actually invented by none other than Elmo Williams for *Tora! Tora! Tora!* (Memo, Elmo Williams to Gordon Stulberg, November 17, 1970 [Elmo Williams Collection, Folder 142; Margaret Herrick Library, Academy of Motion Pictures Arts and Sciences]).

11. Donald Richie, "Donald Richie on Subtitling Japanese Films," *Mangajin* 10 (1991): 16.

12. See, for example, Toda Natsuko, *Jimaku no Naka ni Jinsei* (Tokyo: Hakusuisha, 1994), 27; Okaeda Shiji, *Supa Jimaku Nyumon—Eiga Honyaku no Gijutsu to Chishiki* (Tokyo: Baburu Puresu, 1988), 18; Kamijima Kimi, *Jimaku Shikakenin Ichidaiki* (Tokyo: Pandora, 1995), 22.

13. Toda, *Jimaku no Naka ni Jinsei*, 27. Toda is reporting hearsay; it appears that she has done no real research for her history.

14. Biographies include Toda, *Jimaku no Naka ni Jinsei*, Kamijima, *Jimaku Shikakenin Ichidaiki*, and Shimizu Shunji, *Eiga Jimaku no Gojunen* (Tokyo: Hayakawa Shobo, 1985). The latter is the most famous, but Kamijima's is the most interesting of the three. How-to books are popular among translators looking to add variety to their usual slate of boring business translations; a few of them are apparently used as textbooks in classes offered by some of the more high-profile subtitlers; see Kamijima, *Jimaku Shikakenin Ichidaiki*, Okaeda, *Supa Jimaku Nyumon*, Okaeda Shinji, *Jimaku Honyaku Kogi no Jikkyo Chukei* (Tokyo: Gogakushunjusha, 1989), Shimizu Shunji, *Eiga Jimaku no Tsukurikata Oshiemasu* (Tokyo: Bunshun Bunko, 1988), and Shimizu Shunji, *Eiga Jimaku wa Honyaku de wa Nai*, ed. Toda Natsuko and Ueno Tamako (Tokyo: Hayakawa Shobo, 1992).

15. Toda, *Jimaku no Naka ni Jinsei*, 10. This is quite different than, say, Buena Vista's decision to distribute subtitled versions of *Evita* (1996) in dubbing territories. Both are nods to the aura of the original actors' voices, Madonna and Olivier

or Welles. Buena Vista was making a calculated marketing decision. What was Toda thinking?

16. Shimizu, *Eiga Jimaku wa Honyaku de wa Nai*, 61–62.

17. Robert Paquin, "In the Footsteps of Giants," *Translation Journal* 5.3 (July 2001); www.accurapid.com/journal/17dubb.htm.

18. Okaeda, *Jimaku Honyaku Kogi no Jikkyo Chukei*, 194–95. Far more disturbing is his ignorant homophobia when he prefaces a section on homosexuality and subtitling with a bizarre aside implying that the United States has "homos" and Japan does not, and explicitly blaming AIDS on American homosexuals.

19. Toda, *Jimaku no Naka ni Jinsei*, 11.

20. Okaeda, *Jimaku Honyaku Kogi no Jikkyo Chukei*, 6.

21. According to Shimizu Shunji, Films Inc. in Tokyo held a 35mm print of Tamura's *Morocco*. Unfortunately, the company is now out of business.

22. The subtitler's collaboration with structures of censorship is an important form of corruption I will explore in the next chapter. Suffice to say, subtitles in Japan were strictly censored in both prewar and postwar eras. More recently, censorship has largely been directed at the image exclusive of the sound track. Shimizu served for many years on the board of Eirin, one of the primary censorship authorities in Japan. Okaeda has a curious passage in his "lectures" about subtitling pornography. For example, he warns his students not to translate "Oh, that feels so good" directly over the utterance/sex act because the translation would never pass censorship proceedings; however, if the subtitle appears before or after, as in "I'll make you feel good," there should be no problem. How this practice affects the translation of mainstream texts is left unexplained (Okaeda, *Jimaku Honyaku Kogi no Jikkyo Chukei*, 201–2).

23. Shimizu, *Eiga Jimaku no Tsukurikata Oshiemasu*, 350. In one of his reports from the United States about the time of *Morocco*'s release, Tamura contradicts Shimizu's story by writing that he found 234 titles too few (Tamura Yukihiko, "Amerika Nikki 2," *Kinema Junpo* 390 [February 1, 1931]: 57–58). Shimizu's account says that this version never reached public theaters, but a contemporary article suggests otherwise. In "A Quick Note on the Talkie," Hayashi Chitose went to the trouble of counting lines of dialogue and subtitles. Hayashi's count: 387 spoken lines/229 subtitles with 4 "inserted subtitles," for an average of 32 lines/19 subtitles per reel. Although he notes that the most dialogue-heavy scene of the film uses more subtitles (41 for 52 lines), Hayashi stops his analysis with the basic argument that "less is better." I will argue that this is nothing other than a silent-era-specific conception of cinema carded over the sound barrier. See Hayashi Chitose, "Tokii ni Kan Suru Hashirigaki," *STS* 5 (May 10, 1931): 39. At the same time, Tamura himself contradicts Shimizu. One Japanese journal published the *Morocco* script in 1931, claiming to reproduce Tamura's subtitles. However, two of the frame blow-ups published at the time are different from the lines published in the scenario. Furthermore, some of the utterances are quite long, clearly combining two or more subtitles. Thus, it is less than useful for research purposes ("*Morokko*," *Eiga Kagaku Kenkyu* 8 [April 1931]: 175–233).

24. J. M. Harvey, *Life and Letters Today* (autumn 1936): 166–70; cited in Low, *The History of the British Film 1929–1939*, 100. Furthermore, a subtitle script for the Spanish subtitles of *Halleluia* (script dated March 20, 1930) suggests that MGM was adopting a similar practice; there were only 169 titles for the entire film (Scenario,

Halleluia [Box 1248 f. 37, Turner/MGM collection; Margaret Herrick Library, Academy of Motion Picture Arts and Sciences]).

25. Wadayama Shigeru, "*The Champ*," *Kinema Junpo* 441 (July 11, 1932): 37. These and other *ken'etsu daihon* are preserved in the Makino Mamoru Collection and at the Kawakita Memorial Film Institute, Tokyo. Shimizu Chiyota was, along with Tamura, one of the founding members of *Kinema Junpo*, the premiere film magazine from the teens of the last century to the present day.

26. Longer lines required multiple subtitles, making the total number of subtitles 360. The other *ken'etsu daihon* I inspected appeared to have similar subtitle counts. They may be found in the Makino Mamoru Collection and at the Kawakita Memorial Film Institute. For example, Hitchcock's *The Man Who Knew Too Much* (1934) used only 314 subtitles, while the postwar Japanese videotape has 567. *The 39 Steps* (1935) had 606 subtitles for roughly 876 utterances. Robert Flaherty's *Man of Aran* (1934) had only three subtitles for the entire film. These scripts may be found at the Kawakita Memorial Film Institute, Tokyo.

27. Mura Chio, "Ozu Yasujiro no Geijutsu Taido," *STS* 13 (January 10, 1932): 25.

28. *Ken'etsu daihon, The Man Who Knew Too Much* (*Ansatsusha no ie*, 1934); Kawakita Memorial Film Institute, Tokyo.

29. This was related to me by Komatsu Hiroshi, who saw the print while working at the National Film Center. It appears that this occurred in other parts of the world as well. For example, René Clair's *À nous la liberté*'s (1931) original Czech subtitles were unusual; the spoken titles were in the upper right corner, and the music's stream of lyrics were delivered in a crawl across the lower edge.

30. Toda, *Jimaku no Naka ni Jinsei*, 26–27.

31. Tamura Yukihiko, "Morocco," *Kinema Junpo* (February 1, 1931).

32. This appears to be a worldwide phenomenon. For example, the French translator Bernard Eisenschitz relates the case of W. Montague. A famous British subtitler during the talkies era, he believed that the subtitles should arrive a beat or two after the utterance begins—like a silent film intertitle.

33. Reported by Kitagawa Fuyuhiko, "Setsumei, Saido Taitoru, Supaa Inpozu Sono Hoka," *Kinema Junpo* 451 (October 21, 1932): 45.

34. Ota Tatsuo, "Supa Impozu ni Okeru Nihongo no Hinkon," *Nihon Eiga* 4.5 (May 1939): 51. This process probably began in the early 1930s, as is suggested by Tamura Yukihiko's 1933 comment that he was now using up to five hundred titles per film ("Eiga Fuan o Yorokobaseta Hito," *Tokyo Asahi Shinbun* [May 27, 1933]: 5).

35. *Translation Studies Reader*, ed. Lawrence Venuti (London: Routledge, 2004), 24–25.

36. Philip E. Lewis, "The Measure of Translation Effects," in *Difference in Translation*, ed. Joseph F. Graham (Ithaca, N.Y.: Cornell University Press, 1985), 31–62.

37. Ibid., 36.

38. Ibid., 41.

39. Johann Wolfgang von Goethe, "Translation" ("Übersetzungen"), trans. Sharon Sloan, in *Theories of Translation*, ed. John Biquenet and Rainer Schulte (Chicago: University of Chicago Press, 1992), 61.

40. Antje Ascheid's article on dubbing ("Speaking Tongues") admirably attempts to avoid these traps, but falls into others because of an inadequate theorization of translation itself.

41. See Lawrence Venuti, "Translation, Community, Utopia," in *Translation Studies Reader*, ed. Lawrence Venuti (London: Routledge, 2004), 482–502.

42. To the examples that follow, I would add B. Ruby Rich's anecdotal evidence that distributors, who used to hide the nationality of foreign films, also sense a substantial shift in American audiences' relationship to foreign films and subtitles (B. Ruby Rich, "To Read or Not to Read: Subtitles, Trailers, and Monolingualism," in Egoyan and Balfour, *Subtitles*, 167). The subtitles in verse for *Cyrano de Bergerac* (1990) are worth noting for two reasons. Aside from their abusive use of poetic structure and rhyme, there is a question of authorship. They are usually attributed to the genius of Anthony Burgess; however, the British author's signature hides an invisible subtitler, who simply adapted (and simplified) Burgess's translation for the stage. See Lenny Korman and Denis Sequin, "War of the Words," *Screen International* (July 2, 1998): 10.

43. In 1973, René Viénet created incendiary subtitles for a Hong Kong kung-fu film called *The Crush* (dir. Doo Kwang Gee and Lam Nin Tung, 1972). The credit for the translation went to "Association pour le développement de la lutte des classes et la propagation du matérialisme dialectique," and the release title was *La Dialectique peut-elle casser les briques?* (Can the dialectic break bricks?). Robert Stam and Ella Shohat report that "A sequence of devastating karate blows would be subtitled: 'Down with the bourgeoisie!'" See their "The Cinema after Babel: Language, Difference, Power," *Screen* 26.3–4 (May–August 1985): 35–59. For a contemporary review of this curious translation, see D. S., "*La Dialectique peut-elle casser les briques?*" *Image et Son* 276–67 (October 1973): 110–11. *What's Up, Tiger Lily?* is actually a low-budget Japanese detective film titled *Kokusai himitsu keisatsu: kagi no kagi* (1965) with Allen's parodic dubbing on the sound track. These examples are also curious for their parody, which indulges in the abusive translator's pleasure in experiencing the foreign, while sharing the corrupt translator's domination of the source text.

44. Richie, "Donald Richie on Subtitling Japanese Films," 16.

45. Ibid.

46. Thanks to the brilliant programming of the Criterion Collection, we now have a DVD with Richie's original *Throne of Blood* subtitles. The same disk has a second subtitle track with Linda Hoagland's excellent and scrupulously standard subtitles.

47. Martin, "Words to the Wise," 23.

48. Laura Marks, *The Skin of the Film: Intercultural Cinema, Embodiment, and the Senses* (Durham, N.C.: Duke University Press, 2000), 39.

6. Loving Dubbing

1. Quoted in John Belton, "Technology and Aesthetics of Film Sound," in *Film Sound*, ed. Elisabeth Weise and John Belton (New York: Columbia University Press, 1985), 65.

2. Joinville was also called "Babel-sur-Marne."

3. "Tongue Tied," *Screen International* (November 13, 1992): 11.

4. Martine Danan, "Dubbing as an Expression of Nationalism," *Meta* 36.4 (1991): 606.

5. American consul general, Munich, February 26, 1947, no. 428, letter to U.S. Department of State (U.S. NA Record Group 59, 862.4061, 1945–9 Motion Pictures, U.S. National Archives); quoted in John Trumpbour, *Selling Hollywood to the World: U.S. and European Struggles for Mastery of the Global Film Industry, 1920–1950* (Cambridge: Cambridge University Press, 2002), 98.

6. This is argued convincingly by John Trumpbour in ibid., 102–7.

7. This has been confirmed through statistical surveys in an oft-quoted article by George Luyken, who found that 82 percent of Dutch preferred subs, while 36 percent of Brits prefer dubs. See George Luyken, "In Other Words," *Cable and Satellite Europe* (June 1987): 61. It is probably the best evidence that subtitling and dubbing are nothing other than highly conventionalized forms of film translation.

8. Hans-Jürgen Syderberg, "Germany's Heart: The Modern Taboo," *New Perspectives Quarterly* 10.1 (winter 1993): www.digitalnpq.org/archive/1993_winter/germanys _heart.html.

9. Martine Danan, "Hollywood's Hegemonic Strategies," in *"Film Europe" and "Film America": Cinema, Commerce, and Cultural Exchange 1920–1939*, ed. Andrew Higson and Richard Maltby (Exeter: University of Exeter Press, 1999), 236.

10. See J. Clarke, *"Robotech:* the Rebirth," *Manga Mania* 1.16 (1994): 117–19; Maureen Furniss, *Art in Motion: Animation Aesthetics* (London: John Libbey, 1999), 206.

11. Leslie Garisto, "Dubbing Is Booming," *New York Times,* August 29, 1982, H1.

12. Working dubbing directors seem to disagree with this marketing-driven casting. Director George Gonneau, for one, looks for someone with "the peculiar ability of losing oneself as an actor and becoming someone else. Big-name actors aren't always the best dubbers, because they've spent so much time honing and cultivating their own persona" (ibid., H23).

13. Quoted in Tori Maki, "Ikita Kotoba de Shabera Nakattara Dare mo Kanjite Kuremasen yo," in *Tori Maki no Eiga Fukikae* (Tokyo: Yosensha, 2004), 13.

14. Ibid., 8–15. Much of the information in this paragraph on early dubbing practices comes from this interview with Ohira Toru.

15. For example: Matsuda Sakumi, *Seiyu Hakusho* (Tokyo: Okura Shuppan, 2000); Fukushima Ei, *Seiyu Nyumon* (Tokyo: Shinsuisha, 1997); Nakagawa Nami, *Anime Seiyu Dokuhon* (Tokyo: Gen Shobo, 1998); *Eizo Honyaku Hoso Tsuyaku Kanzen Gaido* (Tokyo: Ikarasu Shuppan, 1999); *Eizo Honyakusha ni Naro,* ed. Nihon Eizo Honyaku Akademii (Tokyo: Nihon Jitsugyo Shuppansha, 1997); *Seiyu ni Naru Tame no Renshu Mondai,* ed. Takahashi Tomoko and Deguchi Fujiko (Tokyo: Raichosha, 2000).

16. The situation in the United States is probably unusual, in that quite a few established actors used the dubbing industry as a source for steady income; however, they suppressed this aspect of their careers for fear that it would taint their reputations. See William Wolf, "Film Voices Anonymous," *Cue* (August 6, 1966): 10.

17. Joel Martinsen, "Update: Stephen Chow Sold for 14,542 Yuan," in *Danwei: Media, Advertising, and Urban Life in China* (blog, postdated August 23, 2005). Shi also recorded a set of English-language instruction tapes using Chow's voice.

18. For information on the dubbing bums in Paris, see Paul Gardner, "A Few Become Dubbing Bums," *New York Times,* July 24, 1966, 68.

19. Ruth Carter, "Rome's Inner-Colony of Those Trained in Sound-Track Dubs," *Variety* (June, 19, 1971): 32.

20. Stanley Kauffmann, "Friends and Romans . . . Dubbing along the Tiber," *New Republic* (January 1960): 10.

21. Ernest Weatherall, "Dubbing 'Tango' for German Mkt," *Weekly Variety* (April 11, 1973): 34.

22. H. G. Knox, "English Gives Way to Babel of Tongues as Foreign Language Film Demand Grows," *Erpigram* (July 1, 1930): 1; quoted in Donald Crafton, *The Talkies: American Cinema's Transition to Sound, 1926–1931* (New York: Scribner's, 1997), 425.

23. "Polyglot Cinemas," *New York Times*, May 7, 1933, XX8.

24. Oscar Godbout, "Screening a Newcomer to the Dubbing Field," *New York Times*, January 4, 1953, X5.

25. Garisto, "Dubbing Is Booming," H23.

26. Lora Myers, "The Art of Dubbing," *Filmmakers Newsletter* 6.6 (April 1973): 57. This translator discovered one of the great secrets about dubbing: like anything built on the force of convention, people accept what they grow accustomed to. This also implies that the conventions themselves change and can be changed.

27. Thomas Herbst, "A Pragmatic Translation Approach to Dubbing," *EBU Review, Programmes, Administration, Law* 38.6 (November 1987): 22.

28. John T. McManus, "The Dialogue Magicians," *New York Times*, December 20, 1936, X6.

29. Myers, "The Art of Dubbing," 56.

30. Tom Rowe, "Help, I've Been Dubbed," *Weekly Variety* (May 3, 1972): 99.

31. This originally came from France, where it is also used. I am deeply indebted to Robert Paquin, Herbert Fielden-Briggs, Jirina Hradecká, Luis von Flotow, and Hélène Lauzon (Audio PostProduction SPR).

32. Richard W. Bloomstein, "Cinematic Works with Altered Facial Displays," United States Patent and Trademark Office Patent number 4,827,532 (filed March 20, 1986).

33. Henri Béhar has called subtitling ventriloquism, but the comparison really does not work: "Subtitling is a form of cultural ventriloquism, and the focus must remain on the puppet, not the puppeteer. Our task as subtitlers is to create subliminal subtitles so in synch with the rhythm and mood of the movie that the audience isn't even aware it is reading" (Henri Béhar, "Cultural Ventriloquism," in *Subtitles: On the Foreignness of Film*, ed. Atom Egoyan and Ian Balfour [Cambridge: MIT Press, 2004], 85). This comparison falters because, like dubbing, the spectator of ventriloquism inevitably eyes the ventriloquist's lips, and thus is always aware of his fakery.

34. Jesse Zenser, "Rub-a-Dub-Dub," 8. (Bibliographic information is incomplete, as article was in the "Dubbing" clipping file at the Academy of Motion Picture Arts and Sciences.)

35. *Borges in/and/on Film*, ed. Edgard Cozarinski, trans. Gloria Waldman and Ronald Christ (New York: Lumen Books, 1988), 62. Aldonza Lorenzo refers to the Spanish peasant girl that Don Quixote creates to imagine his ideal lady, Dulcinea. In a footnote Borges asks the logical question: "Since there is usurpation of voices, why not of faces as well? When will the system be perfect? When will we see Juana Gonzalez directly, in the role of Greta Garbo, in the role of Queen Christina of Sweden?" (ibid.). With new digital special effects, it would seem that we are approaching this moment.

36. Joseph Garncarz, "Made in Germany: Multi-Language Versions and the Early German Sound Cinema," in Higson and Maltby, *"Film Europe" and "Film America,"*

257. These are hardly the only examples of critics complaining about the disembodiment of actors by the dubbing apparatus. For example, while noting that all of Buñuel's films were postsynchronized, Vincent Canby still prefers these hybrid versions subtitled rather than "a version that had been dubbed into a kind of disembodied, electronic English by unknown actors" (Vincent Canby, "A Rebel Lion Breaks Out," *New York Times*, March 27, 1983, H22).

37. Douglas Houlden, *Ventriloquism for Beginners* (New York: A. S. Barnes, 1967), 24, emphasis in original; quoted in Rick Altman, "Moving Lips: Cinema as Ventriloquism," *Yale French Studies* 60 (1980): 78.

38. The following quote provides a taste of Altman's primarily theoretical concerns, which are very different from my own. He writes that in cinema's strategy, "each track serves as a mirror for the other and the spectator for the two together. Neither track accompanies the other, neither track is redundant; the two are locked in a dialectic where each is alternatively master and slave to the other; this arrangement so suits both tracks that they studiedly perpetuate the myth of cinema's unity—and thus that of the spectator—as if (and they are right) their very lives depended on it" (Altman, "Moving Lips," 79).

39. Ibid., 76–77.

40. Ibid., 77.

41. The interview was broadcast on an NHK talk show on May 10, 2000.

42. Paquin goes into fascinating detail regarding this discovery in Robert Paquin, "In the Footsteps of Giants," *Translation Journal* 5.3 (July 2001), www.accurapid.com/journal/17dubb.htm.

43. Interview, February 2, 2001, Ann Arbor, Michigan. All subsequent quotes from Harada come from conversations during his stay.

44. Quoted in Noël Burch, *Theory of Film Practice*, trans. Helen R. Lane (New York: Praeger, 1973), 90. It should be noted that this is also a defensive strategy on the part of the dubbers. A director from Czech TV told me, "We need to add sound whenever lips move because it is what people expect. If we don't, then people will think it is our mistake."

45. Marsha Kinder, *Blood Cinema: The Reconstruction of National Identity in Spain* (Berkeley: University of California Press, 1993), 33.

46. Joe Joseph, "Here Comes That Synching Feeling," *Times Saturday Review*, March 21, 1992, 28–29.

47. Gardner, "A Few Become Dubbing Bums," 68.

48. Jonathan Watts, "Get Me Rewrite!" *Hollywood Reporter*, March 30–April 5, 1999, 15.

49. Harada was even asked to write about his experience for the prestigious journal *Chuo Koron* (Harada Masato, "'Furumetaru jyaketto' Jimaku Tenmakki," *Chuo Koron* 103.5 [May 1988]: 312–19). Later he wrote about the experience of subbing and dubbing *Full Metal Jacket* for the main film journal in Japan: "Supa Jimaku wa Ima," *Kinema Junpo* 109 (July 1, 1993): 118–19.

50. Sheryl WuDunn, "Marilyn Monroe Cooing in Falsetto: Dubbers Bring Foreign Film Stars to Japan's Living Rooms," *New York Times*, February 19, 1996, D4.

51. Gardner, "A Few Become Dubbing Bums," 68.

52. See, for example, Zoé de Linde and Neil Kay, *The Semiotics of Subtitling* (Manchester: St. Jerome Publishing, 1999), 59–73.

53. Dan Lybarger, "All in the Translation: An Interview with Neil Gaiman and Minnie Driver," *Lybarger Links* (November 24, 1999), www.tipjar.com/dan/gaiman&driver.htm. Originally appeared in the *Pitch Weekly* (November 24–December 2, 1999).

54. Herbert Fielden-Briggs, interview, October 8, 2004, Montreal, Canada.

55. William Tuohy "Film Dubbing—In Rome It's the Big Word," *L.A. Times,* January 17, 1975, I1, I2o.

56. The Anchor Bay DVD of the film contains both versions.

57. Michael Watt, "'Do You Speak Christian?': Dubbing and the Manipulation of the Cinematic Experience," *Bright Lights Film Journal* 29 (July 2000): www.brightlightsfilm.com/29/dubbing1.html.

58. Ibid.

59. Ibid.

60. Ginette Vincendeau, "Hollywood Babel: The Coming of Sound and the Multiple Language Version," in Higson and Maltby, *"Film Europe" and "Film America,"* 216.

Conclusion

1. Kristin Thompson, "The Rise and Fall of Film Europe," in *"Film Europe" and "Film America": Cinema, Commerce and Cultural Exchange 1920–1939,* ed. Andrew Higson and Richard Maltby (Exeter: University of Exeter Press, 1999), 66.

2. Initially, Italy's Commission for Censorship actually suppressed the dialogue from foreign films between 1929 and 1931. See Elaine Mancini, *Struggles of the Italian Film Industry during Fascism, 1930–1935* (Ann Arbor: UMI Research Press, 1985), 29–30, 97. Only the music and sound effects were retained, effectively returning the foreign films back to the silent era. Their rationalization was that audiences would be drawn to learn languages other than their own. Apparently, subtitling was disallowed, but a limited number of films included intertitles with translations of the dialogue. The government reversed its decision to suppress dialogue in 1932 in the face of protest from every side, but it made dubbing mandatory at the same time.

3. Subsequently, French politicians went further to limit the number of theaters that dubbed films could be shown in (Kristin Thompson, *Exporting Entertainment: America in the World Film Market 1907–1934* [London: BFI Publishing, 1985], 211–12). In France, 304 French-language films were released in 1935. Of these, 150 were dubbed foreign films, 129 were domestic French productions, and the others were MLVs made mostly in Germany (with 17) and then the United States, Italy, Belgium, Spain, and Czechoslovakia (*Kinematograph Year Book 1935* [London: Kinematograph Publications, 1935], 49). The French had achieved a monolingual cinema only a handful of years after the coming of sound. Hollywood subverted the spirit of these French laws for dubbing, which were designed partly to create domestic jobs in the film industry. For example, a report to the French government on foreigners in the film industry points out that none of the France-based dubbing directors for the Hollywood majors were French nationals. See John Trumpbour, *Selling Hollywood to the World: U.S. and European Struggles for Mastery of the Global Film Industry, 1920–1950* (Cambridge: Cambridge University Press, 2002), 235. This suggests that the French protectionist laws had something to do with linguistic

nationalism, with protecting the language itself. As Danan notes, French spectators "still wanted to see the most prestigious American superproductions and stars as long as they could be reappropriated through language—the most powerful symbol of national identity" (Martine Danan, "Hollywood's Hegemonic Strategies: Overcoming French Nationalism with the Advent of Sound," in Higson and Maltby, *"Film Europe" and "Film America,"* 241). Furthermore, traffic in linguistic nationalism ran both ways. The French legislated dubbing domestically, but favored subbing for their own exports. France's *conseiller commercial* in Rio de Janeiro in the 1930s, Étienne de Croy, wrote to the ministry of foreign affairs that "cinema plays an essential role in the popular diffusion of our language and last year, the number of students at our Alliances (françaises) had nearly doubled upon the simple announcement of the return of French film" (Trumpbour, *Selling Holllywood to the World,* 235). Clearly, the matter was more complicated than simply creating jobs for French workers.

4. Henri Storck writes, "The showing of French films in the Flemish regions of the country was prohibited; in these regions the Propaganda Abteilung allowed only German films or French films dubbed in German. Thus the people of Antwerp were only able to hear their favourite French stars talk German, a handicap that was particularly offensive!" (Henri Storck, "The Cinema Industry in Belgium during the Occupation," *Documentary Film New Letter* 5.6 [1944]: 68).

5. "Film Dubbing Ban Rumor Hit: Mexican Guild Man Explains Situation," *Citizen News,* June 27, 1944, 1.

6. Fred Stanley, "Hollywood–Mexico Incident Closed," *New York Times,* July 2, 1944, X2.

7. *Hollywood Reporter* (February 8, 1954).

8. Danny Chechter, "Screen Text: Read the Book? Now Read the Movie," *Business Mexico* 8.3 (March 1988): 48–51.

9. "Translating Hollywood," *Language International* 12.3 (June 2000): 34; my emphasis.

10. A number of people narrated the history of Czech dubbing for me, but journalist Jan Jaroš was especially helpful. This section was based on a research trip to Prague in 2005, which was made possible with the generous help of translator Jirina Hradecká and meetings with Zdeněk Hruška, Aleš Novák, Petr Pospíchal, Martin Václavík, Jiří Josek, Michael Málek, Zdeněk Coufal, Jana Mertinová, Helena Rejžková, and Josef Eismann. For histories of the MLV era, see Petr Szczepanczik, "Undoing the National: Representing National Space in 1930s Czechoslovak Multiple-Language Versions," *CINEMA&Cie* 4 (spring 2004): 55–65; and Ivan Klimeš, "Multiple-Language Versions of Czech Films and the Film Industry in Czechoslovakia in the 1930s," *CINEMA&Cie* 4 (spring 2004): 89–101.

11. Alfred Adler, "Körperform, Bewegung und Charakter," *Der Querschnitt* (September 1930): 338; quoted in Helmut Lethen, *Cool Conduct: The Culture of Distance in Weimar Germany,* trans. Don Reneau (Berkeley: University of California Press, 2002), 32.

12. Minako O'Hagan, "Greetings from Middle-Earth!" *Globalization Insider* 11.1.6 (March 29, 2002): www.lisa.org/archive/newsletters/2002/. A good resource for the debate is "*Fellowship of the Rings* Distorted in Japanese Subtitles," a Web site that contains lists of examples and reprinted materials from various sources: www.herbs.tsukaeru.jp/english_top.html.

13. Tom Westin, "'Rings' Presents Challenges to Subtitlers," *Daily Yomiuri*, February 28, 2002: accessed via Newsbank.

14. The petition may be read, in English, at www.miyako.cool.ne.jp/cgi-bin/treebbs/treebbs.cgi?log=1834.

15. Matthias Müntefering, "Dubbing in Deutschland: Cultural and Industrial Considerations," *Language International* 14.2 (2002): 15.

16. "Dubbing a Big Biz in Paris Pic Scene," *Variety Weekly* (August 12, 1970): 16; "Fellini Withdraws Bid to Forbid Film Showing," *L.A. Times*, January 9, 1988, Part IV, 2.

17. "Translating Hollywood," *Language International* 12.3 (June 2000): 34.

18. The process is to maximize what you get, and to understand how it works and what can be done to make the process smooth and economical. Each industrial context uses slightly different procedures, but an article that provides many hints to producers in this regard is Michael Bakewell's "Factors Affecting the Cost of Dubbing," *EBU Review* 38.6 (November 1987): 16–17.

Index

Abé Mark Nornes is professor in the departments of Screen Arts and Cultures and Asian Languages and Cultures at the University of Michigan. He is author of *Forest of Pressure: Ogawa Shinsuke and Postwar Japanese Documentary* and *Japanese Documentary Film: The Meiji Era through Hiroshima*, both published by the University of Minnesota Press.